SHAKESPEARE AFTER THEORY

Shakespeare after Theory

DAVID SCOTT KASTAN

Routledge
New York and London

Published in 1999 by
Routledge
29 West 35th Street
New York, NY 10001

Published in Great Britain by
Routledge
11 New Fetter Lane
London EC4P 4EE

Printed in the United States of America on acid-free paper.
Book design by Mark Abrams

Library of Congress Cataloging-in-Publication Data
Kastan, David Scott.
    Shakespeare after theory / David Scott Kastan.
        p.   cm.
    Includes bibliographical references and index.
    ISBN 0-415-90112-X (hb). – ISBN 0-415-90113-8 (pb)
        1. Shakespeare, William, 1564–1616–Knowledge–History. 2. Great Britain–History–Elizabeth, 1558–1603–Historiography. 3. Great Britain–History–James I, 1603–1625–Historiography. 4. Literature and history–England–History–16th century. 5. Literature and history–England–History–17th century. 6. Shakespeare, William, 1564–1616–Criticism, textual. 7. Historicism. I. Title.
PR3014.K37   1999
822.3'3–dc21   98-48531
                                                                                        CIP

CONTENTS

Acknowledgments

A book committed to the proposition that all intellectual work is necessarily collaborative should revel in the opportunity to declare its
own social and intellectual debts; and so I would, had not so many
been incurred in the writing that I fear I will unwittingly omit some
collaborator and also inevitably name at least one who would prefer
not to be identified publicly with what is here presented. Nonetheless, I will go ahead, made most uncomfortable, however, by my
awareness of how inadequate this recompense is for what has been
so graciously given me.

I have been much blessed with my friends. Margreta de Grazia, Margaret Ferguson, Lisa Jardine, Claire McEachern, Franco Moretti, Barbara Mowat, Stephen Orgel, William Sherman, Blair Worden, and Steven Zwicker have been the very best of readers, respondents, and often dinner companions, responsible both for much of my understanding of what I was doing and for much of the fun it was to do. I have benefitted more than is seemly from David Armitage's defection from literary studies, as he has served as an uncommonly thoughtful and patient guide to early modern English history. Even though I always pay for the coffee, I fear I am still in his debt. Jim Shapiro has always been the most generous of friends, and, next to my family, he is doubtlessly the person happiest that this book is at last done. He and Jean Howard are colleagues in the truest sense of the word and make working in the Renaissance at Columbia a constant source of pleasure and pride. Though others mentioned here cannot be held liable for the book's deficiencies, Peter Stallybrass cannot get off so easily; he has inspired, encouraged, provoked, instructed (and, truth be told, often distracted) me as this book lurched toward completion, and I feel confident that most of the book's limitations are somehow his fault.

Other friends provided wonderful occasions to present early versions of this material and to be introduced to other intellectual communities: Marge Garber, Al Braunmuller, David Simpson, Peter Lake, Jennifer Low, Richard McCoy, Steven Pincus, and Roy Ritchie; and further afield, David Trotter in London, Peter Holland in Stratford, Peter Madsen and Niels Hansen in Copenhagen, Daniel Vitkus in Cairo, and István Géher in Budapest (who in fact is responsible for the form the book has assumed). My current and former students, too, have had a significant role in the development of this book, sharing with me the exploration of new interests and reminding me of the enduring delights of academic life. All are remembered fondly, but among those who should be remembered publicly are Heidi Brayman, Douglas Brooks, Pat Cahill, Alan Farmer, William Kolbrener, Jesse Lander, Zachary Lesser, and Chloe Wheatley, indeed "young titans," as they were correctly deemed.

Earlier versions of some materials here have previously been published: a version of chapter 1 appeared in *Textus* 9 (1997): 357–74; a version of chapter 3 in *Shakespeare Studies* 24 (1996): 26–33; a version of chapter 6 in *Shakespeare Quarterly* 37 (1986): 459–75; a version of chapter 7 in *Shakespeare Left and Right*, ed. Ivo Kamps (New York and London: Routledge, 1991), pp. 241–58; a version of chapter 8 in *Renaissance Drama* 24 (1995): 101–21; and a version of chapter 10 in *Critical Essays on Shakespeare's "The Tempest,"* ed. Alden and Ginger Vaughan (New York: G.K. Hall, 1998), pp. 91–106. I thank the publishers of this material for permission to use it here in its revised form. I also wish to thank Bill Germano for his faith in this project and for his patience.

ONE

Introduction

> It is . . . far from the case that the search for intelligibility
> comes to an end in history as though this were its terminus.
> Rather, it is history that serves as the point of departure of
> any quest for intelligibility.
>
> −Claude Lévi-Strauss

Introduction: Reading Shakespeare Historically

This is a book about reading Shakespeare historically—or, more precisely, a book about a particular way of reading Shakespeare historically.[1] It is a book about the forms in which Shakespeare's plays circulated, about the imaginative and institutional circumstances in which they were produced, and about what kinds of meanings were generated as the plays were experienced by their audiences and readers. There are other ways of reading Shakespeare historically; other histories may matter to us, not least, of course, our own. Shakespeare's plays are always situated in and saturated by history. History marks the texts as they are set forth, and the texts continue to absorb new histories as they are performed and read. But this book would restore Shakespeare's artistry to the earliest conditions of its realization and intelligibility: to the collaborations of the theater in which the plays were acted, to the practices of the book trade in which they were published, to the unstable political world of late Tudor and early Stuart England in which the plays were engaged by their various publics.

Perhaps it is, or should be, self-evident why one might wish to do this, but Shakespeare has, almost from the beginning, been thought uniquely able to resist such readings, his putative universality rendering them almost insultingly reductive. It was not the nineteenth century that first thought him timeless, imagining him, with Coleridge, "of no age,"[2] or even the memorializing efforts of the 1623 folio, which, with Ben Jonson, were within seven years of his death proclaiming that he was "not of an age but for all time." While Shakespeare lived, his immortality was already being celebrated: the title-page of the 1609 *Sonnets* declared him "OUR EVER-LIVING POET." Certainly if any poet has a claim to be "ever-living" it is no doubt Shakespeare. The most familiar cliché of Shakespeare studies is that he is our contemporary, though the truth is that, somewhat like the promiscuous Hero of Claudio's tortured imagination, he has been everyone's contemporary.

Every age since Shakespeare's death seems to have claimed him as its own. He is now one of our playwrights, exactly as in the eighteenth and nineteenth centuries he was one of theirs. Any examination of the theatrical repertory would prove this. But though he does live on in subsequent cultures in ways none of his contemporaries do, it is not, I think, because he is in any significant sense timeless, speaking some otherwise unknown, universal idiom. Rather, it seems to me it is because he is so intensely of his own time and place. His engagement with his world is the most compelling record we have of that world's struggle for meaning and value. If he is miraculously able to "looke / Fresh to all Ages," as Leonard Digges claimed in the first folio, it is because he enables each age to see for itself what it has been, and, in measuring its distance from that world, to discover what it has become. In his historical specificity, then, we discover ourselves as historical beings. As Jonson saw, he is the "Soule of the Age" both before and as the condition of being "for all time."[3]

What value Shakespeare has for us must, then, at least begin with the recognition of his difference from us; only then can we be sure that what we hear are his concerns rather than the projections of our own. Other minds have moral relevance for us only when we recognize them as other minds. This is perhaps justification enough for wanting to read Shakespeare historically: history functions as some apotropaic fetish to ward off our narcissism, or at least to prevent the premature imposition of present day interests and values. (The important word here is, of course, "premature"; some such imposition is inevitable and indeed desirable.) The effort to read Shakespeare historically seeks to restore his works to the specific imaginative and material circumstances in which they were written and engaged. It would rescue the works from a history-annihilating focus that, in the name of their greatness, isolates the plays from the actual conditions of their production and reception, thus mystifying their achievement even as it is proclaimed. To read Shakespeare historically would be to read the plays with a robust sense of their particularity and contingency—that is, to read them as Shakespeare's plays, even if that means that they cannot be his alone.

Yet, ironically, the most powerful and productive recent critical models of a historical engagement with Shakespeare—those critical practices that either wear by choice or have had attached to them the labels of New Historicism and Cultural Materialism—have been regularly charged with exactly the narcissism that history should counter. Their historical readings seem to some too overtly self-interested to be compelling as historical accounts, significant more as records of our present needs and anxieties than as reconstructions of those of Shakespeare's time.

This paradox emerges, I would say, not from their historical naïveté but from their theoretical sophistication, which forces them to acknowledge the situatedness of the critic as it determines the questions that are asked of the past. Thus, their "presentist" commitments are not only visible from the first but also part of their very understanding of how the past is logically conceivable. Older historicisms found it simpler to pretend that their constructions were limpid, objective accounts of the past, unfiltered by the interests of the observer. But the past is never just there to be interrogated; indeed, its absence is precisely what makes it past and what insists that our knowledge of it be inescapably partial, in both senses of the word, products both of the traces that have survived and of the shaping concerns of those who study them.

Even at this late date, I will happily confess to admiring and still learning from the New Historicism. Nonetheless, if New Historicism can be understood as a discrete and coherent critical practice, I do not think that it is what I am doing here. I have always understood my work as involved in a somewhat different, though clearly related, project (something that Peter Stallybrass and I, usually gleefully, have come to think of as "The New Boredom"). In part, the difference may amount to little more than a greater delight in particularity, exactly what Adorno criticized in Benjamin as "the wide-eyed presentation of mere facts."[4] I confess, however, that I would always rather be on the side of Benjamin than on Adorno's, situated somewhere near the very "crossroads of magic and positivism" that made Adorno so uncomfortable.

At that crossroads, even the assembly of "mere facts" has value, if only by adding an arresting resolution to the cultural outline. It is, however, a particular elaboration of facts that interests me here, not, as Adorno sought, with the goal of recovering the structures of "the total social process," but with a desire to clarify the relations of text and culture that New Historicism often occludes. In its often dazzling demonstrations of the circulation of discourses through culture, New Historicism has rarely paid much attention to the specific material and institutional conditions of the discursive exchanges it has explored. Its idea of representation is a dynamic cultural semiosis, but one too often lacking both a convincing account of how a text actually enters and exists in the world and any sustained attention to what Roger Chartier calls "the effect, in terms of meaning, that its material forms produced."[5] In the very process of relocating literature from a hermetic literary history into the dense cultural system in which it is seen to function, New Historicism too often re-mystifies it as an effect of discourse, alienating the works it studies from the enabling forms in which they were encountered.

It is this exact tendency that I think has given rise to a familiar critique of its practices: the charge of its abstraction and idealization of power. A sharper focus on the material relations of discourse to the world in which it circulates would give its cultural analysis more historical purchase, fixing it more firmly in relation to the actual producers and consumers of those discourses, locating it, that is, in the world of lived history. Only then is discourse truly enlivened, recognized as a product of human desire and design.

This is what this book hopes to do: to examine Shakespeare's plays as they appeared and circulated both as drama and as texts. Such a focus would see the plays no less as social facts than as aesthetic forms, their meanings products of the density of intentions that saturate them. This is not to evade or dismiss the evidence of Shakespeare's artistry, only to recognize that it is not alone sufficient for the realization of his plays. They came into being not merely as products of Shakespeare's unrivaled imagination but as the result of the sustaining activities of the playhouse and the printing shop, and once in the world they immediately sought attention from the public frequenting the theater and the bookstalls. At every stage, then, Shakespeare's art solicits other intentions that interact with his work to produce the meanings the text conveys. It is the evidence of these richly productive interactions that I would here explore, the evidence of Shakespeare's engagement with his world and of his world's engagement with his work. In these interactions Shakespeare's art becomes literally meaningful, that is, full of meanings deriving not only from Shakespeare's "will" but also from the will of others for whom the plays came importantly, if unpredictably, to matter.

TWO

Demanding History

> It is the critic's job to provide resistances to theory,
> to open it up toward historical reality, toward society,
> toward human needs and interests.
>
> —Edward Said

Chapter 1

Shakespeare after Theory

It has become fashionable, in some circles anyway, to claim that the oft-lamented death of literature—if not the imminent decline of the West itself—has been caused by recent developments in literary studies. Deconstruction, Marxism, Feminism, Cultural Materialism, post-Freudianism have been lumped together as a "School of Resentment,"[1] and regularly identified as the potent destroyers of the literary culture, guilty of politicizing familiar texts and alienating them and critical discourse from the reading public. What apparently is at risk is not merely our habits of reading but our very way of life.

"What we are facing," in the words of an anxious critic, "is nothing less than the destruction of the fundamental premises that underlie both our conception of liberal education and a liberal democratic polity."[2] Seemingly, the barbarians are not at the gate but tenured within the university's ivy-covered walls. "Visigoths in tweed," was Dinesh D'Souza's apoplectic phrase for new critical modes that are seen to imperil the fundamental values upon which Western civilization has been built.[3]

"Theory" is the umbrella term for the perceived danger, naming a category of intellectual interest under which diverse and often contradictory discourses have been homogenized and demonized. Under its unifying rubric, "theory," in this familiar, if somewhat hysterical, account, is seen to attack the great tradition of Western culture (to mix my metaphors) like the crown-of-thorns starfish ravaging the great barrier reef. Theory thrives, we are repeatedly told, only in the polluted waters of the modern academy, sucking the life from common sense, intelligibility, and objectivity. It is held responsible not only for the decline of literary culture but also for the decay of the moral life, and for the disappearance of the very idea of a common humanity.

What always confuses me in these conservative attacks on theory is that they oscillate between what seem obviously incompatible claims, condemning it at once for its insidious and subversive power yet also for its insignificance and laughable unintelligibility. Theory is both self-indulgent posturing, as some have argued, a modern scholasticism important only in the low-stakes game of academic prestige, and a potent cultural agent, a terrifying assault on cultural tradition and authority. It seems, then, that theory is bad both because no one outside the small and self-congratulatory community of theorists understands or cares about its abstruse formulations and because it successfully undermines the claims that great books and their once sustaining truths make upon us. The contradiction seems a little like the old joke about the restaurant that should be avoided because the food is so very bad and the portions so very small.

But the contradiction suggests also that theory cannot be held responsible for the demise of literature. Indeed, the often distorted public debate about theory has given literary studies a prominence they have not often had or even desired. In fact, within literary studies, it is only in the arguments of and about theory that a strenuous and sustained consideration of cultural value has taken place at all. The truth is that literature lost its cultural authority, not as super-subtle theoreticians raised questions about the indeterminacy of

meaning or as they insisted that the very category of literature was historically constructed, but as the book has declined in our society as the predominant
source of information and entertainment, replaced by the enormous mass
appeal of electronic media. Theorists did not make that happen, and theorists
could not have prevented it from happening. Theorists, for the most part,
hardly noticed that it had happened at all, still stuck, for all their passionate
oppositional energy, in the paradigms and protocols of an increasingly marginal literary culture.

Indeed, the pervasive nostalgia for a time when the great books of Western
literature were widely read and valued, somehow guaranteeing the worth of
the societies in which they flourished, that time before literature's "death,"
may be, like most nostalgias, the desire for a paradise not lost but for one that
never was. By 1833, Carlyle already had concluded despairingly: "all art is
but a reminiscence now."[4] Democratic society has always at best uncomfortably accommodated elite culture. About the time of Carlyle's cranky pro-
nouncement, Tocqueville was calling America "the civilized country in which
literature is least attended to," though books were written and purchased in
great number. "In aristocracies readers are fastidious and few in number," he
generalized; "in democracies they are far more numerous and far less difficult
to please....The ever increasing crowd of readers and their continual craving
for something new insures the sale of books which nobody much esteems."[5]

Ignoring the politics of Tocqueville's tendentious "nobody," the recognition that high art will be marginalized in the mass culture seems hardly a surprising or profound insight, but it is worth noting that it does expose a fault
line in the thinking of those who would have the democratic values of the
West shaped and guaranteed by the great books. Whether we like it or not,
the Western canon of elite literature speaks neither to nor for most of the
world's people; I am sad to say, it speaks neither to nor for most people in
North America or in Europe. The forms of high culture are increasingly alien
and inaccessible to their lives, and the insistent claims made for the universality of the great books are belied by the limited audience they find.

The right-wing critique of theory as an attack on democratic traditions
and rationality itself is, for the most part, disingenuous and inaccurate, mask-
ing a political agenda that is uncomfortable with theory's awareness of and
emphasis on the political interests that literature can and does serve. But if
theory cannot reasonably be held responsible for the death of literature, or
the decay of Western civilization, or any of the thousand natural shocks that

both flesh and culture are heir to, another critique of theory is possible and indeed necessary at this time.

First, one needs to acknowledge that "theory" is, of course, only *institutionally* singular. Intellectually it is obviously plural.[6] Theory is actually always theor*ies*, a heterogeneous collocation of paradigms and interests that more or less comfortably cohabit under the same institutional roof but that more often than not are intellectually contradictory and incompatible. Yet if outside the academy theory has been homogenized to enable the anxious narrative of its attack upon Western civilization, from within it has often been similarly homogenized, usually to enable a counter-narrative of how Western civilization might be saved from its own darker side. Theory courses and theory textbooks regularly group together differing explanatory models with no acknowledgment of their contradictions and usually with no effort to reconcile them in any way that might justify the inclusivity. Arguably, theory so conceived can do little significant work beyond naming a space of affiliated intellectual interest and ideological concern.

Nonetheless, driven by a necessarily overdetermined set of institutional and intellectual purposes and pressures, sometime in the 1970s, theory was transformed from a minor and arcane subspeciality into a compelling, if not completely coherent, subject in its own right, with imperial intellectual ambitions and substantial institutional prestige. Theorists replaced the new critics (who had supplanted the literary historians, who had in their turn superseded the philologists, who had themselves succeeded the teachers of oratory) at the cutting edge of the profession. In the face of the apparently irresistible attractions of theory—not least that it was an obvious growth industry—literary studies began aggressively chasing after theory, devaluing, if not actually abandoning, its traditional areas of knowledge (like prosody or the rise of the novel) in favor of abstract meta-critical interests that claimed priority as general accounts of literature's underlying conditions of meaning. Exegesis gave way to hermeneutics.

The success of theory (conceived by some, of course, not as success at all but as the *trahison des clercs*) was in large part achieved and rationalized by virtue of its raising the stakes of literary study that had, at least since the Cold War, seemed a decidedly secondary and "soft" discipline, its judgments subjective and its appeal narrowly elite. It did so first, in its structuralist phase, by claiming the intellectual authority of a disinterested science, as it moved away from readings of individual texts to an exploration of the basic grammar of literature itself, the elemental and invariable laws by which its individual semiotic units were combined into meanings; and then in its poststructural phase, by claiming the moral authority of a committed politics, repudiating structuralism's scientific claims in its recognition of "the involvement of culture in political power" and theory itself as a significant political practice, emancipatory and efficacious, "the continuation of radical politics by other means," as Terry Eagleton has enthusiastically asserted.[7]

But if poststructural theory's insistence that cultural representations are unstable and motivated, that is, incapable of being effectively isolated from the specific circumstances of their production or interpretation, is compelling, its own impassioned claim to political consequence is less convincing. The assertion of what no doubt is true, that what had been assumed to be objective literary facts are actually produced by an interested and subjective value system is not necessarily itself a political act, or is so only by an attenuation of the very idea of politics. And if the logical flaw is apparent on which one main pillar of theory's claim to political consequence rests, the experiential limitation of the claim is no less unsettling, if only from the depressing evidence of how few people care. This is not, however, to denigrate either political commitments or literary theory, only to say that if literary theory is political it is always uncertainly and only indirectly so. If one's ultimate goal is to address the massive evidence of the unequal distribution of wealth and power that is so poignantly available in all parts of the world, publishing an essay in *Critical Inquiry* or *Textual Practice* seems a remarkably indirect and ineffective way of pursuing it. I am not arguing that the academy is an insignificant site of politics, only that literary theory is for the most part isolated from the more significant scenes of political action that exist both above and below its place of articulation.

If theory cannot, then, be accurately condemned as the potent destroyer of Western rationality or enthusiastically embraced as a significantly liberatory political practice, it has decisively rewritten our understanding of cultural signification, a rewriting with profound effects for literary studies. It has appropriately challenged the largely unexamined and naturalized categories of literary analysis, including the category of literature itself. If the author is not actually dead, authorial intention has been recognized as only one of the multiple and often contradictory intentions involved in the text's production; if texts do not in fact allow a total free play of meaning, meaning has been revealed as inevitably plural, "*meanings*" that emerge from the contest over the text's representations; if there is a world of agents and agency "outside of the text," it is nonetheless a world that is largely structured and apprehended in language; and if literature is not an indiscriminate field of signification, including all verbal artifacts, it has importantly been revealed as a historically constructed and historically specific field of interests and values that has changed and will continue to change over time.

However, if theory has successfully spoken the previously unspoken assumptions of literary studies, exposing the mystifications and naturalizations of writing and reading practices that are neither universal nor inevitable, it finally cannot, in its own terms, offer convincing alternatives. Theory can complicate and contest the categories of analysis, but the clarification and correction of those categories, the necessary specification of "the processes by which meaning and value are produced and grounded,"[8] can come only through historical scholarship. If, for example, we take as serious and significant the now standard theoretical claim about the limitations of authorial intention as a determinant of literary meaning, a proper response seemingly must shift the investigation to a materialist rather than a theoretical mode. The original error, naïvely idealizing the category of authorship, was in fact a theoretical one, although usually it has been unrecognized as such but remains, of course, no less theoretical for being so. It is only when the book is dematerialized by assumptions of a literary study that would isolate literary meaning from the enabling forms in which it always and only appears that such a claim for the exclusivity of authorial intention could be made at all.

Once one attends to how books are actually produced and reproduced, the fantasy of authorship that theory would contest is apparent. Indeed, put in its baldest form, whatever authors do, they, as Roger Stoddard insists, do not write books.[9] They do *write*, of course—itself a complexly social act—but what they write are manuscripts or typescripts that get turned into books only with the introduction and interference of any number of new agents and intentions. Editors, censors, publishers, designers, printers, binders all interfere with the author's text before it appears as a printed book, and their multiple and often contradictory agencies are necessarily registered in the text's signifying surface.

Whatever else it implies, this obviously is an argument for the necessity of returning literary studies to history, albeit a history that must itself be inflected by the theoretical initiatives that I've been discussing, aware that the approach to the past can neither be value-free nor immediate. It could be argued that exactly such a return has already been announced and realized in the New Historicism; but New Historicism is neither new enough nor historical enough to serve. New Historicism sees itself as cultural history (or certainly as the "cultural poetics" with which it vainly tried to rename itself). At the heart of its project is the refusal of the traditional isolation of the aesthetic from the material domain, the segregation of art from history, indeed to see these arenas as, in fact, intersecting and in some sense mutually constituting, insisting that literature is at once socially produced and socially productive.

It is an attractive and exhilarating position, though not, it must be said, self-evidently true. This heady claim of reciprocity has never been subjected to serious scrutiny. It is merely asserted and rhetorically, rather than logically, reinforced. No doubt to register the dynamic, if unstable, relations it posits between literature and the culture in which it is produced, New Historicism almost reflexively falls into chiasmic formulation ("the historicity of texts and the textuality of history," in its most telling example), as well as its notorious anecdotalism with its habitual gesture toward historic specificity ("On May 13, 1542. . ."), offering some bizarre incident as the point of generation of a cultural principle that is then discovered in a canonical text. Even a critic as sympathetic to its project as Walter Cohen has complained that its practitioners are "likely to seize on something out of the way, obscure, even bizarre: popular or aristocratic festivals, denunciations of witchcraft, sexual treatises, diaries and autobiographies, descriptions of clothing, reports on disease, birth and death records, accounts of insanity."[10] The response to this charge would, of course, be that these texts and events are significant symbolic and material articulations of a culture and that to see them as "obscure, even bizarre" is merely to reveal how inadequately narrow is our conception of the cultural field.

If indeed we must welcome the expansion of the cultural field to include the extra-literary (as well as the accompanying reminder that boundaries of the literary itself are always under challenge and construction), it is interesting that at least one seventeenth-century historian proleptically voiced Cohen's concern. John Trussell, in his *Continuation* (1636) of Samuel Daniel's *History of England*, proudly acknowledges that in the writing of history he has

pared off these superfluous exuberances, which like Wennes upon a beautifull face, disgrace the otherwise gracefull comlinesse of the countenance, I meane, 1. Matters of Ceremony, as Coronations, Christenings, Marriages, Funeralls, solemne Feasts, and such like. 2. matters of Triumph, as Tiltings, Maskings,

Barriers, Pageants, Gallefoists, and the like. 3. Matters of Noveltie, as great inundations, sudden rising and falling of prizes of Corne, strange Monsters, Iustice done on petty offenders, and such like executions, with which the *Cacoethes* of the Writers of those time have mingled matters of state. (sig. A4ʳ)

Trussell's list of "superfluous exuberances" uncannily seems drawn straight from the pages of new historicist scholarship, and the exclusions he boasts of would deny it precisely that material that has brought it so much attention, indeed deny the focus that signals its practice as "new." Yet for Trussell, history, which as he says "is or ought to bee *a perfect register of things formerly done truely*" (sig. A3ᵛ), is essentially concerned with "matters of state." New Historicism, on the other hand, along with a variety of other new historical interests, insists that history is not identical with the history of national politics, realizing that the history of national politics inevitably and purposefully erases other histories–histories of women, children, the poor, for example–histories whose very existence would contest the story the hegemonic state would tell of itself.

The anecdote does acknowledge these alternative histories, but it does so, too often, only to retotalize the culture. The aberrant, the marginal, the local, the particular are appropriated and homogenized into a unitary culture that effectively contains, in that resonant New Historicist pun, multiple, heterogeneous, and contradictory social and psychological sites. If the anecdote truly represented something aberrant it would be less readily assimilable either by the dominant culture or by the critical practices that explore it, but the unremarked procedure assumes (and, it could be said, *produces* in the very terms of its conceptualization) a society in which nothing is truly variant or discontinuous. The anecdote clearly functions here not as evidence but as trope–a synecdoche–assuming, as the very condition of its functioning, the precise thing it would demonstrate: that the part *can* stand for the whole, that the culture is radically coherent (usually by virtue of its saturation in power); and this inescapable coherence then permits, in fact insists upon, the familiar chiasmic relation of the discursive and the historical which is then triumphantly announced.[11]

That these New Historicist procedures yield so easily to formal analysis suggests what I think is true about them: that they are not properly historical at all but rather formalist practices, discovering pattern and order, unity and coherence, in the culture (which is revealingly imagined and engaged as a "text," even if a "social text") exactly as an earlier generation of formalist critics found them in works of literature, each tending to idealize the form they discover, ignoring the disruptive power of the dissonances and stresses they would have it neatly resolve. New Historicism takes its name in contradistinction to the New Criticism it would and did replace, but the name unwittingly announces their similarities. Drawing on Clifford Geertz's integrative concept of culture, New Historicism found social life to be every bit as well wrought as any poem, shaped and sutured by a common set of symbols and codes.[12] For all of its "density of specification," New Historicism is finally insufficiently historical, both in subject and methodology, and arguably insufficiently "new" in its refusal or inability to theorize its work.[13] If, as one enthusiastic practitioner has written, it "combats an empty formalism by pulling historical considerations to the center stage,"[14] it could also fairly be said to articulate and activate a new, even if arguably richer formalism, by presuming the very reticulations of literature and history that it seeks to demonstrate.

What I am arguing for as a more productive role of literary studies is a set of interests and procedures more rigorously historical than recent theory-driven studies have been, but that, unlike the old literary history, takes to heart (and to mind) the implications of the theoretical movements of the last twenty years. "Theory's day is dying," announced Stanley Fish a bit prematurely more than a decade ago,[15] but I do believe that now its day has passed, that we are in what theorists might term a post-theoretical moment. The great age of theory is over (and evidence, if it is needed, might be gathered from the MLA job listings from which "theory" jobs, after a proliferation in the early 1980s, have now virtually disappeared), but not because theory has been discredited; on the contrary, it is precisely because its claims have proven so compelling and productive.

In exposing the mystifications that have dominated our categories of literary analysis, theory has now brought us to the point where we must begin to respond to its significant challenges, not by producing more theory but more facts, however value-laden they will necessarily be, that will reveal the specific historical conditions that have determined the reading and writing of literature. If theory has convincingly demonstrated that meaning is not immanent but rather situational, or, put differently, that both reading and writing are not unmediated activities but take place only and always in context and action, the specific situations, contexts and actions—that is, the actual historical circumstances of literary production and reception—cannot merely be gestured at but must be recovered and analyzed.

If we think for a moment about the apparent *sine qua non* of literary study, the text, perhaps this becomes clear. "Text" is–or at least was, until academic usage thoroughly normalized it–itself a contested word, entering literary studies from linguistic theory. It replaced the common sense words, "book" or "work," with the structuralist term that exploited its etymology from the Latin for "web" or "woven" to suggest its existence, in Barthes's phrase, as a "triumphant plural," always complexly implicated in the multiple linguistic and discursive contexts that it intersects and is intersected by. If the word "book" suggests the literary work's integrity and autonomy, the word "text" suggests its radical interdependency and indeterminacy. Theory's suggestive claim, however, cannot be demonstrated *at the level of theory*. Only historically does the claim become compelling and reveal the way in which the very idea of a text's integrity and autonomy depends upon an impossible idealization of the processes of composition and publication. Modern editors and publishers do produce *books*, coherent physical objects that offer themselves as complete and autonomous, but their coherence is achieved by erasing the evidence of the multiple and often contradictory intentions (even those of a single author) that in fact produced them, evidence that historical scholarship can at least partially recover and restore to view.

The oft-proclaimed "death of the author"[16] might direct our efforts here, but not in the context of literary theory's insistence upon the text's defiant plurality of meaning. The notorious phrase becomes intelligible rather than merely provocative in the recovery of the actual discourses that circulate around and through the text as well as the historically specific conditions of its writing and circulation, both of which must inevitably compromise and disperse any simple notion of authorial intention. Both discursively and materially, authorship is revealed to be more problematic–that is, at once less single and more constrained–than our conventional notions of artistic autonomy and authorial intention would allow.

The author is, of course, not dead (the theoretical claim to the contrary hardly worth the effort of refutation and spectacularly rendered fatuous by the Ayatollah's *fatwah* pronounced against Salman Rushdie in 1989). But if we must, of course, grant that the author is a historical agent and no mere instrument or effect of a linguistic order, we must also recognize that the author is not autonomous and sovereign, neither the solitary source nor the sole proprietor of the meanings that circulate through the text. This is not to dismiss or denigrate the claims of authorship, only to observe that the act of writing is inevitably fettered and circumscribed. An author writes always and only within specific conditions of possibility, both institutional and imaginative, connecting the individual talent to preexisting modes of thought, linguistic rules, literary conventions, social codes, legal restraints, material practices, and commercial conditions of production.

Shakespeare has emerged in the English literary tradition virtually as the iconic name for authorship itself, but increasingly it is clear that his own literary career strikingly resists the very notions of artistic authority and autonomy that his name has come triumphantly to represent. His playwrighting radically testifies to the multiplication of intentions within the actual conditions of production and to his own lack of interest in the individuating forms of literary authority that modern ideas of authorship assume. Shakespeare, of course, had no specifically literary and small financial interest in his plays. He wrote scripts to be performed, scripts that once they were turned over to the company no longer belonged to him in any legal sense and that immediately escaped his literary authority and control. He oversaw the printing and publication of none of his plays, nor did he hold a copyright on any. Although he prospered in his theatrical career, his money came neither from commissions nor from royalties on his plays but from his entitlement as a "sharer" in the acting company to one-tenth of its profits.

Except that as experienced actor and sharer in the company he could no doubt exert influence over production in a way an independent playwright could not, Shakespeare's relation to the plays he wrote was in no way unusual. In spite of Ben Jonson's efforts to establish his plays as a form of high culture, plays remained subliterary, the piece work of an emerging popular entertainment industry. "Riffe raffe" and "baggage bookes" Thomas Bodley would call them in 1612 and order his librarian, Thomas James, not to collect such "idle bookes" in order to protect his library against the "scandal" that would accrue to it from their presence.[17]

Plays were not autonomous and self-contained literary objects but provisional scripts for performance, inevitably subjected to the multiple collaborations of production both in the playhouse and in the printing house, where, of course, actors, prompters, collaborators, annotators, revisers, copyists, compositors, printers, and proofreaders all would have a hand in shaping the play-text. Even at the level of authorship, although printed title-pages, when indeed they indicate the playwright, tend to attribute single authority to their texts, account books reveal how rarely the plays have an "onlie begetter": nearly two-thirds of the plays listed in Henslowe's diary either begin as collaborations or have additions or revisions undertaken by other writers as companies sought to keep their property current.[18] Indeed, the only manuscript of Shakespeare's playwrighting that has apparently survived, the socalled "Hand D" of the manuscript of *The Booke of Sir Thomas More*, bears witness, if the hand is indeed Shakespeare's own, to Shakespeare as collaborator, merely one of five playwrights that combine in the writing of the play (although, significantly, modern editions of Shakespeare's works ironically have tended to remove him from the collaborative context of this playwrighting by isolating the contribution of "Hand D" from the complete manuscript, reproducing, transcribing, and editing it alone).

Plays were generally written on demand for acting companies, and the completed play-text then belonged to the company that commissioned it. Inductions and epilogues speak regularly of the play not as the author's but as "ours," property and product of the players. And the playwright himself is no less their possession: "our poet" or "our bending author," as the epilogue to *Henry V* has it, an author "bending" not only to the artistic challenges of the material but to the assignment set for him by his contractors, who were then free to treat his creation as they saw fit.

Under certain circumstances, and with no necessary regard for the author's wishes or interests, the companies would sell the rights to a play to a publisher, though publication of play-texts was more the exception than the rule. Whereas about 40 percent of the *known* plays in the period from 1575 to 1642 were published, in all the percentage must have been much lower. Indeed, perhaps as few as one in ten plays written for the companies ever appeared in print. Between June 1594 and June 1595, for example, the Admiral's men introduced eighteen new plays. If we can assume this to be something like a representative rate, between one hundred and fifty and two hundred new plays would be introduced in a decade; but in the ten years between 1595 and 1605, only twelve plays associated with the Admiral's men were in fact published.

Our explanations for this phenomenon usually have emphasized the putative value of the scripts to the players, who are imagined jealously guarding their property from predatory publishers eager to make a quick profit from the sale of playbooks. There are, in fact, a few examples of companies actively opposing publication of their plays, most notably the successful effort of the

King's men to prevent a collection of ten of Shakespeare's plays (actually eight by Shakespeare and two, *The Yorkshire Tragedy* and *Sir John Oldcastle*, falsely attributed to him) that Thomas Pavier and William Jaggard attempted to publish in 1619.[19] The reluctance to bring plays into print, however, seems to rest more with their potential publishers than with the acting companies. Far from a reliable shortcut to wealth for publishers, plays were risky business ventures, as Peter Blayney has shown: "no more than one play in five would have returned the publisher's initial investment inside five years. Not one in twenty plays published would have paid for itself during its first year."[20]

If publishers, therefore, were understandably reluctant to print plays (and it should be remembered that on average no more than six a year were printed), the acting companies were indeed themselves generally unenthusiastic about the circulation of their property in published form. In 1608, the articles of association of the King's Revels players explicitly barred its members from publishing any of the company's plays, though it is worth noting that within the year a number of their plays were registered for publication and also the company soon broke up. The actors "thinke it against their peculiar profit to haue them come in print," as Heywood writes generally of play-texts in the preface to *The English Traveller*, presumably, however, less from fear of losing audiences to readers than to prevent other companies from gaining access to their repertory (though there is little evidence of repertorial piracy among companies apart from the notorious episode, recounted in its induction, of *The Malcontent* being acted by the King's men in retaliation for the Children of Chapel's theft of *Jeronimo*).

Yet when a play was printed it was usually, as its title-page often announces, "as it hath been lately acted," or "as it was played," not an authorial text but a theatrical version, whose textual authority and commercial appeal derived not from the playwright but from the company of actors who performed it.[21] Where authors' names were present on title-pages, the theatrical auspices are still as likely as not to be included, while the authorial ascriptions, though becoming ever more common through the seventeenth century, are not necessarily reliable or inclusive attributions of intellectual property. The title-page of *The Yorkshire Tragedy* (1608), for example, declares that it was "*Written by* W. Shakespeare"; *The Witch of Edmonton* (1658) assigns the writing of the play to "divers well-esteemed Poets; *William Rowley, Thomas Dekker, John Ford,* &c"; and an edition of Marston's *The Malcontent* (1604) thoroughly confuses the issue of authorship in its choice of verb assignments,

claiming on its title-page to be "Augmented by *Marston./* With the Additions
played by the Kings/ Maiesties Servants./ Written by *Ihon Webster.*"

Whatever the title-page assertions, the literary ambitions of playwrights
were rarely a factor in publication. (Ben Jonson is, of course, the exception
that proves the rule, the 1616 folio's characteristic "The Author, B. I." on its
individual title-pages revealingly anomalous; indeed, until the 1630s, Jonson
is the only performed playwright identified as an "author" on a title-page.[22])
The conditions of playwriting alone militated against literary tradition. Plays
were written quickly to fulfill the demands of the theatrical repertory
(Heywood, for example, claims in his preface of *The English Traveller* that it
was but one of "two hundred and twenty, in which I haue had either an entire
hand, or at least a maine finger"); and the very nature of play production
denies the playwright any exclusive claim upon the finished product, denies,
in the fluidity of performance, even any firm sense that the product could ever
be finished.

Nonetheless, this is not to say that playwrights were indifferent to the
appearance of their work in print. While it is true that, other than the example of Jonson, there is little evidence of dramatists being interested in publication much before 1605, numerous seventeenth-century playwrights,
including Chapman, Ford, Glapthorne, Heywood, Marston, Massinger,
Middleton, Shirley, and Webster, oversaw the publication of some of their
work. Some of course apologized for their decision "to commit [their] plaies
to the presse," as Heywood did in his epistle for *The Rape of Lucrece* (1608),
which he claims he agreed to have published only because so many of his
plays had "accidently come into the Printers handes" in texts "so corrupt and
mangled" and printed "in such sauadge and ragged ornaments" that he was
himself "vnable to know them." There is, no doubt, something disingenuous
in the explanation; after nine of his plays had already found their way into
print, Heywood still protests, in his *Apology for Actors* (1612), that he has
"beene euer too iealous of [his] owne weaknesse, willingly to thrust into the
Presse" (sig. A4[r]).

Increasingly, however, playwrights did so thrust, and they did so with the
aim of asserting the integrity of their work against the collaborative claims of
the theater. Barnabe Barnes, for example, contributes a dedication to *The
Devil's Charter* in 1607, and the title-page, which announces that the play was
performed before the King by "his Maiesties Seruants," also insists that the
printed text has been "exactly reuewed, corrected, and augmented since by

the Author, for themore pleasure and profit of the Reader." And Webster insists on including a marginal note in the 1623 quarto of *The Duchess of Malfi* opposite the italic setting of the song of the churchmen: "The Author disclaimes this Ditty to be his" (sig. H2^r).

Shakespeare never displays this sense of artistic propriety. He seems to work comfortably within the collaborative economies of the theater, never purposefully turning to print to assert or clarify his literary achievement. He oversaw none of his plays through the press, and his name did not even appear on a title-page until 1598, when Cuthbert Burby included it on the title-page of his quarto of *Love's Labour's Lost*. Shakespeare's name gradually did come to mark the editions of his plays. The title-page of the 1598 quarto of part one of *Henry IV*, for example, did not include his name, but the next edition in 1599 declares that it was "Newly corrected by *W. Shakespeare*." The assertion, however, does not establish Shakespeare's artistic authority over this new edition. The edition is a mere reprint of the earlier one, and the claim of its addition of its author's name, is a marketing tactic designed to promote sales. It seems to have been successful, because *1 Henry IV* was an early bestseller, appearing in seven editions before the folio of 1623. But other plays of Shakespeare succeeded in the bookstalls without his name gracing their title-pages. *Henry V*, for example, appears in two editions (1600 and 1602), and again in the "Pavier" quarto of 1619 and falsely dated 1608, without Shakespeare's name.

Shakespeare appears on early title-pages not as an affirmation of his artistic or legal authority over the text but merely when publishers believed his name would help sell books. When, for example, Nathaniel Butter's "Pide Bull" quarto of *King Lear* emblazoned Shakespeare's name across the title-page in a type face substantially larger than any other, it may seem that the modern author has fully emerged and is being celebrated in its most heroic form; but Shakespeare's name functions on that title-page less to identify the playwright than to identify the playbook. The "Shake-speare" of the "Pide Bull" title-page is the publisher's Shakespeare, a simulacrum invented to individualize and protect Butter's property (who, incidently, three years earlier had offered *The London Prodigall* as "By William Shakespeare," ironically confirming the claim of the 1622 quarto of *Othello*: "The Authors name is sufficient to vent his work"–at least if the name is "Shakespeare" whether or not the "work" is indeed his own).

The category of authorship remains understandably precious to

Shakespeareans (and the recent emphasis upon revision seems a way of attempting to preserve it from the evidence of multiple texts[23]), but it is only by attending to the actual conditions of playwrighting in early modern England that the historical Shakespeare can be saved either from the mystifications of idealist criticism or from the no less mystifying moves of poststructural theory, where instead of disappearing into the putative unity and self-sufficiency of form he would disappear into the assumed priority of the linguistic order itself. Historical scholarship at once disperses and reconstitutes Shakespeare, revealing him to be something more than a product of the text and something less than its exclusive producer. If the conditions of the playhouse and printing house inevitably work to deconstruct and decenter Shakespeare, scattering him in the necessary collaborations of play and book production, he is, as the title-pages reveal, effectively reconstructed in the early modern bookshop, firmly established by and for commerce. If authors do not write books, at the very least they do, by the early seventeenth century, seemingly enable them to be sold.

Focus on the forms, both symbolic and material, in which the text appears importantly clarifies the claims of authorship and authority. Such a focus insists that the literary work is not monolithically created by an intention but is collaboratively produced within specific conditions of possibility.[24] It seeks to understand the text both as an imaginative construct and a physical artifact, in both aspects a product of multiple intentions that determine its form as well as its meanings. The work of literature cannot be understood as an autonomous, self-sufficient totality, what Pierre Macherey calls "the mythical product of some radical epiphany," for this would be "to isolate it into incomprehensibility,"[25] to deny it any principle of realization. The notion of such self-sufficiency demands an idealization of authorial intention that must find the material text always inadequate, a defective version of what is imagined. Rather, the work of literature might better be understood as an actual product of an author working in (and against) specific discursive and institutional circumstances; and literary study, in turn, might better be defined not as the uncovering of the author's uniquely privileged meaning concealed somehow within the text but as the discovery of the text itself as it speaks the corporate activities that have brought it into being, the "complex social practices," as Margreta de Grazia and Peter Stallybrass write, "that shaped, and still shape, [its] absorbent surface."[26]

Both materially and imaginatively the text is, of course, a product of collaborative energies and exchanges. If its circumstantial materiality obviously involves effective agencies other than the author's, its seemingly essential symbolic dimension is no more a realm of authorial autonomy and freedom. Writing, understood as an imaginative act, is inevitably less an invention than an *inter*vention, a motivated entrance into a preexisting set of linguistic and discursive possibilities. It makes little sense, then, for literary interpretation to assume as its primary task the recovery of an authorial intention, which by definition is insufficient to produce the text (in either its symbolic or material aspect). The author cannot be credibly understood as the sole determining source of the text's meaning, which is produced by multiple impulses and operations, only some of which originate with the author or are even accessible to his (or, belatedly, her) control. Meaning, therefore, should be sought precisely in the webs of engagement that permit a text to be written, printed, circulated, and read. Indeed if authorship is to retain a significant, rather than a merely nominal position in our accounts of literary meaning, it must be restored to its enabling and inhibiting circumstances.

This is not, however, as some would claim, to reject literature for history or to reduce literature to history. It is merely to insist that literature is ineluctably historical; that is, literature is always produced, as well as read (indeed the category itself is always even defined) in historically specific forms of imaginative, discursive, and institutional possibility. Its meanings are not, of course, fixed at the moment of its origination. Imaginative writings, more than other discursive forms, do have the capacity to live on in time, but on each occasion that they are reproduced, reengaged, and reimagined they are so in admittedly different, but no less historically specific terms.

The text's historicity, then, is not to be thought of as a contamination of its essence but as the very condition of its being, a historicity that locates creativity within determinate conditions of realization. Rather than seek to escape this full, complicating historicity by attempting to penetrate the text's signifying surface in search of the author's original intentions (admittedly, themselves a historical fact, however difficult to determine), we should energetically confront that surface, which is, in fact, the only place where the activity of literary production can be engaged. This is not to deny the creativity of the author but rather to understand it; for the material text is where the conditions and constraints of authorship become legible, where its authority is at once asserted and undermined, as the author's dependency upon other agents becomes obvious and the literary object reveals its inevitably multiple histories and significations–histories and significations that in fact extend beyond the text's verbal structure. All aspects of the text's materiality signify and its inescapable materiality is witness to the collaborative nature of the text and textuality.

Such an understanding, however, must necessarily redirect attention away from "the principle of thrift" that is the author[27] to the plenitude implicit in the networks of dependency in which meaning is actually produced. It should, indeed, shift the very axis of the activity of interpretation from the vertical to the horizontal,[28] moving us from a critical practice that would look *through* the surface of the text in search of the authentic–and authorial–meanings supposedly lurking somewhere (where?) below to one that aggressively looks *at* the text, where meanings are in fact collaboratively made and engaged, constructed and contested. This is not, I would insist, to evade the necessity of reading by replacing a fantasy of authorial presence with a new one of self-evident materiality; it is only to clarify what it is that is read. Perhaps, after all, it is true, as Oscar Wilde quipped, that it is only superficial people who do not judge by appearances.

This emphasis upon the dispersal (though not the denial) of authority in the production of literature seems to me both appropriate and useful for Shakespeare scholarship and for literary scholarship in general. It is a way of fully acknowledging authorial intentions while still recognizing that these are never solely determining but necessarily function within a fabric of *other* intentions–not least those of its readers–that motivate and sustain the activity of writing; or, put differently, it is a way of resisting the romantic idealization of authorship as the sovereign source of literary meaning and returning it to the actual collaborative economies that are the essence of all intellectual and social practice. This focus on the sustaining collaborations of Shakespeare's art is not to elevate them above–or to substitute them for–the artistic intelligence, intentions, or should we merely say, *will* of the playwright; though it is to insist that this will becomes manifest only in the context of other wills, other intelligences and intentions, that are obviously necessary to produce the play either on stage or as a book.

Nonetheless, I anticipate three main objections to what I am arguing (and no doubt will be surprised by a number of others): first, that this move beyond theory merely returns literary studies to the positivism of an older, untheoretical historiography. In the face of the growing awareness of the mediated nature of perception and cognition, history can no longer pretend to recover and recount the past "as it actually was," but it need not, therefore, abandon the desire for definitive and usable historical knowledge. Knowledge of the past is, of course, affected by the contingencies of the present, but it does not follow that the past is therefore merely an effect of these. *We* are not the producers of the past; we are only, but not insignificantly, producers of the past *as past*, that is, producers of the meanings the past has for us. The past *exists* (for us now) as we construct it, but of course it *existed* independent of any of our representations; and that existence imposes an obligation upon and value for our constructions. To say that this existence cannot be apprehended except in mediated form—the mediations both of the records that preserve it and the mediations of the interests of the observer—is to say only that it is past, as well as to admit that history, like all other forms of human knowledge, is inevitably contingent but not obviously any more so or any more incapacitatingly than any other act of human understanding.

The second objection is not, in fact, hypothetical but actual (it was raised by a graduate student at a university where I presented an earlier version of this essay): that the approach urged here returns the study of literature to an elitism it has struggled to escape, demanding access to rare book collections and scholarly training. My first response is that it is not elitist nor does it demand elite access to make clear the constructedness of the texts we read, their contingencies that tie them to history. And if the alternative is to ignore the processes and practices by which the literary work is produced and read, we are left with an honorific and toothless formalism that offers in exchange for its apparently democratic principle of access a profound lack of consequence for literary study. Literature that can be apprehended immediately, that is, a literature unaffected by the material and historical formations of either its texts or its readers, is a fantasy of the literary text as self-sufficient and self-contained[29] that would, by virtue of its willful isolation of the text from the necessary conditions of its production, rob it of its actual ties to a social world of meaningful and multiple human agency (and, not incidentally, disturbingly erase that labor from the calculus of literary value).

The final anticipated objection is much simpler and therefore perhaps the most powerful: that the focus on history, even the history of the enabling conditions of literary activity, still deflects attention from the literary text itself. The problem I see with this is largely with the phrase "the literary text itself," for it is that very idealization, that assumed self-sufficiency of the literary object, that set literary studies off in search of theory to begin with. The text itself never exists—that is, it never exists apart from the various materializations that have made it present.

"Texts are worldly," Edward Said has written, "to some degree they are events, and even when they appear to deny it, they are nevertheless a part of the social world, human life and of course the historical moments in which they are located and interpreted."[30] It is, however, only by turning to history from theory that this can be shown to be true and meaningful, that the particular forms and particular effects of a text's "worldliness" can be discovered and demonstrated. A recognition of the historicity of the play—as book and as performance—a focus on the specific conditions of its production and reception, returns it to the world in which and to which it is alive; increasingly, literary criticism is learning that what it attends to are the marks of this worldliness. Reading those marks, recognizing that a play's materializations, in the printing house and in the playhouse, *are* the play's meanings rather than merely passive and sometimes embarrassing conveyors of them, is what I take to be the almost inevitable practice of Shakespeare studies after theory, no longer *chasing* after it but working powerfully and productively in its wake.

> Literature, we may say, must in some sense always be
> an historical study, for literature is an historical art.
>
> —Lionel Trilling

Chapter Two

Are We Being Interdisciplinary Yet?

Several years ago I was invited to participate on a panel at the North American Conference on British Studies. I will confess here to a somewhat unseemly delight in the fact that "real historians" seemed to want to listen what I had to say, but I was surprised to discover that the session was entitled "After the New Historicism."[1] Had this been the meeting of the Midwestern MLA it would not, of course, have been so unexpected, since New Historicism did indeed take root in English studies, and the internal dynamics of the profession made it inevitable that we would soon choose to see ourselves as aggressively "after" rather than merely abjectly belated. (This book is, of course, written "after theory.") But my genial assumption has been that historians have always been less affected by fashion than literary scholars and, more to the point, that to historians the New Historicism little mattered, except perhaps as the source of reassuring evidence that literary scholars don't really understand history, either as a subject or a discipline. Why, then, a group of historians should have cared if or even noticed that we might be now *after* the New Historicism is still not exactly clear to me.

What is, however, clear is that the title, like the makeup, of the panel in Chicago (which included two historians—that is, people teaching in history departments—and two . . . well, what? The absence of an agreed-upon name for the work done by inhabitants of English departments is indeed part of the story here) testifies to a general belief that historians and literary scholars (will that do?) should speak to each other, but also to the conviction that the New Historicism is not the proper meeting ground for that conversation. I do not want to engage here in New Historicism bashing.[2] First of all it is too late in the day for that to matter much; and second, I think that New Historicism in fact has been an unusually healthy and productive commitment in literary studies, restoring literature to a vital relationship to the world in which it is written and read.

Its efforts to register the dynamic, if unstable, relations between literature and the culture that motivates (and in turn is modified by) it should at very least be recognized as a serious attempt to bridge the institutional and intellectual distance that exists between the disciplines. Literature and history often seem to belong to entirely different, if dependent, realms of being. Even when the disciplines reach toward each other they awkwardly miss connection: history becomes an effect of discourse as literature becomes an epiphenomenon of history. Never do the two realms seem to inhabit the same plane of reality. New Historicism, however, took as its project precisely the leveling of this inequality, refusing to segregate the aesthetic from social, economic, and political processes, refusing to isolate the discursive from the material domain, indeed to see them as intersecting and in some sense mutually constituting, to recognize the literary work as at once shaped by and, more actively, shaping the culture in which it is produced.

Nonetheless, New Historicism, for all of its efforts to locate literary texts in relation to social practices and political institutions, has had significant influence only within literary studies. Though its primary commitment is to see the literary text as at once socially produced (thus breaking out of the aestheticism of traditional literary criticism) and socially productive (breaking out of literary studies all together), New Historicist accounts have little affected historians' cultural understandings. In literary studies, of course, they have had unmistakable influence. Though from the first, New Historicism provoked a strong critique from both left and right in the politicized world of English departments, by the mid-1980s it had, nonetheless, supplanted deconstruction as literary study's dominant (i.e., most visible) critical practice, its conspicuous success deriving in no small part from its energetic championing of the very history that deconstruction erased from texts and textuality.

From historians, however, there has been at best indifference, at worst, contempt. Historians apparently don't see its representations as history at all.[3] Usually they dismiss the practices of New Historicism as arbitrary and uninformed, finding its use of evidence cavalier and its understanding of key historical concepts naïve. In truth, for the most part they find literary studies in any of its modes of little disciplinary interest. They generously offer to instruct us (see, for example, Glenn Burgess's gracious offer to help us see "what students of Renaissance literature might gain from a more intimate liaison with their colleagues, the historians"[4]), but they rarely seem to think a more intimate liaison with us might be of consequence for their practice.

Nonetheless, on both sides of the disciplinary divide we usually continue to smile and gesture at each other, much like junior high school students at a school dance, and if the gym of the New Historicism, we now agree, makes too slippery a dance floor for us to meet comfortably, we still engage in our rituals of dread and desire hoping to find a comfortable common ground. On the one hand, literary critics repeat, almost as a mantra, Fredric Jameson's oddly transhistorical imperative, "Always historicize"[5]; and on the other, historians obligatorily echo Hayden White's insistence upon "The Historical Text as Literary Artifact."[6] That is, literary scholars are urged to recognize not only that the works they study are produced and read at particular times and under specific intellectual and institutional conditions that affect their meanings but also—and for Jameson most crucially—that history is both literature's ground and ultimate referent; and historians are led, almost certainly less enthusiastically, to admit that the works they write are not exactly true. The facts they deploy, of course, are true (or they couldn't otherwise be called facts), but obviously the narratives in which these are embedded cannot be said to correspond to something in the past in the same manner as the repre-

sented facts can be. The structure of the history we write can only be "by accident" the same as the reality it would articulate; but, more disconcerting, as
Louis Mink has said, is that we cannot in any case know if it is the same, since
to know it so would require "knowing the structure of historical actuality independently of any representation of it."[7]

But it isn't clear that our disciplinary gestures toward one another have
brought the practices or even the interests of the two disciplines any closer
together. Certainly what has been achieved in rapprochement is not something that can properly be thought of as *interdisciplinary*. It is true that historians have come to see literature as one of the potentially useful archives of
their own study and have increasingly come to recognize the inescapable textuality of both the written records they study and their own historical
accounts. Nonetheless, there is no sense that either the resulting scholarly out-
put or the object of inquiry is, as a result, anything other than what has always
been confidently understood as "history." Similarly, literary scholars have
increasingly (or, more properly, once again[8]) insisted that literary texts are not
autonomous and self-contained, and have sought their meanings not only in
terms of the formal relations of the work itself but also in its necessary connections to a cultural context that the literary work seemingly both requires
and alters. Turning to history to recover these contexts, literary scholars have
often brilliantly connected the internal structures of the literary work to the
wider cultural environment that motivates and sustains it. But the resulting
scholarship, however impressively it may remark and measure the social
energy of a literary work, too often provides less evidence of a commitment
to interdisciplinarity than to a policy of disciplinary *Lebensraum*.[9] Literary
study has relentlessly extended its chosen object of study from literary texts
to textuality to the symbolic operations of culture itself, which is inevitably
imagined as a "cultural text" to justify the aggressive expansion of focus, but
with literature still enthroned as its most compelling and comprehensive
interpreter.

To some degree, of course, the widespread appeal to interdisciplinarity
heard all through the academy is a reflection of our dissatisfaction with the
fragmentation of knowledge, where disciplinary boundary-lines work to segregate amateurs from professionals, and professionals from one another.
Within literary studies, however, the import of the interdisciplinary gesture
may, too often, be recognizable as an unconscious effort on the part of the discipline to retain its own traditional preeminence in the project of a liberal arts

education in the face of the growing difficulty, especially in America, of having the canon of English literature uncritically form its core. However idealistically motivated, the move toward what could be called cultural studies is a canny institutional strategy, possibly preventing departments of English from shrinking in size and prestige as have departments of Religion and Classics that themselves once enjoyed English's centrality in the liberal arts curriculum.

Something truly interdisciplinary, I take it, would expose the limitations of disciplinary knowledge formations and work to undermine the authority of the disciplinary culture of the modern academy, though usually the most successful examples of real interdisciplinary work (say, biochemistry) quickly constitute themselves as new disciplines rather than stand as counterdisciplinary forces. No doubt this is in large part a function of the reward structure of higher education, which generally assigns administrative authority—hence control over curriculum, hiring, and promotion—only to departments. So it isn't entirely clear that interdisciplinarity can survive the institutional contexts in which it must live. But even where interdisciplinary work is encouraged to maintain itself in its intellectual and administrative hybridity, one might at least consider whether it is always a good thing to undertake it, whether every subject will productively yield to the interface of interdisciplinary practices. In general I am all for breaking down the disciplinary boundaries that are less natural structures of intellectual activity than institutional inheritances deriving largely from nineteenth-century German universities; but the commitment to interdisciplinarity has now become as reflexive and sentimental as was the commitment to disciplinary integrity. There may be something still to be said for traditional disciplinary interests and procedures, and, in any case, anything that my dean and provost are so enthusiastic about certainly makes me want to take a second look.

In literary study, the pressures toward interdisciplinarity are, however, almost irresistible. "Literary criticism is always becoming 'something else,'" Leslie Fiedler wrote almost fifty years ago, "for the simple reason that literature is always 'something else.'"[10] Its meanings are historical, psychological, ethical, philosophical, and ideological. Its order is rhetorical, linguistic, and aesthetic. It is a commodity and a fetish. Unable to be defined adequately by intrinsic literary properties that might precisely distinguish it from other discursive forms, literature inevitably offers itself to the interested gaze of many disciplines, and literary study in turn has poached upon the theories and methodologies of these (usually, however, only as the particular theory has been repudiated by its home discipline[11]) in order to understand the various rationalities of the literary text. Nonetheless, literary scholarship, however it fancies or fashions itself, still has as its archive only the body of literature that has always been its subject, although the lineaments of the body have indeed been substantially stretched in recent years.

Literary study has come to understand that the very category of literature is unstable, at different times encompassing different classes of utterances. It is less a coherent system of representations than a constantly rearticulated ensemble of signifying acts. What counts as literature at any moment in our disciplinary culture is in fact what literary scholars study, an academic version of Duchamp's assertion that "art is what is introduced into an art context." This recognition has allowed the broadening, almost to the point of elimination, of the canon. There is still (*pace* Harold Bloom and William Bennett) a generally agreed upon set of literary works existing as the core of necessary disciplinary knowledge—those books, as Geoffrey Hartman says, that we agree to "start reading straightaway"[12]—but there is also a much wider sense of what is appropriate to study as literature, both in terms of previously ignored authors and traditionally devalued genres.

Indeed, it is cultural value itself that has emerged as a major object of interest within the field, refocusing attention from the internal, formal relations of the work of art to the ways in which it both produces and absorbs cultural meanings. Texts and contexts are no longer seen as the inside and outside of literary utterance but rather as interdependent factors exerting influence upon and contained within one another. The meanings of the literary work are therefore not intrinsic to it, not properties solely of its internal structuring, but functions of its mediation of and by the cultural contexts in which it is located.

Literary meaning, then, becomes inescapably historical, and literary scholars have turned to history, not as in the past, to provide inert data to illuminate certain textual details, but now to explore the very conditions in which cultural meanings are articulated and circulate. Yet what is dismaying to many literary scholars is that, having elegantly formulated and explored the productive interrelation of literature and history, the historians consistently ignore it and us, unconvinced that our formulations of cultural value have any import for their historical understandings. We regularly read their work but historians rarely read ours. Any check of footnotes in scholarly books in the two disciplines would confirm this.

There is, however, a reason for the general neglect of literary scholarship by historians, and it is not, I take it, disdain. I will grant that most historians are perfectly prepared to acknowledge that some of us are very fine literary scholars, but, much like physicists and economists who are equally willing to acknowledge the existence of impressive literary scholarship, they do not see that this is work that in general has much immediate relevance for their own. The reason, no doubt, is that, from the viewpoint of many historians, even when literary scholars are interested in historical issues they generally do not read history at all; they read historians. So the work of these literary scholars has no immediate claim upon the attention of the historians who have already read—and perhaps are in fact themselves—the historians that the literary critics read.

Part of the misunderstanding between the disciplines is that, as here, crucial words mean different things in each, not least that notoriously slippery signifier, "history" itself. When we (that is, literary scholars) use the word "history" we generally are referring to the body of scholarship produced by historians; historians tend to mean the object of inquiry itself. So we are being historical by our lights when we read historians, and we believe our narratives of cultural meanings are historical, hoping (against hope) that historians might also think them so.

It is not, however, merely that we have a different understanding of what it means to do history; it is that we want to do something different. One reason that historians are so dismissive of what they see as the irresponsible use of historical evidence by literary scholars is that they have assumed an identity of interest between the two disciplines—demanding a parallel identity of procedure—that is illusory. The two disciplines are in fact asking different questions of the past and have each found an effective (though clearly different) protocol to find convincing answers. Historians regularly bewail the arbitrariness of literary scholarship's deployment of evidence. One reference in the dispatch of the Venetian ambassador serves happily as a hanger for a whole wardrobe of cultural understanding. A historian would, of course, demand more before being confident of the claim the quotation would prove (though how much more is interesting: would two references validate the point—five, ten? What is the necessary density of reference for conviction?). But this fact, rather than demonstrating that historians are more scrupulous and demanding scholars than their literary counterparts, proves only that different evidentiary standards exist for different projects. If the goal is to discover if something was *thought,* a single reference might well be considered inadequate, too easily explained as idiosyncratic and aberrant; if, however, the goal is to discover if something was *thinkable* at a certain moment, then one example demonstrates the case quite nicely.

The thinkable is a perfectly legitimate scholarly interest, and reliable protocols of argument and evidence exist to pursue it. Whether this is or should be of interest to historians is another matter. To a literary critic interested in the individuality of a particular work, that some idea is demonstrably thinkable is of consequence (although this is precisely the reason that to most historians a literary critic's reading of a text, however alert and ingenious, is of little concern, as the text derives its value from its very idiosyncracy); to a historian interested in what was thought, the exemplarity of a work is the source of its value (which is why to most literary critics the readings of historians seem insufficiently attentive to the particularities of the text and ultimately somewhat obvious). Nonetheless, if we can agree that, for better or worse, historians in general don't read literary critics,[13] we must admit that they increasingly do read literary texts. But they tend to read them not as literature but as documentary evidence of something else, usually as the most elegant example of some idea that has been oft thought but ne'er so well expressed.

Clearly this begs the question of what it means to read a text as literature, but, whatever else it may mean, it certainly means that one cares that it is a work of literature. This is not I think a tautology; it is rather to claim that context matters, that ideas and phrases cannot be removed from the aesthetic structures in which they are embedded, any more than they can from the historical circumstances in which they are produced, without changing their intended meanings. Too often, however, what happens is that a revealing word or phrase is used to prove an intentional commitment of the author to a political or philosophical position with too little sense of how the language functions in its particular context. A republican sentiment in the mouth of a literary character does indeed provide evidence that republican sentiments were thinkable; it does not necessarily prove that the author thought them or used the text to advance them.

Now perhaps this is only to say that historians don't do literary criticism very well, exactly as historians say literary scholars don't do history very well. Or more likely it is only to say that historians aren't doing literary criticism at all, any more than we are, according to the accepted procedures and protocols of that discipline, doing history. Sixteenth-century historians may well find Spenser's writings, for example, useful to explain something about six-teenth-century history, as Spenserians regularly these days find sixteenth-cen-tury history relevant to explain things about Spenser's writings. In one case, history is explained by reference to the text; in the other, the text is explained by reference to history. But these are different projects, demanding different scholarly procedures and evidentiary standards. The projects intersect, of course, but that does not make either interdisciplinary. A purely instrumental use of the insights and techniques of another discipline cannot be what any-one means—or should mean—by interdisciplinarity. Historians do at times use literature for the purposes of various forms of historical scholarship, just as lit-erary scholars at times use history for the purposes of various forms of liter-ary scholarship. I think that this formulation is true, but, I confess, it isn't a very interesting assertion. And I think there is something more productive to be said about disciplinary relations than merely that historians are historians and literary critics are literary critics, even if we can admit that these discipli-nary identities are not essential or immutable.

Perhaps returning to intellectual history (for this is a field of interest in which historians do engage directly with written texts with a primary goal of interpreting them) may clarify what this might be. Part of my objection to how many historians of ideas use literature is not that they use it in nonliterary ways—that, as I have just said, is to be expected; it is rather that they often use it in what are insufficiently historical ways. That is arguably less to be expect-ed, but the philosophical and political vocabularies that they would recon-struct seem to me a kind of idealism, strangely isolated both from the specif-ic texts in which they appear and from the specific events that motivate them. Common vocabularies do not necessarily imply common purposes. Indeed, I would argue that even if different authors can be shown to make use of a similar vocabulary, the shared phrases inevitably function differently in their different texts, crucially modified by what surrounds them; and that the dif-ferent circumstances that motivate the writing will inevitably insure that the words mean something different. Certainly the word "king" used after 1649 can't quite mean what it did before.

In part this suggests that what is missing from the accounts of much intel-lectual history is a sense of the productivity of the verbal medium itself, the inability of authors to control fully the lability of the texts they write. Or, put differently, what is missing is an adequate notion of intentionality itself. Historians of ideas tend to idealize authorial intentions, that is, to see them as transparent in and fully controlling the meanings of a text. But meaning cannot be reduced to an author's intentions, except tautologically. One can, of course, simply insist that the intended meaning of the author *is* the meaning of the text, and bracket off all unintended meanings as something other than "meaning" ("significance," say, as E. D. Hirsch argued[14]). But texts inevitably generate meanings unintended by their authors, and to eliminate these from the field of meaning is to misconstrue the nature of writing, reading, and the text itself.

This is not to resurrect the familiar, if misleading, structuralist assertion that meaning is an effect of language rather than of its users. I believe firmly that meanings are produced intentionally, but also that no single intention determines the meaning of a text. Multiple and often contradictory intentions are present in the texts we read. This is true materially, for the book is literally produced by agents who have (non-authorial) intentions that are visible on the signifying surfaces of the text; discursively, for every text, it could be said, is more a composite than a composition, an engagement with other texts that themselves leave traces as ideological fault lines through the authorial text; and phenomenally, as it is experienced by readers reading purposefully, their relationship to the text determined at least as much by their own unpredictable motives as by the author's. Form, it might be argued, is the author's effort to insist on an exclusivity of intention, but it is an effort that must fail.

The history of ideas is, understandably, not interested in this failure. It is, almost by definition, concerned with the degree to which the effort succeeds, the degree to which an author can be seen to draw upon and manipulate successfully the available vocabularies and conventions to produce an intended meaning. Even in its most sophisticated and productive form, the work of Quentin Skinner and his followers, this is the commitment. Powerfully drawing on linguistic theory, particularly the linguistic pragmatics of Wittgenstein and the speech-act theory of Austin and Grice, Skinner endeavors to recover the "historical meaning" of the texts he studies by exploring the ideological contexts in which it is situated. Recognizing that it is not enough to understand only the "locutionary" or propositional force of the argument, this project insists on considering also the "illocutionary," or purposive force of the utterance; that is, it is necessary to understand not only what the crucial terms of an utterance mean as they operate within the conventions chosen by the author but also what motivates the author's very engagement with them.[15]

This understanding of historical meaning marks a welcome break with earlier forms of intellectual history that tended to focus either on the particularities of some exceptional work understood as a "self-sufficient object of inquiry and understanding," or on some given idea, which achieves coherence only by ignoring the particular uses made of it.[16] For Skinner, neither the great books approach to intellectual history nor the focus on key concepts is "genuinely historical."[17] The one confronts us with singular figures thinking "at a level of abstraction and intelligence unmatched by any of their contemporaries"; the other with concepts reified into "ideas" only by ignoring the historical specificity of their use. Skinner, instead, urges a historical pragmatics. What did an author say and why? And the answers are found in the author's deployment of certain crucial words and phrases that reveal the ideological position inhabited by the work.

But the focus on the motivated use of available political vocabularies, by design, returns the project to a history of concepts rather than of the works in which they are embedded, and the ease with which phrases are disarticulated from their immediate textual environment and from other determining contexts, both textual and historical, in order to locate them within coherent genealogies of thought has the effect of flattening out both the discourse and the works that deploy it, finding a least common denominator at the expense of the specific densities of the individual work and of the historical moment in which it is produced.

To understand a work historically does mean, I would agree, to see it as it was intended, but these intentions, as I will argue all through this book, are always both textually and historically overdetermined in ways that traditional forms of intellectual history, more interested in ideas than in events (even textual ones), cannot easily accommodate. Of course, if one's goal is the recovery of historical meaning, one must attend to who writes and why, but answers to those questions do not explain how a text is produced or experienced; that is, they offer only an attenuated sense of both the range and the producers of a text's meanings.

A more capacious understanding of intention, I would argue, is necessary for a "genuinely historical" understanding of a text, one more fully engaged with the actual conditions under which meaning is generated. This, of course, means thinking about the author's intentions, however difficult they are to untangle from the internal dynamics of the work that would embody them. But this very difficulty is the sign of the work's radical historicity, unmistakable evidence of how the inescapable circumstantiality of the text, its existence not only as aesthetic structure but as object and event, brings authorial intentions into contact (and often conflict) with other desires and actions, desires and actions that, no less than the intentions of the author, are responsible for the meanings that the text conveys.

If scholars are to attend to meaning in its historical dimension, they must consider not only the text as it is linguistically and aesthetically structured but also the institutional and material conditions that determine how it is available to be experienced, as well as the circumstances, competencies, and concerns of those who engage it (recognizing the reader, that is, as a historical agent rather than merely as an effect of the text). Meaning cannot be grasped apart from a consideration of the forms in which the work circulates and the conditions under which it is encountered.[18] "Who reads and what" is as relevant a question as "who writes and why," and both must be answered if we are to consider meaning as a genuinely historical concern.

A text's meanings, as they emerge in history, are not produced solely by its author's intentions, which in various ways get disrupted and dispersed as the text is materialized and encountered; rather, its meanings are generated in the complex negotiation between the pressure it exerts, as both a formal and material structure, and the often perverse productivity of its readers or spectators (in the case of a play), who experience the text with unpredictable desires, expectations, and abilities. Inevitably, then, the text's meanings are plural and mobile rather than single and stable, grist more for the mill of the cultural critic interested in the stresses that culture would suture than for the intellectual historian interested in a shared conceptual inheritance.

The text must be understood as a verbal construct, a physical artifact, and an event, in all aspects a product of multiple intentions that determine its form as well as its meanings. This understanding at once acknowledges the intentions of a text's author but recognizes that these are not powerful enough in themselves to explain either its materialization or its effects; that is, an exclusive focus on intention cannot finally account for either the text's literal presence or variable activity in the world. Only by thinking of textual meanings as products of multiple intentions—and not least those of readers or spectators—do these meanings become historical, alive with human purpose.

Here is at least one place where literary and historical studies can meet on the same plane, in the study of the literary work as both text and object, as a structure of words and ideas and also as the material vehicle in which it enters and acts in the world. Such a focus is genuinely interdisciplinary, responsive both to the productivity and the production of the text, to its formal organization and its material form, to the intentions that motivate its writing and the institutional and technological mediations necessary for these to be encountered. Here the skills and procedures of the literary critic and the historian find a common project, as the text is understood not as "a world of plenitude above history,"[19] but as a world of plenitude that is radically historical, a form of social knowledge and of social experience.

I am not, of course, supposing that this is the only possible interface of literary studies and history, only that this is a particularly exciting and rewarding one. Thinking about a particular work as it is produced within the rich web of intentions that shapes its intelligibility, thinking about it, that is, as a verbal structure, as a cultural gesture, as a material object, and as a commodity, restores it to history, clarifying how it produces and conveys meaning. Such attention may well be what comes "after the New Historicism" to fulfill the promise of its desires, returning texts and the ideas that circulate through them to a world replete with meaningful human activity.

THREE

The Text in History

We commend a study of the text of *Richard III* to those, if such there be, who imagine that it is possible by an exercise of critical skill to restore with certainty what Shakespeare actually wrote.

—W. G. Clark and W. A. Wright,
The Cambridge Shakespeare, 1864

I've always heard it can't be done, but sometimes it doesn't always work.

—Casey Stengel, 1964

Chapter 3

The Mechanics of Culture: Editing Shakespeare Today

Everyone seems to be doing it these days, or thinking about doing it, or most often—it is the nineties, after all—thinking about why he or she is not doing it. Editing, that is. Editing has suddenly become hot, or, if not exactly hot as an activity to undertake (it does, after all, involve a lot of very tedious, numbingly cold work), at least a hot topic (arguably *the* hot topic in Shakespeare studies) to debate. Never has the materiality of the texts we study seemed so compelling, so unavoidable, and so exhilaratingly problematic.

In no small part because the emergent electronic technology now threatens the hegemony of the printed book (though not, as some have claimed, its actual existence, for the advantages of the codex form become increasingly obvious as the electronic alternative presents itself), the achievements of print culture have become objects of intense interest in their own right. It shouldn't, of course, have required the electronic revolution to focus our attention upon the medium of print, but the processes of textual production are newly visible and urgent. The materializations of the text are no longer inevitable or transparent, and scholars are no longer indifferent to the historical formations of the literary works they study.

For years, however, we just read whatever edition we happened to have at hand, confident that the text was accurate and authoritative. It was part of the democratic legacy of the New Criticism, or at least the New Criticism as it was practiced in the college classroom. No need for rare books, for access to archives, for arcane knowledge of printing house practices or paleography. Cheap, reliable editions available for all to read closely were the cornerstone of English studies in the American academy in the anti-elitist educational environment that followed World War II.

Occasionally we heard the *caveat lector*: Matthiessen's notorious discussion of the discordia concors of *White Jacket*'s "soiled fish of the sea," when in fact Melville described the sea snake, more accurately if less poetically, as "coiled"; or the transposition in the text of "Among School Children" in early editions of the *Collected Poems* turning Yeats's Aristotle into a "soldier" from the "solider" of the original.[1] But we had no need to worry. The Shakespeare texts we read had no errors of that kind. We read *King Lear* and lectured patronizingly about the 150 years or so when Shakespeare's play was known on stage only in Tate's sentimental redaction ("Then there are gods, and virtue is their care!"), proud that our age could bear the play *itself* in all of its authentic murderousness.

But, of course, "the play itself" turned out to be the problem. That play we (used to) read—*King Lear*, ed. Kittredge; *King Lear*, ed. Harbage; *King Lear*, ed. Muir or Fraser or Bevington—was not exactly what we thought. It was what we have learned to call "conflated" or "constructed," a product of editorial labor almost as much as of authorial design. We are now told that *King Lear* is not one play but two, and that editors have been combining bits of both to make a text that Shakespeare never wrote or imagined. The 1608 quarto and the 1623 folio text are seen to represent distinct and discrete versions of the play, one "as Shakespeare originally wrote it," as the editors of the Oxford

Shakespeare claim, and one "as he substantially revised it" apparently some years later after the first version had been performed.[2]

And this wasn't exactly a new claim. As early as 1927, Granville-Barker was "sure" that the folio text recorded "some at least of Shakespeare's own reshapings."[3] In 1931 Madeleine Doran argued at length (though later she modified her view) that Q1 was derived from Shakespeare's manuscript and that the folio text derived from prompt copy that had been revised, abridged, and censored.[4] Indeed, as early as 1725, Pope had declared the probability that the folio texts contained "Alterations or Additions which *Shakespear* himself made."[5] But it wasn't until the publication in 1983 of *The Division of the Kingdoms* that an old heresy became the new orthodoxy.[6] *King Lear* then became definitively *King Lear*s, and the implications of the knowledge seemed to many to argue powerfully against the familiar editorial practice of conflating the two versions, each now understood as self-sufficient and, in many regards, incompatible.[7]

Nor was the argument for revision, and the concomitant argument against editorial conflation, limited to *Lear. Hamlet, Othello, Troilus and Cressida, 2 Henry IV*, and *Richard II*, it has been argued, similarly show evidence in their various early printings of extensive revision (though not, it must be said to the revisionists' dismay, demonstrably or necessarily Shakespeare's own; once the play enters the repertory it inevitably escapes the author's exclusive control).[8] Those comfortable, old paperbacks, with their underlinings and marginal notes, that we've taught from for so long no longer seem quite so authoritative nor appear so reliable. Shakespeare's *King Lear* and Shakespeare's *Hamlet*, as their covers proclaim, turn out to be something less than truth in advertising. They are more properly Alfred Harbage's *King Lear* or Kenneth Muir's, Harold Jenkins's *Hamlet* or Maynard Mack's, the editorial work of selecting and consolidating material from the variant evidence of the early textual witnesses producing a text that, ironically, in its very commitment to Shakespeare's authority (a commitment to "the principle," as the Victorian editor Charles Knight said, "that not a line which appears to have been written by Shakespeare ought to be lost"[9]) is different from any that Shakespeare ever intended, as well as different, by virtue of its individual editorial decisions, from any other edited version.

But the problem of authority does not emerge only in regard to plays that exist in more than one substantive version. The texts of those plays that have no early quarto printing and were printed only in the folio (with its promise

of plays "cur'd, and perfect," as Shakespeare "conceiued the[m]") are themselves not stable. Even these are not self-authorizing, seemingly demanding
editorial activity that, quite literally in the name of Shakespeare, removes the
text from the circumstances of its production and denies it its integrity.
Traditionally, editors have understood their task as the effort, in Fredson
Bowers's loaded phrase, to "strip the veil of print from a text"[10] in order to discover the authentic reading of the manuscript that underlies the visible surface of the printed book. Editions offer themselves as reconstructions of the
play that the author wrote before it suffered the inevitable contamination of
playhouse and printshop. "Corruption somewhere is certain," write the editors of the Oxford Shakespeare in the *Textual Companion*; the "text is diseased."[11] And the activity of editing is, therefore, generally understood as a
process of purification, returning the work of art to its innocent and whole-
some state before it fell into print.

However, not least of the difficulties of an editorial theory designed to
restore the reading before the text was corrupted by print is that often, as in
the case of Shakespeare, the untainted original does not exist. None of
Shakespeare's manuscripts survive to compare with and correct the printed
editions, and the appeal to their nature can be no more than hypothetical and
in fact often seems disturbingly circular: that is, the manuscript is reconstructed or, more accurately, imagined by reference to an imperfect printed
text whose imperfections are discovered in relation to the hypothesized manuscript. Editors, nonetheless, continually invoke the authority of the no longer
extant manuscript, variously conceived, as witness to the intentions of the
playwright. Thus, the authority of the so-called good quartos is taken to be
their derivation from the author's "foul papers" (i.e., a holograph draft ready
to be copied or printed), though no foul papers of any of Shakespeare's plays
have survived, and in fact there is no surviving example of such a manuscript
for any playwright of the period. Indeed, Paul Werstine has compellingly
argued that the very category of "foul papers" as it is used by Shakespearean
editors is "a product not of reason but of desire—our desire to possess in the
'good quartos' Shakespeare's plays in the form which he, as an individual
agent, both began and finished them."[12]

But the desire for innocence and authenticity, however understandable, is
possibly misplaced. Not only is it doomed to frustration (not merely because
of the frustrating absence of any manuscripts of Shakespeare's plays, but also
because of the double bind that Greg himself noted that would inevitably viti-

ate their authority: if the hypothetical manuscript is imagined as the playwright's own it would no doubt contain "unresolved textual tangles"; if it is imagined as a theatrical fair copy, there can be no certainty that it represents only the work of "the author himself"[13]), but also, like so many desires, this may be a longing for an inappropriate object. What is sought are the intentions of the writer, but the drama, of all literary forms, is the least respectful of its author's intentions. Plays always register multiple intentions, often conflicting intentions, as actors, annotators, revisers, collaborators, scribes, compositors, printers, and proofreaders, in addition to the playwright, all have a hand in shaping the play-text; but *editions* of plays tend to idealize the activity of authorship, actively seeking to remove it from the conditions of its production, from the very social and material mediations that permit (both authorial and nonauthorial) intentions to be realized in print and in performance.

In itself, the focus on authorial intention is, of course, neither an inappropriate nor an unprofitable concern. The author's intentions are certainly one of the interpretive horizons of the play and, however evanescent, undeniably a historical one at that. (I have to confess it seems odd that any defense of intentionality is required, even one as qualified as mine is here.) Works of literature in some obvious sense originate with an author, and the task of scholarly editing has usually been understood as the effort, in G. Thomas Tanselle's disarmingly simple phrase, "to discover exactly what an author wrote."[14] Editors study the surviving textual witnesses, consider the process of their transmission, and, by selection and emendation, construct a critical edition that offers itself as "authoritative," that is, as the author intended it in spite of the inability of any of the surviving, substantive texts perfectly to realize and represent those intentions.

Thus editors will inevitably seek to correct some of what the printed texts avow. Sometimes this seems utterly unobjectionable: turned letters are silently righted (for example, with the folio's "turu'd" in *Much Ado About Nothing,* 2.3.20, TLN 852, which one could at least hope was a bored compositor's desperate in-joke), and obvious typos are corrected (e.g., the folio's "ptayers" for "prayers" in *Antony and Cleopatra,* 2.3.3, TLN 967), practices that indeed could be said to "purify" a text, ridding it of manifest error.

But other changes are more problematic. "Emendatory criticism is always hazardous," as Samuel Johnson insisted. "There is danger lest particularities should be mistaken for corruptions, and passages rejected as unintelligible, which a narrow mind happens not to understand."[15] The perceived need to emend may reflect not some textual deficiency but only our ignorance of syntactic, semantic, or stylistic possibilities, and even in cases where some editorial response is indeed required by an unmistakable defect in the printed text, the emendation itself can never in its own terms be said to be definitively correct. An editor's knowledge of paleographic or printing house habits may well be brought to bear to suggest a credible explanation for the putative error and a viable substitution that will satisfy the aesthetic and ideational demands of the line; but even Theobald's inspired "a babbled of green fields" for the folio's "a Table of greene fields" (*Henry V*, 2.3.16–17, TLN 839) can at most claim, for all its obvious attractions, to be *plausible*. Indeed other reasonable emendations have been suggested here: "talkd," for instance, for "Table" (which is no less graphically possible and gains some additional support from the quarto reading where the Hostess reports that Falstaff did "talk of floures"). Theobald's "babbled" seems, of course, almost irresistibly "Shakespearean," a stronger word choice than the commonplace "talked"; though this very fact only confirms that it is on subjective, critical grounds rather than would-be objective, bibliographic ones that the preference finally rests. The emendation cannot with absolute certainty be said to restore an authentically Shakespearean reading, even if it does produce a line that gratifyingly conforms to our sense of Shakespeare's imaginative habits.

This is perhaps only to say that a critical edition is indeed critical; but, even granting the limitations of what certainties can be achieved in such an edition, in so far as an author's intentions are themselves the desired object of study, such idealizing, or, as it usually known, "eclectic" editing is of obvious value and its conventional procedures necessary and appropriate. The surviving texts will almost certainly not fully and faithfully represent the intended work, and the task of the editor who has chosen to focus on such intended forms (that is, forms that exist, however immaterially, both prior to and independent of any of the work's physical manifestations) is to restore what is understood to be deficient in the documentary record, recovering and representing intentions that previously were frustrated in the process of their earlier materializations. Nonetheless, though the author's intentions are unquestionably one, and even, it might sensibly be claimed, the single most important determinant of the form in which the literary work appears, an exclusive focus on intention—at least the author's intention to *mean*, as opposed to the intention to *do*[16]—inevitably works to sever the activity of writing from the most immediate historical contexts that motivate and sustain it, leaving the author implausibly isolated in single and sovereign splendor.

One could, of course, shift the focus away from the playwright to the theater itself as a way of socializing those intentions. As performance was the only form of publication that Shakespeare sought for his plays, one might argue that editions should center on the theatrical rather the authorial text, effectively restoring the play to the multiple intentions of performance. Indeed, the recent Oxford Shakespeare claims to do just that, seeking to present the "texts of Shakespeare's plays as they were acted in the London playhouses which stood at the centre of his professional life."[17] But how are we to know how "they were acted"? How can this information be recovered from the witness of the early printed play texts?

The Oxford editors attempt to do so by applying the principles of critical editing to the available documentary evidence but reversing the traditional valence of presumptive manuscript authority, now valuing those printed texts putatively showing evidence of having derived from or been influenced by "promptbooks" over those based upon authorial "foul papers." But an appeal to the promptbook can no more certainly be used to reconstruct a performance text than an appeal to the playwright's "foul papers" can be used to reconstruct authorial intentions, not least because the promptbook is itself no less a category of desire than foul papers are. No early promptbook of any Shakespeare play survives, and none exists for any play of the period that would suggest that it was intended as a definitive playing text. The few surviving play manuscripts and printed playbooks that do show markings by a bookkeeper have, as William Long has shown, almost none of the textual characteristics that bibliographers have attributed to promptbooks.[18] Though obviously not without enormous value for our effort to understand the early modern theater, the surviving "promptbooks" indicate more the bookkeeper's concern with backstage activity than with what is spoken or acted on stage.

But in any case, the play as performed is not a single or stable thing. It would, of course, vary with the circumstances of every performance, and no company's promptbook could anticipate the changes that specific performances might demand: adjustments in staging to suit differing playing venues, revisions of the text to keep it current or to be sure it would not offend, lines forgotten or botched, or even some inspired improvisation responding to an intrusive spectator in the yard. Indeed, none would try, as the equivocal stage direction from the so-called prompt copy of Heywood's

The Captives indicates: "Eather strikes him wth a staffe or Casts a stone" (ll. 2432–34). As Werstine remarks, "the quest for a stable entity called a 'performing text' thus becomes as quixotic as the abandoned quest for authorial intention."[19] Released into the context for which it was intended, the play-text becomes thoroughly malleable, responsive to various shaping intentions competing with those of the author.

Playwrights certainly recognized this fact, and some turned to publication to reclaim what was, from their perspective, inevitably lost in performance, if only as the performance text was cut to keep the playing time within the somewhat elastic "two hours traffic" to which an audience could be expected to attend.[20] As James Saeger and Christopher Fassler have shown, during the seventeenth century the familiar title-page authorization–"As it hath been lately acted by . . ."–which often specified both the theatrical company and the theatrical venue, gradually gave way to a declaration of authorship, as playwright's names began to appear on title-pages with ever greater frequency.[21] But just as significant as the changing authorization of the text is a changing conception of the text itself. It is not only that the text is increasingly offered as the achievement of the playwright rather than of the acting company, but often it is a different text that is made available, no longer one as "it hath been played" but a fuller, authorial one, "Containing more than has been Publickely Spoken or Acted," as the title-page of Jonson's *Every Man Out of His Humour* has it.[22]

The implications of this, or at least the dilemma it poses, for editing seems obvious. If one edits to recover and represent the playwright's intentions one would almost certainly have to include material that never appeared on stage; if one edits to recover and represent the play as a performance blueprint one would as certainly have to omit material that the playwright indeed wrote and quite obviously valued.[23] Each corresponds to one of the two prevailing views of Shakespeare, who is seen either as the consummate man of the theater or as the quintessential literary personality. But if one's interests are in the play as a theatrical document, the edited text has less obligation to the playwright's intentions than to the acting company's use of them. The theater inevitably absorbs and alters its playwright's words, adapting them to its own possibilities and needs, and more than occasionally improving them in the process. The difficulty is that most of what has happened on stage has not been recorded; the variable performance text never exists in any written form, and no edition can come close to representing the disparate renderings of the play on stage.

Whether or not, then, it is possible for a critical edition to register the process adequately, in the professional theater the playwright's intentions are inevitably subordinated to the demands of performance. We have come, however, to see not merely playwrighting but all forms of authorship as something more problematic—that is, both less individual and more constrained—than traditional notions of artistic integrity would assert. The author certainly is not dead, but every act of writing is now understood to be inevitably compromised and fettered rather than some free and autonomous imaginative activity. An author writes always and only within available conditions of possibility, both imaginative and institutional, and the text is realizable through (and inevitably altered by) the labor of other agents. Increasingly, textual criticism, if not editing itself, has attempted to uncover the full network of agents involved in the production of the text, restoring the literary work to the collaborative economies necessary for its realization and recognizing in the evidence of these collaborations not the causes of the text's deterioration as it escapes the purity of the author's imaginings but the enabling circumstances of its actualization, whether on stage or in the printing house.

Yet if this social conception of textuality (a notion identified most immediately with Jerome McGann and D. F. McKenzie[24]) has had enormous influence upon the field of textual scholarship, it has not—and arguably cannot—have the same effect on editing itself. To recognize that authorial intentions not only operate alongside of but in fact demand nonauthorial intentions for their materialization is to restore the text to its full historicity. But the commitment to this historicized text radically complicates, if not thoroughly undermines, the traditional basis of editing. If the study and presentation of the text are designed to reveal the historically determined and meaningful collaboration of authorial and nonauthorial intentions, there are no longer grounds on which one version of a text might be thought superior to another. For an editor interested in Shakespeare's intentions, Q1 *Hamlet* is of less value than Q2, but for the textual scholar interested in the social text, Q1 speaks the material and institutional conditions of its production every bit as fully as Q2 or the folio text (and is a "bad quarto" only if goodness is understood as proximity to an authorial manuscript). Indeed if one's interests are in the social construction of the text rather than in some authorial version, there seemingly is no reason to edit at all, since the unedited text, even in its manifest error, is the only and fully reliable witness to the complex process of the text's production and to the necessary resistance, as William Morris would have said, of its materiality.

The logic of the sociological focus seems to point to the abandonment of edited texts altogether in favor of facsimiles of the early printed editions, which supply a richer field of signifying material offering evidence of the social contexts of their production. *Macbeth* could be studied in a facsimile of the folio that provides the only substantive text of the play, *Lear* in facsimiles of both the 1608 quarto and the folio, and *Hamlet* in facsimiles of all of its three early printings, each of which advertises itself as a different sort of play emerging from a different institutional logic. Such facsimiles would indeed provide readily available and reasonably cheap copies of early texts that cannot be easily examined in their original, permitting a more carefully reticulated understanding of the work of art within the conditions of its original production than an eclectic edition that seeks to remove all signs of what Bowers dismissed as "non-authorial accretion."[25]

But facsimile, for all its obvious ability to reproduce many of the significant visual characteristics of the original texts, performs, in both printed and electronic modes, its own act of idealization. It reifies the particulars of a single copy of the text, producing multiple copies of a textual form that would have been unique (as a result of early modern printing house practice in which the binding of corrected and uncorrected sheets makes it unlikely that any two copies of a sixteenth-century book could be identical). And in this idealized form, facsimile limits the focus on the material text merely to the bibliographic codes structuring the verbal medium. It is obviously unable to reproduce the text's complete materialization in paper, ink, and binding, material aspects that, as is proven by Prynne's outrage in *Histrio-mastix* (1633) that Shakespeare was printed on "farre better paper than most Octavo or Quarto Bibles" (sig. **6^v), are unquestionably part of the text's significance.[26]

If edited versions, then, usually idealize the activity of authorship, facsimile versions work to idealize the printed text; and it becomes clear that no decision about the presentation of a literary work can be made that does not involve some loss of desirable information. In part this is a result of the codex technology itself. Concerns about size and cost of the printed book force choices upon us that are neither inevitable nor desirable, and the electronic future may in this regard offer some relief. Certainly, the most inclusive form of one of Shakespeare's plays will be a hypertextual edition that will include digitized versions of all the early substantive printings (as well as, in theory, any number of critically edited texts). But hypertexts, for all that they allow an escape from the physical limits of codex production, are, of course, dependent upon the same physical idealization of the individual printed versions as any facsimile and have their own disadvantages, not least those of their very capaciousness. The hypertext is less an edition than an infinitely expandable and promiscuous archive, and, if that is indeed the point, it should be noted that it is one thing to have such (hyper)textual richness available and quite another to read it.

In truth, most of us will for the foreseeable future continue to read Shakespeare's plays and teach them in edited versions, in book form rather than off a computer screen, with spelling and punctuation modernized.[27] If we occasionally—even more than occasionally—may lament that fact, recognizing what we have given up in accepting the text that has been constructed for us by an editor, we know also how much we have gained. If we must admit that in actuality there is no fully acceptable way to edit Shakespeare, at least no way to edit without losses that, depending upon one's interests and needs, will at times vitiate the advantages of the text's accessibility in whatever form it is presented, we also must admit that reading an edited text is a remarkably convenient way to engage the play, especially for students who, however naïvely, merely want to read it (to say nothing about for actors who require a single and stable text to perform). But in reality there is no other way to engage the play, for from its very first appearance as printed text it has been edited, mediated by agents other than the author, and intended for the convenience of its readers.

It is this sense of the impossibility of editing and yet the inescapability of it, that, I think, creates and explains the excitement of textual studies today. This paradox is the sign of the text's complicating historicity. We have come to understand that a text may no more be definitive and authentic than it may have an "onlie begetter." The text is always constructed in accord with a set of cultural values and textual assumptions, and its making and remaking are not evidence of its contamination but are, in fact, the very conditions of its being. This is not to say that it makes no difference in what form the play appears, only that no specific form of the play represents (what can only be a fantasy of) the true original, exactly as the advertisement of the first folio uncannily suggests, promising printed texts "according to the True Originall Copies." The play exists in its materializations, of the printing house and of the playhouse, and these *are* the play's meanings rather than passive and sometimes inadequate conveyors of them. It is always as text that literature enters and acts in history, and a focus on the material and linguistic conditions of its textuality firmly locates it in the world in which and to which it is alive. Recognition of this may perhaps dull our desire to "strip the veil of print from a text," but it is, after all, the nineties.

> All speculation over man the creator is intended to eliminate real knowledge.
>
> —Pierre Macherey

Chapter 4

Shakespeare in Print

What I want to argue here is perhaps as simple as saying that Shakespeare didn't write the books that bear his name. This is not, however, to enlist on one side of the familiar controversy about authorship, disputing whether or not someone other than Shakespeare wrote the plays while hiding behind the identity of the glover's son from Stratford. That argument has little to recommend it, except its unintended humor. One of the early proponents of the Earl of Oxford's authorship was infamously named J. Thomas Looney (although, as Oxfordians never fail to point out, the common

Manx pronunciation was in fact "Lone-y").[1] An article maintaining that the plays of Shakespeare were actually written by Daniel Defoe (in spite of the fact that Defoe was born about thirty-seven years after the Shakespeare folio was printed in 1623) was written by the no more happily named George M. Battey; and more recently a New York lawyer took up the cause of Marlowe's authorship in a privately printed dramatic fantasy. His name, alas, was Sherwood E. Silliman.[2] I sometimes take all this as *ad hominem* proof that there is a God.

Like most of us, I don't doubt for a moment that there was a Shakespeare, and that (sometime before he was discovered as a writer for Hollywood) he was indeed a playwright writing for the London stage. He was the leading dramatist of the Lord Chamberlain's men, later the King's men, turning out on average two plays a year for eighteen years, ensuring his company a steady stream of actable scripts, which in performance reliably succeeded in attracting theater-goers in substantial numbers to the Globe and the other venues where the company played. Whatever literary ambitions he harbored were secondary to the demands of the theater, where the achievement of the playwright is at once realized and obscured in the achievements of the actors on stage. Shakespeare held the copyright on none of his plays, and, though eighteen were published in his lifetime, he supervised none of them through the printing process. Performance was the only form of publication he sought for them.

This was, of course, normal behavior for a professional playwright. Plays in the period were essentially subliterary, and most, probably about 80 percent, never reached print at all. (As an indication, only about 30 of the 282 hundred and eighty two plays mentioned by Henslowe were published at any time in the sixteenth or seventeenth century.) And the plays that did find their way into print for the most part did so as the ephemera of an emerging entertainment industry rather than as valued artifacts of high culture. "Hardly one in fortie" was "worthy the keeping," Thomas Bodley would write to his librarian, Thomas James, about playbooks. "The more I thinke about it, the more it doth distast me, that such kinde of bookes, should be vouchesafed a rowme, in so noble a Librarie."[3]

Plays were generally mere piece-work, commissioned by the acting companies (for one-time payments to freelance playwrights, usually between £5 and £8), though sometimes companies entered into contractual arrangements with a playwright for a set number of plays per year, like that between Queen

Henrietta's company and Richard Brome, where the playwright promised to write exclusively for the company, furnishing three plays a year in exchange for fifteen shillings weekly plus one day's profits for each new play.[4] The commissioned script belonged to the company, and once in their hands it was subjected to the multiple collaborations of production, as staging requirements and actors' temperaments inevitably enforced their changes upon it; and, as the play remained in the repertory, it might well be subject to further revision, often at the hands of some new playwright, as the acting company sought to keep its property current. In 1601, Ben Jonson received forty shillings for "adicians" to *The Spanish Tragedy*; the following year, Samuel Rowley and William Birde shared four pounds "for ther adicyones in doctor fostes."[5]

Theater thus frustrates literary aspirations, dispersing authority for the play among various agents—collaborators and revisers, bookkeepers and prompters, musicians and carpenters, and, of course, the actors themselves—all of whom bear some responsibility for the play's eventual shape and success. Plays as written are rarely identical with plays as played; practical theatrical considerations (of cost, of time, of personnel, of the available resources of the theater itself) enforce changes upon them, and any professional playwright not only knows this to be the condition of having one's work performed but also knows that production considerations often improve what was originally penned.

Shakespeare's cultural preeminence usually obscures for us the fact that he too wrote in such circumstances, that his artistry was indeed embedded in commercial, institutional, and material conditions that subordinated his literary talent to practical and pragmatic theatrical concerns. He was unusual only in that for most of his career he wrote only for a single company and worked not as a piece-worker, as did most professional playwrights, nor even as an "ordinary poet" like Richard Brome under contract to a company of actors, but as a "sharer" in the company that performed his plays. Although he prospered in his theatrical career, his earnings came neither from commissions nor royalties for his writing but from his entitlement to one-tenth of the company's profits—a share handsome enough to permit him considerable investment in real estate: in 1597 buying the substantial freehold house in Stratford known as New Place, the second largest dwelling in town; in 1602 purchasing about 125 acres of land in the nearby manorial fields to the north of Stratford for £320, and three years later a half interest in a Stratford tithe farm for an additional £440.

If, then, as a sharer Shakespeare achieved a material success far greater than most of the theater professionals of the day, as a playwright his experience was in most respects exactly like other professional playwrights. He wrote scripts that were designed to be played, scripts that legally no longer belonged to him once they were turned over to the company and that artistically were subject now to the shaping pressures of performance. As a sharer in the company and one of its experienced actors he could, of course, influence production in a way that no freelance playwright could ever hope to, but, like any playwright, he knew that what he wrote would be modified as it came to life on the stage.

When his plays appeared in print, they did so neither as testament to his literary achievement nor to his literary ambition. They were printed without his involvement, and without any apparent desire on his part that they so appear—and in truth they were not, strictly speaking, his to publish in any case. In the absence of anything like our modern copyright law (which dates only from 1709), the acting companies effectively owned the scripts they commissioned, and their ownership extended even to publication. Brome's contract with the Salisbury Court specifies that he "should not suffer any play made or to be made or Composed by him . . . to bee printed by his Consent or knowledge" without prior approval from the company.[6]

And such approval was not always readily forthcoming. The epistle in the second state of 1609 *Troilus and Cressida* asserts the reluctance of "the grand possessors" to let their play be published, and there is occasional evidence of companies acting aggressively to prevent their scripts from coming into print. In March of 1600, the Admiral's men borrowed forty shillings to "geue vnto the printer to staye the printinge of patient Gresell," and on three occasions the King's men, believing that publication would work to their "detriment and prejudice" seemingly used their influence to have the Lord Chamberlain issue a directive to the Stationers to print none "of the playes or interludes of his maiesties servants without their consents."[7] Of course, a member of the company was the usual conduit by which a script reached the publisher, and the contract between the sharers in the Whitefriar's theater therefore insisted that "noe man of the said company shall at any time hereafter put into print any manner of playe booke now in use, or that hereafter shalbe soulde unto them, upon the penaltie and forfeiture of ffortie pounds starlinge or the losse of his place and share of all things amongst them."[8]

Nonetheless, many plays were printed, often as companies sold off scripts to publishers to raise money or to publicize themselves, but often from other sources: from individual actors who may have prepared a text from memory, from their friends who had come into possession of a manuscript copy of a play, even on occasion from the playwrights themselves, engaging in what Heywood elsewhere calls "a double sale of their labours, first to the Stage, and after to the Presse" (*The Rape of Lucrece*).[9] Publishers would purchase playscripts from various sources, worrying little about the nature or indeed the source of the text they received. What was purchased, as Peter Blayney reminds us, was "a manuscript, not what we now call a *copyright.*"[10] The legal issues, in essence, concerned material property not intellectual property, ownership not authorship. A publisher bought the transcription of a play from any one of a number of people who might legitimately claim that it was theirs to sell, and it was then his[11] to publish in the form he acquired it, which was rarely, if ever, identical with the form of the author's imagining.

All the plays of Shakespeare that were published in his lifetime appeared in small and inexpensive formats. The texts are of varied quality and provenance, some seemingly printed from manuscripts that seem to be authorial, others showing the inevitable cuts and interpolations of the theater, still others printed from transcriptions of reported texts, either witnessed or even acted by their reporters. A number of these—*Romeo and Juliet* (1597), *Richard III* (1597), *Henry V* (1600), *Merry Wives of Windsor* (1602), *Hamlet* (1603), *Pericles* (1609), as well as *The First Part of the Contention* (1594) and *Richard Duke of York* (1595), versions respectively of *2* and *3 Henry VI*—reveal such extensive stylistic and structural differences from what is taken to be the authentic form of the play that they have usually been considered, following Pollard, "bad quartos" (or, in the case of *Richard Duke of York*, more properly a "bad" octavo).[12] Seen as defective and perhaps stolen texts in the familiar bibliographic narratives, arguably these merely reveal a normal process of textual change in the theater and in the printing house. In any case, not one of the early printings, whether "bad" or "corrected," as some title-pages insist, displays any sign whatsoever of Shakespeare's interest or involvement in its publication. For none has Shakespeare provided a dedication or an epistle to the reader or worked to ensure the accuracy of the printed text—or, indeed, protested its inaccuracy, unlike, for example, Heywood, who, however disingenuously, claims that he allowed his plays into print only because "some of my plaies haue (vnknown to me, and without my direction) accidentally come into the Printers handes, and therfor so corrupt and mangled (coppied onely by the eare) that I haue been vnable to know them. . . ."[13] On the other hand, the two long poems Shakespeare wrote, *Venus and Adonis* (1593) and *The Rape of Lucrece* (1594), printed by fellow Stratfordian Richard Field, are obviously carefully produced, and each is issued with a signed dedication to the Earl of Southampton. The plays reached print without any similar care or sign of the playwright's involvement.

All this is, of course, well known. Equally well known is the fact that Shakespeare has, nonetheless, become the most recognizable, almost inescapable, author in the world. He can today be read in more than ninety-five languages, and copies of his plays can be purchased in almost every country on the earth. Indeed, he has emerged as the most often read (or at very least the most often assigned) author in English. Shakespeare with his quill in hand is easily recognized as a symbol of artistry even by those who have never read or seen any of his plays. Yet however gratifying, his literary reputation no doubt would have come as a great surprise to Shakespeare had he lived to see it. Working comfortably in the communal structure of the professional theater, his playwrighting career strikingly resists the very notions of literary authority and autonomy that his name has come triumphantly to represent.

Ben Jonson was different. Writing within the same professional conditions as did Shakespeare, Jonson assiduously worked to become a man in print. He published his plays from the first, apparently with the consent of the King's men (who were content to reemploy him, even after plays written for them, like *Every Man Out of His Humour* [1600] or *Every Man In . . .* [1601], appeared in print). Not only did he collect nine of his plays for inclusion in an impressive folio volume published in 1616, entitled *THE WORKES OF Benjamin Jonson* (a title that provoked derision from those who claimed that mere plays were unworthy of such dignified treatment, that Jonson had obviously forgotten the difference between play and work), but the texts themselves were carefully prepared and presented to rescue them from the intrusions and imperfections of what Jonson called the "loathed stage," monumentalizing them as high art and individualizing them as, however improbably, completely his own.[14]

But the process of individuation, of Jonson's self-conscious creation of himself as author, did not begin only with the 1616 folio. For example, in his epistle "to the reader" in the 1605 quarto of *Sejanus,* Jonson proudly asserts that the published text differs from what was played on stage, "wherin," he admits, "a second pen had a good share." Belatedly, Jonson becomes the play's sole author, systematically erasing the hand of his collaborator, substituting new lines never played, in order to present to his readers a text that is his own, one indeed "Written by Ben; Ionson," as the title-page says, rather than the play that was actually played in London. Jonson regularly corrects, or in this case, actually reconstructs his texts, removing them from the collaborations of the playhouse, establishing them as readerly texts rather than printed scripts, even supervising them through the printshop to claim control over the text's accidentals, trying, that is, to make precise and true his title-page claim: "the Author B. I."

For Shakespeare it was decidedly otherwise. His interest in his plays always remained theatrical, and he released them with no apparent apprehension into the sustaining collaborations of the theater.[15] He displayed no commitment to or anxiety about the claim of authorship, and no obvious desire to see his plays in print at all. He might well have brought them to his townsman Field, as he apparently did with the narrative poems, but he did not.

In 1756, Samuel Johnson, in his proposal for a new edition of Shakespeare's plays, found in the fact of Shakespeare's lack of interest in print publication the first link of a chain of circumstance that determined the dispiriting quality of so many of the early printings: "It is not easy for invention to bring together so many causes concurring to vitiate a text," he wrote; Shakespeare

> sold them not to be printed, but to be played. They were immediately copied for the actors, and multiplied by transcript after transcript, vitiated by the blunders of the penman, or changed by the affectation of the player; perhaps enlarged to introduce a jest, or mutilated to shorten the representation; and printed at last without the concurrence of the author, without the consent of the proprietor, from compilations made by chance or by stealth out of the separate parts written for the theatre; and thus thrust into the world surreptitiously and hastily, they suffered another deprivation from the ignorance and negligence of the printers, as every man who knows the state of the press in that age will readily conceive.[16]

Johnson gets some of his facts wrong, not least those that lead to his wholesale contempt for the art of printing at that time, but his recognition that Shakespeare's plays were printed in editions that were largely indifferent to their author's intentions is correct. What is misplaced is only Johnson's breathless dismay.

The drama is, of all literary forms, the least respectful of its author's artistic intentions. Play-texts are written for the theater and so unsurprisingly show the marks of theatrical attention, adaptation, and abridgement. When in 1647 Humphrey Moseley publishes the first folio of the collected plays of Beaumont and Fletcher, he admits that "When these *Comedies* and *Tragedies* were presented on the stage, the *Actours* omitted some Scenes and Passages (with the *Author's* consent) as occasion led them; and when private friends desir'd a Copy, they then (and justly too) transcribed what they *Acted*" (sig. A5ʳ). Moseley claims that in his edition the full play-text, all that was written, both what was acted and what was omitted, would be printed, but his recognition that cutting is the norm of performance (and that it is done "with the Author's consent") and that transcripts were made of these performance texts ("and justly too") is an important correction to the familiar bibliographic narratives that find incompetence at best and unscrupulousness at worst behind the "deprivation" of the Shakespeare quartos.[17]

The limitations of the early Shakespearean printings are almost never the result either of dishonest publishers seeking pirated texts on which they hoped to make a killing or of negligent or ignorant printers careless of their copy or their craft. Rather, the early quarto and octavo editions, even in their imperfections, accurately reflect the commercial conditions existing in the playhouse and the printing house, the conditions in which the plays were literally produced. But if the plays were changed in the playhouse largely by design, in the printing house they were changed largely by contingency.

Publishers in the period for the most part worked opportunistically, printing texts that became available to them on which they hoped to make a profit. When they obtained a play-text, if no other stationer had previously registered the title, they were usually free to publish, with no obligation to inquire into the state or provenance of the text, whether it was theatrical or authorial, memorially transcribed or an author's foul papers. The printers themselves, of course, tried to produce an accurate text, and for the most part succeeded; but in places crowded or illegible copy forced compositors to guess at readings; where copy was clear, occasional auditory and compositorial errors distorted it; pieces of type would get damaged; type occasionally slipped; inking could be imperfect. Proofreading was done, but if read against copy at all, it was likely, especially with a playbook, to have been done quickly, whether by a corrector employed by the press, by an available printer, or, even, as it was on occasion and then no doubt somewhat less hastily, by the playwright himself.[18] Once presswork began, an early pull would be read in house (this time not usually against copy); but as the presses were not normally stopped as this reading took place, when corrections were finally made, printed sheets would exist in both corrected and uncorrected states.

The normal activity in the playhouse and the printing house thus insures that the play that appeared in the bookstalls was always something other than the play Shakespeare wrote (the practice of stop-press corrections assures that no two copies of the printed playbook were themselves likely to be identical); but the printed text, if it inevitably vitiates, in Dr. Johnson's word, the intentions of the playwright, accurately registers the various factors in the text's production. Plays and playbooks are always produced by many people in addition to the author: playwrights write play scripts that are turned into plays by theater companies and are turned into books by stationers. Many others affect the design of the playbook that finally appears, and their activity is necessarily registered in the text's signifying surface.

Today we take it for granted that the texts we read are by Shakespeare. We buy *The Arden Shakespeare*, *The Oxford Shakespeare*, *The Norton Shakespeare*, although in some cases—*Two Noble Kinsmen*, for example or *Henry VIII*—the work of another hand seems surely present (*The Arden Shakespeare and Company?*); and even in cases where such conventional forms of collaboration seem unlikely, the very process of producing the play, on stage and in print, insures that hands other than Shakespeare's own have affected the shape of the text.

But the truth is that Shakespeare's earliest publishers didn't seem much to care one way or the other. John Danter's edition of *Titus Andronicus* in 1594 completely omits Shakespeare's name from its title-page; rather, its title-page provides various other information, not least about its printing and where it can be bought. The play-text is advertised—and title-pages were explicitly forms of advertising, functioning as banners fastened to the bookstall[19]—not as by William Shakespeare but by the acting company that had performed it: "As it was Plaide by the Right Honourable the Earle of Darbie, Earle of Pembrooke, and Earle of Sussex their Seruants." And even when it is reprinted, first in 1600 and then again in 1611, neither bibliographic scruple nor mercenary interest leads the publisher to add Shakespeare's name to the title-page.

Indeed, throughout the sixteenth century most printed plays were advertised exactly as Danter's text announces, "As it was plaide" or "as it hath been lately acted"—that is, not as an authorial text but as a theatrical version, a book whose textual authority and commercial appeal derive from the company of actors that had performed it rather than from its author.[20] The early printings of Shakespeare's plays reveal no sustained or systematic interest in their authorship. *Titus Andronicus*, as we have just seen, is published without Shakespeare's name identifying the play, as are the first editions of *2* and *3 Henry VI*. But these, it might be contended, are immature efforts of a young playwright, whose achievement arguably does not yet merit the recognition nor permit a publisher to capitalize on his name on the title-page. Yet editions of later and more successful plays also refuse to exploit—or even acknowledge—Shakespeare's authorship. *Romeo and Juliet* appears in 1597 without Shakespeare's name on the title-page; instead the play is offered "As it hath been often (with great applause) plaid publiquely, by the right Honourable L. of Hunsdon his Seruants"; its next two printings, in 1599 and 1609, suggest that it has now been "Newly corrected, augmented, and amended" but make no mention of either its author or its putative corrector, only that it again "hath bene sundry times publiquely acted, by the right Honourable the lord Chamberlaine his Seruants." In 1597, the first quarto of *Richard II* was similarly offered to its potential readers only "As it hath beene publikely acted by the right Honourable the Lord Chamberlaine his seruants," and the 1598 quarto of *Henry the Fourth* also makes no mention of Shakespeare on its title-page.

Seven plays appeared in quarto before one was issued with a title-page that includes Shakespeare's name. Not until 1598, when Cuthbert Burby prints *Loues Labors Lost,* does Shakespeare make his first appearance on the title-page of a play; the title-page, however, does not triumphantly proclaim the author but sets his name modestly in small italic type, identifying the play as "Newly corrected and augmented By *W. Shakespere.*" This is not even necessarily an assertion of authorship, though on other evidence it seems certain that Shakespeare is indeed the play's author. The claim that the quarto was "newly corrected and augmented," whether or not literally true, was most likely designed less to advertize Shakespeare's hand than to differentiate this edition from an earlier, now lost printing of a defective text (especially as Burby uses almost the same phrase to differentiate his edition of *Romeo and Juliet* in 1599 from John Danter's flawed text of *Romeo and Juliet* in 1597). But in any case the muted assertion of authorship on the title-page suggests that Burby is not counting on "Shakespere" to sell his book.

The unequivocal evidence of the early printings is, then, that Shakespeare had no interest in their publication, and, what is perhaps more surprising, that his publishers had as little interest in him—either as an author or as a commodity. At least this latter would soon change. In 1608, the "Pide Bull" quarto of *King Lear* does enthusiastically assert Shakespeare's authorship: "M. William Shakespeare: / *HIS* / True Chronicle Historie of the life and / death of King LEAR and his three / Daughters." Here the play is being confidently displayed and celebrated as Shakespeare's, yet the printed text shows no more sign of Shakespeare's involvement in the publication process than any of the earlier quartos. It is no more exclusively "HIS" than any of the others that had previously escaped his control. Indeed, it is a poorly printed quarto (it was the first play-text that the printer, Nicholas Okes, had ever undertaken in his shop), and Shakespeare clearly did not oversee its publication. Verse is mislined, sometimes printed as prose; speeches are misassigned; the compositor seemingly misreads the manuscript that he prints from, printing "crauing" for "cunning," "confirming" for "conferring," guessing at a nonce-word "crulentious" for "contentious." Sometimes he apparently mishears the copy that is read to him, for example when he prints "in sight" for "incite," and "a dogge, so bade in office" for "a dog's obeyed in office," errors that must be auditory rather than misreadings of copy or compositorial mistakes.[21]

The quarto *Lear* is presented as William Shakespeare's play, but in truth it is Nathaniel Butter's, the publisher who owns the text and chooses now to assert Shakespeare's authorship to help market his play, trying either to capitalize on Shakespeare's growing reputation (though, as we have just seen, neither the publisher of the 1609 *Romeo and Juliet* nor of the 1611 *Titus Andronicus* seemingly thought that reputation to be of sufficient merit to justify the inclusion of Shakespeare's name on either of those title-pages), or, more probably, to differentiate this play from the anonymous publication of 1605, *The True Chronicle Historie of King Leir*.[22] In either case, Shakespeare's name functions literally, although in different senses, as a mark of distinction. Nonetheless, it should be noted that the next play to appear, the 1609 quarto of *Troilus and Cressida*, printed by George Eld for Richard Bonian and Henry Walley, seems notably less confident about the tactic. It does indeed identify the play as "Written by William Shakespeare" but this appears in the smallest typeface on the title-page. Unlike the 1608 *Lear*, which trumpets Shakespeare's name, *Pericles* whispers the identity of the playwright. Indeed it seems almost as if, as Peter Stallybrass has written, the title-page assertion was purposefully designed "to deflate any grand pretensions of authorship."[23]

But Shakespeare never had any such pretensions. It is only with the pub-

lication in 1623 of the book usually referred to as the first folio that
Shakespeare truly enters English literature as an author, and that, of course,
was hardly his own idea. He had died in 1616, seven years before the folio
appeared, and to the end showed no signs of any specifically literary ambition, content to produce plays for the theater. But the folio assumes that
Shakespeare is an author to be read, not merely the provider of scripts to be
acted—or perhaps, more accurately, assumes that he is an author not necessarily to be read but one whose writings are at very least to be purchased and
displayed.

The folio was a physically impressive book and proved a complicated
printing project, though it is not by any means an elegant production.[24]
Printing began early in 1622 and took about twenty-one months to complete.
The published book is large, consisting of over 900 pages measuring about 13
by 8 inches. It was printed in pica type in double columns on medium quality, hand-made rag paper. The volume contained thirty-six of Shakespeare's
plays, eighteen of which had never been published before (or seventeen, if the
1594 *Taming of A Shrew* is considered to be an early version of Shakespeare's
Taming of The Shrew), a dedication and an epistle, prefatory verse, as well as an
engraved title-page, with a three-quarter page portrait of Shakespeare and a
facing poem. It sold for a pound when bound in plain calf, somewhat less in
other bindings, and unbound, as many books were purchased, it sold for
about fifteen shillings. Its very appearance in folio marks the volume as a
major shift in the cultural positioning of Shakespeare, a shift confirmed within a few months of its publication when the library established by Thomas
Bodley (who had died in 1613, a year after ordering his librarian not to collect play-texts) did accept a copy and had it bound in fine leather and stamped
with the Oxford coat of arms.[25]

It isn't clear whose idea the collected volume was, or even what was the
precise motivation behind it. Certainly, Edmund Blount and William and
Isaac Jaggard were the principal stationers involved. William Jaggard, however, died in November of 1623, perhaps within days of the volume's completion, his son Isaac succeeding to his business. It is Isaac's name that
appears with Blount's on the imprint, although the colophon, printed somewhat earlier at the time *Cymbeline*, the final play in the volume, was completed, asserts the volume was "Printed at the Charges of W. Iaggard, Ed. Blount,
I. Smithweeke, and W. Aspley." John Smethwick and William Aspley, who
owned the rights to six plays between them, became minority shareholders in

the venture rather than leasing or selling their rights.[26] The volume was printed at the Jaggards' printing house, and presumably Blount was its principle
bookseller from his shop at the Black Bear in the churchyard of St. Paul's.

The publishers apparently contracted with the King's men for the playhouse manuscripts of the plays that had not yet been printed, Isaac Jaggard
and Blount's entry of 8 November 1623 of sixteen plays "as are not formerly
entred to other men,"[27] establishing their copyright to these plays; and they
obviously worked to secure the publishing rights to those that did belong to
other publishers. Contacting the publishers who held title to the various printed plays, Jaggard and Blount would have sought to acquire the rights (presumably not seeking outright title to these plays but merely permission to
publish them in the folio collection[28]), either by leasing or buying or having
them otherwise assigned, as with the six plays that Smethwick and Aspley
controlled and allowed to be printed seemingly in exchange for some percentage of the enterprise. Thomas Pavier had acquired the rights to three
plays (*2* and *3 Henry VI* and *Henry V,* although all three had been published
only in flawed texts, which, however, had no bearing upon his title), and he
held at least half a share in another: *Titus Andronicus.* Matthew Law also held
multiple titles, *Richard III, Richard II,* and the first part of *Henry IV,* all of which
had been transferred to him from Andrew Wise in 1603.

No other publisher held the rights to more than a single play. One of this
group, Henry Walley, who owned the rights to *Troilus and Cressida,* apparently refused at first to grant the syndicate permission to publish his play, though
work had already begun on its printing. As a result, *Troilus and Cressida* does
not appear at all in the folio's "Catalogue," and some copies of the folio were
in fact printed and sold without the play. Agreement was eventually reached
with Walley, but by that time the play, originally intended to follow *Romeo and
Juliet,* had been replaced there by *Timon of Athens* and work on the volume
had continued through to the end with the colophon printed. When *Troilus*
belatedly became available, it could not, therefore, be simply added on, and
it had to be awkwardly fit in at the beginning of the section of tragedies. The
already printed sheet, containing the last page of *Romeo* and the first three of
Troilus with their original page numbers, was used, with the last page of *Romeo*
merely crossed out, and the rest of the play freshly printed and left unpagi-
nated. At least five copies of the folio have survived in this form. Eventually,
no doubt because this was so manifestly a makeshift solution, a theatrical prologue, absent from the 1609 quarto, was uncovered and printed to replace the

crossed-out page of *Romeo*, and this single cancel leaf, with this prologue on one side and a reset first page of *Troilus* on the other, replaced the old first page that had the crossed-out final page of *Romeo and Juliet* as its recto. There are, thus, as Peter Blayney has shown, three discrete issues of the folio, though most surviving copies of the book are in this final, corrected state.[29]

Negotiations with Walley were not the only ones that left their mark upon the book. The syndicate apparently had similar troubles reaching an agreement with Law who in his three histories owned three of the period's best-sellers. Eventually a deal was struck, but not before the printing of the histories had to be stopped and work moved ahead in the volume. Once agreement was reached with Law and it was possible to return to these plays, the printers discovered that an inadequate amount of space had been allotted; an additional quire of eight leaves had to be added to complete the printing of *2 Henry IV*, though the text didn't quite fill all of the new pages, no doubt accounting for the anomalous final leaf with its unusually large type for the epilogue and a list of roles on the verso.

With Pavier, the other multiple title-holder, it was simpler. At least negotiations with him didn't involve interruptions to the printing or resettings of the text. Pavier seemingly agreed to sell or lease his rights immediately. He was a friend of the Jaggard family, and he might well have been part of the syndicate were it not for his own involvement four years earlier with a plan to publish a quarto collection of ten of Shakespeare's plays (in fact eight by Shakespeare and two, *The Yorkshire Tragedy* and *Sir John Oldcastle*, falsely attributed to him) that was derailed when the King's men successfully implored the Lord Chamberlain to order that "no playes that his Ma^{tyes} players do play shalbe printed w^{th}out consent of som[m]e of them."[30] The intervention seemingly stopped the planned–for collection, but, as printing had already begun, Pavier and William Jaggard apparently decided to continue printing but issue the texts individually with falsely dated title-pages, presumably so they would seem old stock that could be safely sold at Pavier's shop in Ivy Lane.[31]

It is, in many ways, a puzzling episode. Jaggard was the printer of the Shakespeare folio, his son one of its publishers, so the players' willing involvement with him in the production of the 1623 folio suggests either that they were unaware of his role in the events of 1619 or unconcerned about it once the collection had been forestalled–or perhaps merely forgiving. Pavier himself was not an unscrupulous publisher, as some historians have claimed; on the contrary he was more than usually successful and well respected.[32] His publishing ventures had shifted from the newsbooks and plays of his early career to devotional literature in the period of his involvement with this project, and he had recently been elected to the governing courts of the Stationers' Company. Yet whatever the motives, a collection of Shakespeare's plays had been attempted three years before printing on the folio began, and, with its collapse, its would-be publisher sold or leased his rights to the new syndicate.

Whatever else they may show, these publishing arrangements reveal again how marginal the author was to this process of constructing the Shakespeare folio. Only publishers had rights that needed attention, and the physical form of the book was affected by business dealings as much as by literary considerations. Nonetheless, the volume remarkably presents itself as Shakespeare's own. "Mr. William / **SHAKESPEARES** / COMEDIES, / HISTORIES, & / TRAGEDIES. / Published according to the True Originall Copies" proclaims the title-page, and offers the stark, unadorned engraving by Martin Droeshout as witness to its authenticity. Hooded eyes engage us from a large head floating oddly above the unfashionable ruff. The short poem opposite, however, asks us to look away, contesting the portrait's power to arrest us with its image. "O, could he but haue drawne his wit / As well in brasse, as he hath hit / His face, the print would then surpasse / All, that was euer writ in Brasse. / But, since he cannot, Reader, looke / Not on his Picture, but his Booke." It is the book we should look to, the book where we are told we will discover not only what is authentically Shakespeare's but indeed what is authentically Shakespeare.[33]

But what is in that book? We have seen that Shakespeare is there somewhere, but certainly not whole and unadulterated; the texts themselves are based on scribal copies and foul papers, annotated quartos and prompt books; they reflect both first thoughts and later theatrical additions. They reveal his active engagement in the collaborations of the theater company and his passive acceptance of the collaborations in the printing house. The volume, however, would tell a different story. Shakespeare is no longer a mere collaborator but here, as Ben Jonson's commendatory poem names him, "The AVTHOR Mr. William Shakespeare." The theatrical authorizations that mark the quartos are gone; there is no mention that any text is here "as it was played"; indeed, the acting companies are never mentioned by name. (The names of the principal players are, of course, printed, though interestingly enough on a page that is part of an afterthought to the preliminaries.) The texts themselves are offered as new and improved, or, rather, as original and still uncontaminated, the title-page promising that the plays are "Published according to the True Originall Copies." An odd phrase, that: "True Originall Copies," "copy" apparently meaning here a text to be copied rather than a copy of that text; but the phrase sounds disturbingly oxymoronic (if it is original can it be a copy; if it is a copy can it be original?), unwittingly rendering the claim of originality problematic, as all claims of originality inevitably are.

Still, the volume pursues its project of creating Shakespeare as the author he never wanted to be. Some recent critics have claimed this as the project only of later editors, eighteenth-century scholars like Capell and Malone; in fact, it started with his first. John Heminges and Henry Condell were friends of Shakespeare and fellow sharers in the company (in Shakespeare's will he left each of them, along with Richard Burbage, the three surviving members of the shareholders of the Globe when it was built in 1599, 26s.8d to "buy them ringes," further evidence, if any is necessary, of how little Shakespeare chafed against his existence in the community of the acting company). It was the two actors who apparently provided the publishers the manuscripts of the eighteen plays that had not yet reached print; Leonard Digges, in a commendatory poem addressed to Shakespeare, commends also the labor of the two "pious fellowes" who have given "The world thy Workes." And at least one other contemporary toasted their editorial activities, in a poem entitled "To my good freandes m^r John Hemings & Henry Condall":

> To yowe that Joyntly with vndaunted paynes
> Vowtsafed to Chawnte to vs thease noble straynes,
> How mutch yowe merrytt by it, it is not sedd,
> But yowe haue pleased the lyving, loved the deadd,
> Raysede from the woamb of Earth a ritcher myne
> Than Curteys [i.e., Cortez] Cowlde with all his Castellyne
> Associattes, they dydd butt digg for Gowlde,
> Butt yowe for Treasure mutch moare manifollde.[34]

As the senior members of the King's men, Heminges and Condell had access to the play scripts and, if they had no proprietary rights themselves to the plays, they were certainly the logical candidates to negotiate for the acting company with the publishers. As the only two surviving members of the original fellowship of actors that Shakespeare had joined (Burbage having died in 1619), they would know better than any how the manuscripts they delivered to Blount and Jaggard would have modified the manifold treasure of Shakespeare's words. In spite of the folio's claims that its play-texts are "truely set forth, according to their first ORIGINALL," only three of the eighteen previously unpublished plays seem to be printed from something that might reasonably be thought to be Shakespeare's foul papers. The others derive either from scribal transcripts or the bookkeeper's marked playbooks. Scribal versions tend to rationalize texts, cleaning up inconsistencies, regularizing speech headings, spelling, punctuation, even, on occasion, metrics; theatrical copies would inevitably have registered interpolations and cuts made to enable the scripts to play (as is evident, for example, in the text of *Macbeth*). Nonetheless, in their epistle addressed "To the great Variety of Readers," Heminges and Condell pretend otherwise. The texts now "collected & publish'd" are said to be set forth exactly as they flowed from their author's imaginings. "Where before," they say, readers "were abus'd with diuerse stolne, and surreptitious copies, maimed, and deformed by the frauds and stealthes of iniurious imposters that expos'd them: euen those, are now offer'd to your view cur'd, and perfect of their limbes; and all the rest, absolute in their numbers, as he conceiu'd the[m]."

Scholars have, understandably, aggressively mined this sentence for evidence about the earliest transmission of Shakespeare's plays, and have constructed influential narratives based upon Heminges and Condell's distinction between the "diuerse stolen, and surreptitious copies" that were "maimed, and deformed" and "all the rest." The consensus shaped by the groundbreaking work of the new bibliographers (i.e., those scholars working mainly in the first third of the twentieth century like Pollard, Greg, and McKerrow, who did successfully revise our understanding of early modern English printing and publishing practices) holds that the first set of terms does not apply to all the pre-folio quartos but only "to plays of which the Quartos have bad texts and the Folio good ones."[35] This now common understanding has it that Heminges and Condell differentiate those quarto texts (like Q1 *Hamlet* or Q1 *Romeo*) that seemingly derive not from Shakespeare's manuscripts but from unauthorized transcripts of the play made by a reporter or one or more actors (hence "maimed, and deformed") and that were published without the authority of the acting company (hence "stolne, and surreptitious") from "the rest" of the plays in the folio, a group that in turn encompasses two further categories of texts: the "good" quartos, i.e., those editions printed from legally acquired copy that was either Shakespeare's own manuscript or a transcript of it, and the playhouse manuscripts of the previously unpublished plays.

Though the distinction is neat and underpins a number of the most influential ideas of the new bibliography, it seems to me unlikely. First of all, it is a strained reading of the sentence, insisting upon three categories of texts where Heminges and Condell offer only two: the previously "deformed" texts that are now offered "cur'd" of their defects and "all the rest" that are still exactly as Shakespeare "conceiu'd" them. And, second, it projects an implausible and anachronistic sense of bibliographic sophistication upon the two actors. An author might well complain–and indeed some did (though never Shakespeare)–about an unauthorized printing, but an actor would be unlikely to notice or to care, having always worked in contexts where theatrical requirements inevitably took precedence over the integrity of authorial design and where the publication of plays was generally an irrelevance, if not an inconvenience. Even in those cases where the King's men had opposed the publication of their plays the quality of the texts was not the concern.

Perhaps if it could be proven that the texts for the "good" quartos were purchased directly from the company, while those for the "bad" quartos were inevitably pirated editions, then there would at least be a profit motive that would explain the sensitivity; but the familiar bibliographic distinction owes far more to scholarly desire than to the facts of the case.[36] There is little basis for assuming that a "bad" text was necessarily irregularly published (cf. Millington's version of 2 Henry VI, which, however defective, was properly registered) or that a "good" one necessarily reached print with the acting company's consent (cf. Bonian and Walley's Troilus and Cressida, which they happily admit was published in spite of the opposition of the play's "grand possessors").

I take it, rather, that Heminges and Condell distinguish only two kinds of texts: one, the "stolne, and surreptitious copies," simply consists of the group of plays that has already been set out in print, "good" and "bad" quartos together; and the other, "all the rest," is comprised of the previously unpublished play scripts to this point safely held in the hands of the actors. In the folio Heminges and Condell bring both groups together "to keepe the memory of so worthy a Friend, & Fellow aliue, as was our SHAKESPEARE," as they say in their dedication to the Herberts. Those vagrant play-texts, previously "maimed, and deformed" in the process of their publication, have been "cur'd" (through some unspecified editorial labor); where before they were "exposed" to the reading public in their deformity, now they are displayed "perfect of their limbes." The playhouse manuscripts, on the other hand, having been continuously sheltered from the depredations of the publishing process, already perfectly reveal Shakespeare's intentions and can be printed exactly as "he conceiu'd the[m]."

What prevents this straightforward explanation of Heminges and Condell's sentence from being readily accepted is that the new bibliographers had quite correctly observed that all the early quartos were not, in fact, irregularly published and defective texts. Their research proved without a doubt that publishers in most cases acquired their copy legally from those who owned it, published it according to the normal professional procedures, and produced a text that was reasonably accurate and reliable. Still, perhaps as many as ten of Shakespeare's plays had appeared in versions that could possibly be considered "bad texts": *2* and *3 Henry VI, Richard III, Romeo and Juliet, Loves Labor's Lost* (though the "bad" quarto, if there was one, has not survived), *Henry V, The Merry Wives of Windsor, Hamlet, King Lear,* and *Pericles* (which, of course, is not included in the 1623 folio). Thus, though some of the pre-folio versions could be thought "surreptitious" and "deformed," others clearly could not, and these in many cases had served as the copy for the folio texts. If Heminges and Condell are accurately describing the nature of the early texts, their claim about the "diuerse" editions that had previously circulated obviously cannot refer to all of the earlier printings, and, so the new bibliographers, in their desire to affirm the integrity of the folio editors and the texts they set forth, interpret the sentence to mean what their knowledge of the facts demands.

But their very insistence that Heminges and Condell have provided an exact description of the characteristics of the early texts works to undercut their interpretation of the two editors' claim. At most, two of the plays appearing in the folio might be thought to satisfy their account of a text now "perfected" and published regularly that before existed only in a version that was both "surreptitious" and "maimed." The "bad" quartos of *Loves Labor's Lost* (if there was indeed an earlier, defective printing), *Romeo and Juliet,* and *Hamlet* had already been superseded by better texts and indeed ones that the folio versions of these plays in various ways depend upon. The early texts of *2* and *3 Henry VI,* both of which are generally considered somehow defective, were seemingly fully authorized publications, part two of *Henry VI* registered in 1594, the registration apparently also covering part three, as the rights to both parts were transferred to Thomas Pavier from Thomas Millington in 1602. *Richard III* (1597) and *King Lear* (1607) also were both properly registered, *Richard III* to Andrew Wise on 20 October 1597 and *Lear* to Nathaniel Butter and John Busby on 26 November 1607; and while both texts differ markedly from their folio versions, containing lines absent from the folio and missing lines there present, neither displays the kind of textual corruption usually thought to be characteristic of a "bad" quarto.

The quarto versions of *Henry V* and *Merry Wives*, however, may more plausibly be considered nonauthorial texts (though certainly Q1 *Henry V*, perhaps abridged for performance, is entirely coherent, its deficiencies largely a function of its inadequate stage directions; Q1 *Merry Wives* seems more likely to be a reported text), and in both cases some abnormality surrounds their publication. *Henry V* was published in 1600 by Thomas Millington and John Busby without registration and in the face of a "stay" against its printing recorded on 4 August 1600. *Merry Wives,* however, was registered; John Busby enters it on 18 January 1602, but its rights were immediately assigned to Arthur Johnson. The unusual practice has appeared to some as telling evidence of Busby's shrewd if not shifty effort to avoid liability for the purchase of unauthorized copy, although it seems far more likely to have been a perfectly legitimate method of generating a small profit with very little risk by selling the rights to a play rather than undertaking its publishing.[37]

In any case, if at most only two of the thirty-six plays of the folio can be considered to have earlier been published in a form both "surreptitious" and "maimed" (and even of these two, one is arguably not "surreptitious" and the other arguably not "maimed"), it hardly seems enough to bear the full weight of the radical differentiation of authorized (and "perfect") and unauthorized (and "deformed") texts upon which Heminges and Condell's sanction of the folio versions rests. Instead, it's more likely that their contested sentence means exactly what it seems to say; the plays in print at the time of the publishing of the folio are what Heminges and Condell deride and what they distinguish from the putatively authentic texts that appear in their volume.

I am not, however, suggesting that we should, therefore, ignore the compelling research of Pollard, McKerrow, and Greg, and return to Malone's unduly pessimistic conclusion about the early quartos: that "undoubtedly they were *all* surreptitious, that is stolen from the playhouse, and printed without the consent of the author or the proprietors."[38] Undoubtedly the early printings were not all unauthorized or defective. What I am claiming, however, is that Heminges and Condell *say* they were, perhaps because to men of the theater a cheaply published playbook could be nothing else, but mainly, no doubt, to increase the appeal of the newly published folio volume. The two actors simply assert that "before" the folio was available readers were "abus'd" with corrupted texts and that "now" they may enjoy Shakespeare's plays "perfect of their limbes" and "absolute in their numbers, as he conceiu'd the[m]."

It is the classic "before and after" advertiser's tactic, and can hardly be taken as a definitive account of the early texts. It is moving testimony to our desire for the authentic Shakespeare that it was ever thought to be so. Rather than be understood as an authoritative textual history, Heminges and Condell's bibliographic claim should be recognized as a motivated fantasy of textual production, and, interestingly, one exactly like the image of Shakespeare's process of creation: "His mind and hand went together: And what he thought, he vttered with that easinesse, that wee haue scarse receiued from him a blot in his papers."[39] Shakespeare seemingly writes without labor, and these texts, unlike any previous ones, reproduce his effortless creation also without flaw or blemish. Writing and print go together exactly as did his "mind and hand." In their epistle, Heminges and Condell establish Shakespeare as an author by erasing the very conditions of his art, the principles of its realization. The multiple agencies of the theater and the printing house, even the agency of his own work, are denied. The epistle insists that the plays are set forth as Shakespeare "conceiu'd them," but the processes of their materialization improbably leave no trace. In Heminges and Condell's account, Shakespeare's absolute authority is left uncontested and intact—or, more exactly, their account doesn't *leave* Shakespeare's authority unchallenged, it is the very means by which that authority is invented. Shakespeare never had it, and unlike Jonson, never tried to claim it.

Arguably, today much more is at stake in the assertion of Shakespeare's unique authorship, for he has come to play another role he never sought, as the witness and guarantor of Western moral and social values; for Heminges and Condell, and the publishing syndicate that put together the volume, it was perhaps much simpler. Heminges and Condell offer the book to its hoped-for readers and invite them to judge as they see fit: "Iudge your sixepen'orth, your shillings worth, your fiue shillings worth at a time or higher, so you rise to the iust rates, and welcome. But, what euer you do, Buy." "Read him," they urge; and "again and again"; but the bottom line (suggesting

Blount's anxious hand in the epistle) is: "What euer you do, Buy."

The commercial context of the folio must not be forgotten. Today it seems obvious to us that the volume was the necessary and appropriate memorial to England's greatest playwright, but at the time all that was clear to Blount and his partners was that they had undertaken an expensive publishing project with no certainty of recovering their considerable investment.[40] If Shakespeare the writer must inevitably be found decentered and dispersed in the communities and collaborations of early modern play and book production, he has been purposefully and powerfully reconstituted as an AVTHOR in the commercial desires of the early modern book trade.[41] Indeed, if Shakespeare cannot with any precision be called the creator of the book that bears his name, that book might be said to be the creator of Shakespeare. Ben Jonson, driven by a powerful literary ambition, actively sought his role as an author. Shakespeare, as we have seen, was largely indifferent to such individuation, comfortably working in the collaborative ethos of the theater. But it is Shakespeare, of course, who has emerged as the towering figure of individual genius, never, however, having sought his greatness but having it thrust upon him seven years after he died.

The struggle for tne text is *the text.*

−R. Cloud

Chapter 5

"Killed with Hard Opinions": Oldcastle and Falstaff and the Reformed Text of *1 Henry IV*

No doubt, as has long been recognized, Shakespeare did not originally intend Hal's fat tavern companion to be named "Falstaff." As early as the 1630s, Richard James had noted that

in Shakespeares first shewe of Harrie ye fift, ye person with which he

vndertook to playe a buffone was not Falstaffe, but Sr Jhon Oldcastle,

and that offence beinge worthily taken by personages descended

from his title, as peradventure by manie others allso whoe ought to

haue him in honourable memorie, the poet was putt to make an igno rant shifte of abusing Sr Jhon Fastolphe, a man not inferior of Vertue though not so famous in pietie as the other, whoe gaue witnesse vnto the truth of our reformation with a constant and resolute martyrdom, vnto which he was pursued by the Priests, Bishops, Moncks, and Friers of those dayes.1

Apparently objecting to the defamation of the well-known Lollard martyr, the fourth Lord Cobham (as Oldcastle became through his marriage to Joan Cobham in 1408), William Brooke, the tenth holder of the title,[2] seemingly compelled Shakespeare to alter the name of Sir John, acting either in his own right as Lord Chamberlain (as Brooke was from 8 August 1596 until his death on 5 March 1597) or through the intervention and agency of the Queen (as Rowe claims: "some of the Family being then remaining, the Queen was pleas'd to command him [Shakespeare] to alter it"[3]).

Pale traces of the original name, of course, seem to remain in the modified text. Hal refers to Falstaff as "my old lad of the castle" (1.2.41), the colloquial phrase for a roisterer seemingly taking its point from the name of its original referent; and a line in act two–"Away, good Ned. Falstaff sweats to death" (2.2.107)–is metrically irregular with Falstaff's name but arguably not with the trisyllabic "Oldcastle"[4] (and the image itself is grotesquely appropriate for a man who notoriously did virtually sweat to death, being hanged in chains and burned at St. Giles Fields, the spectacular martyrdom grimly memorialized in one of the woodcuts in Foxe's *Acts and Monuments*). Also, in the quarto of *2 Henry IV*, a speech prefix at 1.2.114 has "Old" for "Falstaff," a residual mark somewhat like phantom pain in an amputated limb[5]; and the Epilogue insists that "Oldcastle died a martyr, and this is not the man" (l. 32), a disclaimer that is meaningful only if it might reasonably have been assumed on the contrary that "this" might well have been "the man."

I do not have any substantive quarrel with this familiar argument.[6] I have no new evidence that would confute it nor indeed any to confirm it. It seems certain that Shakespeare, in *1 Henry IV*, originally named his fat knight "Oldcastle" and under pressure changed it. The printing of the quarto in 1598 was perhaps demanded as proof of Shakespeare's willingness to respond to the concerns of the authorities.[7] Oldcastle thus disappeared from the printed texts of the play, though it is less certain that he disappeared in performance: Rowland White, for example, reports a production by the Lord Chamberlain's company in March of 1600 for the Flemish ambassador, apparently at Lord Hunsdon's house, of a play referred to as *Sir John Old Castell*. Though some have thought this to be *The First Part of the True and*

Honorable History of the Life of Sir John Oldcastle by Drayton, Hathaway, Munday, and Wilson, it is almost certainly Shakespeare's *1 Henry IV* rather than the play belonging to the Admiral's men, which was unquestionably still in that company's possession (and so unavailable to the Lord Chamberlain's men) at least as late as September 1602, when Henslowe paid Dekker ten shillings "for his adicions."[8]

Yet whatever play was performed for the ambassador, clearly the character we know as Falstaff was sometimes known as Oldcastle. In Nathan Field's *Amends for Ladies*, published in 1618, Seldon asks, obviously referring to Falstaff's catechizing of honor in act five of *1 Henry IV*: "Did you never see / The Play, where the fat knight hight *Old-Castle*, / Did tell you truly what this honor was?" (sig. G1ʳ). Presumably Field, for one, did see that play with "Falstaff's" catechism in Oldcastle's mouth, as seemingly did Jane Owen, who in 1634 similarly recalled "Syr Iohn Oldcastle, being exprobated of his Cowardlynes" and responding: "If through my persuyte of Honour, I shall fortune to loose an Arme, or a Leg in the wars, can Honour restore to me my lost Arme, or legge?"[9]

I am concerned here with what Oldcastle's elimination from and subsequent haunting of *1 Henry IV* means—both for a critic of the play interested in its religio-political valences in the late 1590s, and for an editor of the text, necessarily concerned with questions of composition and transmission. Gary Taylor has recently argued that at very least what this history means is that editions of *1 Henry IV* should return "Oldcastle" to the play, restoring "an important dimension of the character as first and freely conceived."[10] And, notoriously, the complete Oxford text does just that; although somewhat oddly the individual edition of *1 Henry IV* in the Oxford Shakespeare, edited by David Bevington, pointedly retains Falstaff's name, arguing sensibly that as Falstaff reappears in other plays, depending on familiarity with the name and character of the fat knight in *1 Henry IV*, he must be considered, as Bevington writes, "a fictional entity, requiring a single name. Since that name could no longer be 'Oldcastle,' it had to be 'Falstaff,' in *1 Henry IV* as in the later plays."[11]

I share Bevington's resistance to Taylor's provocative editorial decision (though for reasons somewhat different than Bevington's and on grounds that he might not accept), and hope that my argument here, which attempts to reconsider the historical circumstances, both ideological and textual, of the act of naming, will lend it support. Nonetheless, Taylor's position has at least one solid stanchion. It cannot be denied that the name of Shakespeare's knight was initially "Oldcastle"; and therefore it may be helpful to consider that original act of naming. Critics who have commented on the "Oldcastle" name have usually focused on the perceived slight to the honor of the Cobham title and speculated either that Shakespeare intended an insult to William Brooke (usually, it is argued, because of Brooke's putative hostility to the theater[12]); or that Shakespeare intended no insult but unluckily chose his character's name, as Warburton argued in 1752: "I believe there was no malice in the matter. *Shakespear* wanted a droll name to his character, and never considered whom it belonged to."[13]

It seems to me unlikely that Shakespeare set out to mock or goad Lord Cobham, not least because, if the play was written, as most scholars assume, in late 1596 or early in 1597, Cobham, who became Lord Chamberlain in August of 1596, was a dangerous man to offend; and no one has put forth any credible motive for the pragmatic Shakespeare to engage in such uncharacteristically imprudent behavior.[14] But Warburton's formulation can't be quite right either: that Shakespeare "*never* considered" to whom the name "Oldcastle" belonged. If the play does not use the fat knight to travesty the Elizabethan Lord Cobham, certainly it does use Sir John to travesty Cobham's medieval predecessor. Contemporaries seemed to have no doubt that Shakespeare's character referred to the Lollard knight. The authors of the 1599 *Sir John Oldcastle* consciously set out to correct the historical record Shakespeare had distorted: "It is no pampered glutton we present, / Nor aged Councellour to youthfull sinne, / But one whose vertue shone above the rest, / A Valiant Martyr, and a vertuous Peere" (Prologue, ll. 6–9). Thomas Fuller similarly lamented the travestying of the Lollard martyr by "Stage poets," and was pleased that "Sir John Falstaff hath relieved the memory of Sir John Oldcastle, and of late is substituted buffoon in his place."[15] George Daniel, in 1649, was another who saw through Shakespeare's fiction, like Fuller commending "The Worthy S^r whom Falstaffe's ill-us'd Name / Personates on the Stage, lest Scandall might / Creep backward & blott Martyr."[16]

If Shakespeare's fat knight, however named, is readily understood to "personate" the historical Oldcastle and "blott martyr," one might well ask what is at stake in his presentation as a "buffoon." Whatever Oldcastle was, he was hardly that.[17] Oldcastle had served the young Prince Henry in his Welsh command but had remained a relatively undistinguished Herefordshire knight until his marriage, his third, to Joan Cobham, the heiress of the estate of the third Baron Cobham. At last wiving wealthily, Oldcastle became an influential landowner with manors and considerable land holdings in five counties. He was assigned Royal commissions and was called to sit in the House of Lords.

However, for all his new-found political respectability, Oldcastle remained theologically "unsound." Clearly, he held heterodox views. He was widely understood to be a protector of heretical preachers, and was himself in communication with Bohemian Hussites and possibly sent Wycliffite literature to Prague. Perhaps inspired by the decision of the council at Rome early in 1413 to condemn Wycliff's work as heretical and certainly encouraged by the newly crowned Henry V's need for ecclesiastical support, the English Church began vigorously to prosecute the Lollard heterodoxy, and Oldcastle himself was tried before Archbishop Arundel in September of 1413 and declared a heretic. Oldcastle was, however, given forty days to recant his heresy, no doubt because of his long friendship with the King, and during this period of confinement he succeeded in escaping from the Tower. Following his escape, a rebellion was raised in his name and an attack on the King was planned for Twelfth Night. The King learned of the uprising and surprised and scattered the insurgent troops mustered at Ficket Field. Oldcastle fled and remained at large for three years, hiding in the Welsh marches. On 1 December 1417, news of his capture reached London. Oldcastle was carried to the capital, brought before parliament, indicted and condemned. He was drawn through London to the newly erected gallows in St. Giles Field. Standing on the scaffold, Oldcastle, it was "popularly believed,"[18] promised that on the third day following his death he would rise again, whereupon he was hanged in chains and burned, as Francis Thynne writes, "for the doctrine of wiclyffe and for treasone (as that age supposed)."[19]

Although it took considerably longer than three days, Oldcastle was finally resurrected. As the English Reformation sought a history, Oldcastle was rehabilitated and restored to prominence by a Protestant martyrology that found in his life and death the pattern of virtuous opposition to a corrupt clergy that underpinned the godly nation itself. Most powerfully, in the five Elizabethan editions of Foxe's *Acts and Monuments* (1563–96), Oldcastle emerged, as Foxe writes, as one "so faithful and obedient to God, so submiss[ive] to his king, so sound in his doctrine, so constant in his cause, so afflicted for the truth, so ready and prepared for death" that he may "worthily be adorned with the title of martyr, which is in Greek as much as a witnessbearer."[20]

Foxe, however, must explain away the charge of treason if Oldcastle's life is to bear compelling witness to the truth of the emerging Protestant nation. For Oldcastle to serve not just as a martyr whose life testifies to the perpetual struggle of "the true doctrine of Christ's gospel" against the "proud proceedings of popish errors" (vol. 2, p. 265) but also as the saving remnant on which the godly nation is built, his spiritual faith cannot be in conflict with his political loyalties. The heresy of his proto-Protestant Lollardy is easily dismissed by an emergent Protestant historiography but, since the Protestant cause in sixteenth-century England was inevitably tied to the monarchical claims of authority over the Church, the charge of treason is less easily accommodated. Oldcastle's putative participation in a rebellion against the King puts at risk what Peter Lake has called "the Foxian synthesis" of "a view of the church centered on the Christian prince and one centered on the godly community."[21]

Foxe, of course, successfully locates Oldcastle within this synthesis. He erases the tension produced by the insurrection by erasing from the chronicle accounts of Oldcastle's involvement in it.[22] Indeed, the erasure is literal, though Edward Hall rather than Foxe is the agent. Foxe reports how Hall had echoed earlier chroniclers in writing of Oldcastle's conspiracy "against the king" and was preparing to publish his account, but, when a servant brought him "the book of John Bale, touching the story of the lord Cobham," which had "newly come over" from the continent, Hall, "within two nights after . . . rased and cancelled all that he had written before against sir John Oldcastle and his fellows" (vol. 3, pp. 377–78). For Foxe, the account of Hall's erasure of Oldcastle's treason is a conversion narrative that serves to guarantee Foxe's own debunking of the chronicle accounts of the Oldcastle rebellion.

Oldcastle's rebellion is finally for Foxe not an inconvenient fact but an outright invention of biased historians. He shows the inconsistencies and contradictions in the earlier accounts and concludes that it is merely "pretensed treason . . . falsely ascribed unto [Oldcastle] in his indictment, rising upon wrong suggestion and false surmise, and aggravated by rigour of words, rather than upon any ground of due probation." The invention, continues Foxe, is ideologically motivated, the charge rising "principally of his [Oldcastle's] religion, which first brought him in hatred of the bishops; the bishops brought him in hatred of the king; the hatred of the king brought him to his death and martyrdom" (vol. 3, p. 543).

But even if Oldcastle is innocent of treason, Foxe still must inconveniently admit "the hatred of the king," thus exposing the fault line in a historiography that would appropriate Lollardy as the precursor of the national Church. If Oldcastle is, as a Lollard, a martyr of the Protestant faith, he is, also, as one hated by the King, an uncomfortable hero of the Protestant nation. The unavoidable tension between Oldcastle's faith and Royal author- ity makes impossible the identity of the True Church and the godly nation that Elizabethan England officially demanded.

Perhaps it is on this note that one can begin to assess the question of why it is that Shakespeare should ever have chosen to portray the historical Oldcastle as the irresponsible knight of his play. In 1752, an article in *Gentleman's Magazine*, signed only P. T., asked, "could *Shakespeare* make a pam- pered glutton, a debauched monster, of a noble personage, who stood fore- most on the list of *English* reformers and Protestant martyrs, and that too at a time when reformation was the Queen's chief study? 'Tis absurd to suppose, 'tis impossible for any man to imagine."[23] P. T. undertakes to explain away the evidence that Falstaff ever was Oldcastle in Shakespeare's play, but since that evidence seems as incontrovertible as the evidence that Oldcastle, as P. T. says, "stood foremost on the list of *English* reformers and Protestant martyrs," one must assume that Shakespeare deliberately engaged in the very character assassination P. T. finds impossible to imagine.

Gary Taylor, committed to the original and the restored presence of Oldcastle in the play, has argued that Oldcastle's notoriety as a proto- Protestant hero is precisely that which demanded Shakespeare's travesty. John Speed, in *The Theatre of the Empire of Great Britaine* (1611), had objected to the presentation of Oldcastle as "a Ruffian, a Robber, and a Rebell" by the Jesuit Robert Parsons (writing as N. D.), complaining that his evidence was "taken from the Stage-plaiers" and railing against "this Papist and his Poet, of like conscience for lies, the one euer faining, and the other euer falsifying the truth" (p. 637). Marshalling evidence that purports to establish Shakespeare's sympathy to Catholic positions if not Shakespeare's commitment to the Catholic faith itself, Taylor, like Speed, takes the caricature of Oldcastle to suggest at very least Shakespeare's "willingness to exploit a point of view that many of his contemporaries would have regarded as 'papist.'" Noting other dramatic facts that admit of such an interpretation, Taylor concludes: "In such circumstances, the possibility that Shakespeare deliberately lampooned Oldcastle can hardly be denied" ("Fortunes," p. 99).

It can hardly be denied that Shakespeare has deliberately lampooned Oldcastle, but I think Taylor has somewhat misjudged the "circumstances" in which Shakespeare was writing and in which his play would be received. Whether or not Shakespeare was a Catholic or Catholic sympathizer,[24] Shakespeare's audience in 1596 or 1597 was far more likely to see the lampooning of Oldcastle as the mark of a Protestant bias rather than a papist one, providing evidence of the very fracture in the Protestant community that made the accommodation of the Lollard past so problematic. Lollardy increasingly had become identified not with the godly nation but with the more radical Puritans, the "godly brotherhood," as some termed themselves, that had tried and failed to achieve a "further reformation" of the Church of England. If in the first decades of Elizabeth's rule the Lollards were seen (with the encouragement of Foxe) as the precursors of the national Church, in the last decades they were seen (with the encouragement of Bancroft and other voices of the Anglican polity) as the precursors of the nonconforming sectaries who threatened to undermine it.

No doubt recognizing that the radical Protestants were the inheritors of the doctrine and the discipline of the Lollards, as well as their reputation for sedition, John Hayward, in his *Life and Raigne of King Henrie IIII*, notes, as Daniel Woolf has observed, "with some regret the growth of Lollardy." The nonconformist community, the "favourers and followers of Wickliffes opinions," were consistently at odds with the crown, "which set the favour of the one and the faith of the other at great separation and distance." The political tensions existing at the end of Richard's reign and continuing through Henry's insure that Lollardy does not, in Hayward's history, comfortably anticipate the Protestant nation. "For Hayward," writes Woolf, "quite unlike John Foxe, Lollards were not early protestants but progenitors of Elizabethan Brownists, violators of the Reformation principle *cuius regio, eius religio.*"[25]

But if Hayward recognized the nonconformist genealogy, he was not alone in doing so. In 1591, an almanac, written by a conforming astrologer identifying himself as "Adam Foulweather," predicted that "out of the old stock of heresies" would soon "bloom new schismatical opinions and strange sects, as Brownists, Barowists and such balductum devises, to the great hinderance to the unitie of the Church and confusion of the true faith."[26] And the separatist leader, Francis Johnson, writing defiantly from the Clink in 1593, himself confirmed his ties to "the old stock of heresies," proudly asserting that his opinions were identical to those that "were accounted Lollardye and heresye in the holy servants and martirs of Christ in former ages," like "the Lord Cobham (who was hanged and burnte hanging). . . ."[27]

Under the leadership of John Field (the father of Nathaniel Field, the author of *Amends for Ladies*), nonconforming Protestants had in the 1580s attempted the establishment of Presbyterianism by parliamentary authority, but by the mid-1590s, the government, led by Whitgift's rigorous promotion of uniformity and the Queen's continuing insistence "upon the truth of the reformation which we have already,"[28] had succeeded in its campaign against the radicals. Christopher Hatton's appointment as Lord Chancellor, as Thomas Digges remembered, marked a change of policy whereby not merely papists but "puritans were trounced and traduced as troublers of the state,"[29] and by the early 1590s, radical Protestantism, conceived of by the government as a threat to the polity, was in retreat, at least as a political movement. The "seditious sectaries," as the 1593 "Act to retain the Queen's subjects in obedience"[30] termed the nonconformists, were driven underground or abroad; and advanced Protestantism, even as its evangelical impulse thrived, was, in its various sectarian forms, thoroughly "discredited," as Claire Cross has written, "as a viable alternative to the established Church in the eyes of most of the influential laity who still worked actively to advance a further reformation."[31] Whatever Shakespeare's own religious leanings, then, certainly most members of his audience in 1596 would most likely have viewed the travesty of a Lollard martyr not as a crypto-Catholic tactic but an entirely orthodox gesture, designed to reflect upon the nonconformity that the Queen herself had termed "prejudicial to the religion established, to her crown, to her government, and to her subjects."[32]

Yet even if Taylor has mistaken the probable political implications of the lampooning of Oldcastle in 1596, what is for Taylor the more central bibliographic argument in favor of restoring the censored name "Oldcastle" to the text of *1 Henry IV* seemingly remains unaffected. Taylor argues that "the name 'Falstaff' fictionalizes, depoliticizes, secularizes, and in the process trivializes the play's most memorable character" (p. 95), and that argument would hold regardless of what the political valence of the suppressed "Oldcastle" actually is. Taylor's insistence that restoring "Oldcastle" effectively rehistoricizes the character of Sir John is compelling (even if I would rehistoricize it differently). However, what is to me troubling about the editorial implications of this argument is that restoring "Oldcastle," if it rehistoricizes the character, effectively *de*historicizes and in the process dematerializes the text in which he appears.[33]

Whether or not the travesty of Oldcastle would have shocked what Taylor calls "right-minded Protestants" ("Fortunes," p. 97)–and the answer clearly must depend upon what is understood to make a Protestant "right-minded"– whatever meanings attach to Shakespeare's fat knight, as Taylor's own argument shows, are not functions of an autonomous and self-contained text but are produced by the intersection of Shakespeare's text with something that lies outside it, a surrounding cultural text, what Roland Barthes calls "the volume of sociality,"[34] that the literary text both mediates and transforms. Yet if Taylor's critical response to the censored name "Oldcastle" ingeniously acknowledges the interdependency of the literary and social text, his reintroduction of "Oldcastle" to the printed text paradoxically works to deny it.

Taylor insists that we should restore the name "Oldcastle" to the play since the change "was forced upon Shakespeare," and the restoration allows us to return to "Shakespeare's original conception" ("Fortunes," p. 88). "Oldcastle" is what Shakespeare initially intended and, therefore, argues Taylor, what modern editions should print. "So far as I can see," Taylor writes, "the chief, indeed the *only* objection to restoring the original reading (Oldcastle) is that the substituted reading (Falstaff) has become famous" ("Fortunes," p. 89, emphasis mine). But there is at least one other substantive objection to the restoration: that is, that all the authoritative texts print "Falstaff" and none prints "Oldcastle." "Oldcastle" may return us to "Shakespeare's original conception," but literally "Oldcastle" is not a "reading" at all.[35]

To disregard this fact is to idealize the activity of authorship, removing it from the social and material mediations that permit intentions to be realized in print and in performance. It is to remove the text from its own complicating historicity.[36] The restoration of "Oldcastle" enacts a fantasy of unmediated authorship paradoxically mediated by the Oxford edition itself. Taylor here privileges "what Shakespeare originally intended" ("Fortunes," p. 90) over the realized text that necessarily preserves multiple (and sometimes contradictory) intentions. While Taylor's commitment here to authorial intention is obviously not in itself an unknown nor unproductive theoretical position,[37] what is undeniably odd about this particular exercise of it is that it seemingly rejects what is the central achievement of the Oxford Shakespeare, which differentiates itself from its predecessors by acknowledging the fact that dramatic production in Shakespeare's England was never an autonomous authorial achievement but a complex social and theatrical activity in which authorship was only one determinant, the Oxford Shakespeare is, in Taylor's words, "an edition conspicuously committed to the textual and critical implications of the recognition that Shakespeare was a theatre poet, whose work found its intend-ed fruition only in the collaborative theatrical enterprise for which he wrote."[38]

Obviously, Gary Taylor understands better than most editors that dra-matic texts are produced by multiple collaborations, and the Oxford edition uniquely attempts to register these, presenting not "the literary, pretheatrical text" but a text as it appears "in the light of theatrical practice."[39] Yet what allows him in the case of the disputed name of Falstaff/Oldcastle to privilege Shakespeare's original intention over the operations of "the collaborative the-atrical enterprise," the necessarily multiple and dispersed intentionalities of Renaissance playmaking, is Taylor's certainty that the change from "Oldcastle" in *1 Henry IV* was "forced upon" the playwright; that is, the replacement of "Oldcastle" is taken as evidence of an unsolicited and irre-sistible interference with the author's intentions rather than as a symptom of the inevitable compromise and accommodation that allow a play to reach the stage or the book shop. For Taylor the issue is clear: "The change of name is not an instance of revision but of censorship" ("Fortunes," p. 88). And as an instance of censorship it is a "depredation" to be editorially undone.

Indeed, it does seem certain that Shakespeare originally intended to call his character "Oldcastle," and it seems equally obvious that Shakespeare was, in some fashion, compelled to change the name. But the necessary vagueness of that "in some fashion" suggests a problem with the appeal to intention. If Taylor is correct to say that we "know what Shakespeare originally intended," his secondary premise is more vulnerable: that we know "why that intention was abandoned" ("Fortunes," p. 90). In fact we do not. If it does seem clear that political pressure was applied, it is less so in what form it was exerted. Taylor speaks confidently of "the censor's intervention" ("Fortunes," p. 85), but there is no record of any such action. It seems probable that Richard James's account is largely correct, that the Elizabethan Lord Cobham took "offence" at the travesty of a former holder of the title. But it is worth remem-bering that the scholarly James is writing well after the fact and with no obvi-ous connection to any of the participants; and, although Nicholas Rowe's tes-timony is offered as "independent confirmation that the Cobhams were responsible" for the censorship ("Fortunes," p. 87), Rowe is writing at an even further remove from the events, and Rowe, as we've seen, actually says that "the Queen," not the Cobhams, commanded the alteration, suggesting anoth-er source of pressure and muddying our sense of the nature of the interfer-ence with Shakespeare's text.[40]

My point is not to deny that governmental authorities were unhappy with the parody of the Lollard martyr, Oldcastle, but only to indicate that the available evidence does not allow us to say precisely why "Oldcastle" disappeared from the text of *1 Henry IV*. An influential family seems unquestionably to have objected to the name "Oldcastle," but it is less certain that the elimination of that name was a result of the operations of a process we can confidently and precisely identify as censorship. This is not to split hairs but to move to the heart of the bibliographic argument. If we have an example of the external domination of authorship, any edition of *1 Henry IV* that was committed to the recovery of Shakespeare's artistic intentions might well introduce—though certainly not *re*introduce—"Oldcastle" into the printed text; although an edition, like Oxford's, that insists "that Shakespeare was a theater poet" could plausibly, even in the case of such censorship, have found "Falstaff" to be the appropriate reading, since censorship was one of the inescapable conditions of a theater poet's professional existence.

But we do not in fact know that the replacement of "Oldcastle" with "Falstaff" was an effect of governmental imposition rather than an example of the inevitable, if arguably undesirable, compromises that authors make with and within the institutions of dramatic production. In the absence of documentation, we cannot tell whether we have a text marred by forces beyond the author's control or a text marked by the author's effort to function within the existing conditions in which plays were written and performed. It does seem certain that Lord Cobham objected to the scurrilous treatment of Oldcastle in the play, but we do not have the evidence that would tell us whether "Falstaff" is evidence of Shakespeare's subsequent loss of control over his text or of his effort to keep control of it; that is, we cannot be certain whether "Falstaff" resulted from the play's censorship or from its revision.

But the very uncertainty is as revealing as it is frustrating, suggesting that often no rigid distinction between the two can be maintained. Authority and authorship were usually not discrete and opposed sources of agency but instead were interdependent activities that helped constitute the drama in Elizabethan England.[41] No doubt some form of interference from above led Shakespeare to change Oldcastle's name to "Falstaff," but scrutiny and regulation were among the determining circumstances of playmaking no less than were boy actors in the theater or casting off copy in the printing house. Playwrights worked with and around censors to get their texts to the stage and into the shops. Finding what was acceptable to the censor was as necessary as finding out from the actors what played well. We cannot then say that "Falstaff" represents the "domination of the author's meaning" ("Fortunes," p. 92). "Falstaff" seems rather the evidence of the author's desire to have his meanings realized on stage and in print. Certainly, the use of "Falstaff" in subsequent plays suggests that Shakespeare, however happily, accepted the compromise of his artistic integrity, brilliantly incorporating it into his own intentionality.

Obviously we do not know what Shakespeare and his company thought about the change of name in *1 Henry IV*, but, claims Taylor, "the later intentions of Shakespeare and his company only matter in relation to a single question: would he (or they) have restored 'Oldcastle' to Part 1 if given the chance" ("Fortunes," p. 90). For Taylor the answer is "yes," confirming his decision to print "Oldcastle" in the edited text of the play. The stage history that apparently shows *1 Henry IV* occasionally performed "with the original designation intact," even after *2 Henry IV, The Merry Wives of Windsor,* and *Henry V* were written with the character of Sir John named "Falstaff," serves for Taylor as evidence that Shakespeare or Shakespeare's company continued to imagine the fat knight of *1 Henry IV* as "Oldcastle" ("Fortunes," p. 91).

But the argument from the stage history is at best inconclusive. Even ignoring the fact that intentions other than those of Shakespeare or his company might determine the choice of name, especially in a private performance, simply on the basis of the frequency of allusions to Falstaff in the seventeenth century (more than to any other Shakespearean character[42]), it seems clear that the play was far more frequently played with the new name in place than with the residual "Oldcastle." The popularity of the character known as Falstaff was virtually proverbial. Sir Thomas Palmer remarks Falstaff's ability to captivate an audience as one benchmark of theatrical renown: "*I could . . . tell how long* Falstaff *from cracking nuts hath kept the throng,*" he says in a prefatory poem to the 1647 Beaumont and Fletcher folio, to indicate a standard against which to measure the collaborators' putatively greater success.[43] And Leonard Digges writes: "When let but *Falstaffe* come / *Hall* [sic], *Poines,* the rest—you shall scarce have a roome / All is so pester'd."[44] Sir Henry Herbert's office-book registers Falstaff's impressive cultural currency, referring to the play itself, as performed by the King's men at Whitehall on "New-years night" of 1624–25, as *The First Part of Sir John Falstaff.*[45]

Nonetheless, a bibliographic argument against Taylor's claim that Shakespeare or at least his company continued to think of Sir John as

"Oldcastle" seems finally more compelling even than the theatrical one: his friends and fellow sharers were in fact "given the chance" to restore the censored name and manifestly decided *not* to return "Oldcastle" to the play. With the decision to collect and publish Shakespeare's plays in a folio edition, Heminges and Condell had the perfect opportunity to reinstate "Oldcastle." Indeed as we have seen in the last chapter, they advertise the virtue of the 1623 Folio as repairing the defects of the earlier quartos, curing texts previously "maimed, and deformed" and printing them now "as he [Shakespeare] conceiu'd the[m]."[46] At the time of the printing of the First Folio, no Cobham was around to enforce the change of name demanded by the tenth Lord's sensitivity in 1596: Henry Brooke, the eleventh Lord Cobham, had been found guilty of treason in 1603 for his activity in a plot to place Arabella Stuart on the throne, and he remained confined in the Tower until his death in 1619. The Cobham title then remained unfilled until 1645. Yet in 1623, with the Cobham title discredited and vacant, Heminges and Condell did not see the restoration of "Oldcastle" to the text of *1 Henry IV* as a necessary emendation to return the text to the uncontaminated form in which it was first "conceiu'd."

Taylor offers a conjectural argument that perhaps they "tried unsuccessfully" to reinstate the "Oldcastle" name: "The delay in printing Folio *Henry IV* could easily have risen because of an attempt to secure permission from the new Master of the Revels . . . to restore the original surname." Taylor, however, is forced to concede: "If Heminges and Condell did attempt to restore 'Oldcastle,' they obviously failed. . . ." Yet in the absence of any evidence that they in fact did try to restore the name or any that they were likely to have failed had they so tried, it is hard to resist the all-too-obvious conclusion that Taylor strenuously works to avoid: "that Heminges and Condell, as Shakespeare's literary executors, were happy enough to perpetuate 'Falstaff' in *Part 1*" (p. 92). But so it seems they were. With no obvious impediment to reinstating "Oldcastle," Heminges and Condell retained the name "Falstaff," providing evidence not of Shakespeare's original intention, no doubt, but of the complex interplay of authorial and nonauthorial intentions that allowed *1 Henry IV* to be produced (and that allows *any* text to be produced), providing evidence, that is, that the play is not autonomous and self-defined but maddeningly alive in and to the world. "Falstaff" is the mark of the play's existence in history, and, perhaps in their most telling bibliographic decision, Heminges and Condell wisely left his "rejection" to Hal.

FOUR

The Text as History

> No man can have in his mind a conception of the future, for the future is not yet. But of our conceptions of the past, we make a future.
>
> —Thomas Hobbes

Chapter 6

"Proud Majesty Made a Subject": Representing Authority on the Early Modern Stage

Freud offers as an example of humor the story of Louis XV and one of his courtiers renowned for his wit. The King commanded "the cavalier to concoct a joke at his [the King's] expense. He wanted to be the 'subject' of the witticism. The courtier answered him with the clever *bon mot*, '*le roi n'est pas sujet*'"[1]—the king is not a subject. If this is not a brilliant comic moment, it is at least a skillful political maneuver. The courtier's own subjection to the King's authority demands the pun in order to permit him simultaneously to satisfy and to decline the assignment. The wordplay is ingeniously responsive to the uncertainty of whether the greater danger lies in the risk of offending the King by refusing to provide a jest or in the risk of offending him in actually providing one.

In mid-seventeenth-century England, however, any similar jest would inevitably have had a bitter flavor. To be sure, Renaissance absolutism had insisted that the king was not a subject. "A subject and a sovereign are clean different things,"[2] Charles I defiantly claimed, but the words were among Charles's last, spoken in 1649 as he stood on the black scaffold against the Banqueting House awaiting his execution.

Charles's trial and beheading testify unequivocally to the fact that in England the king had become a subject, no longer privileged as "a little GOD," in his father's phrase, "to sit upon [God's] throne and rule over other men."[3] The English king was held subject to "the authority of The Commons of England," as John Bradshaw, who presided at the King's trial, repeatedly asserted.[4] Alvise Contarini, a Venetian ambassador, sympathetically wrote to the Doge:

> The poor king of England has at last lost both crown and life by the hand of the executioner, like a common criminal, in London, before all the people, without anyone speaking in his favor and by the judicial sentence of his own subjects.[5]

In France, on the other hand, with Louis XV's power intact, the king could be the subject only of a witty courtier's jest, of a grammatical rather than a judicial sentence.

I am interested in what in England permits the king to be subjected to his subjects' power and authority, in what, that is, permits the erasure of the distinction between sovereign and subject that had been at the center of the English political formation. In Shakespeare's *Richard II,* Carlisle asks angrily as Richard is forced to abdicate his throne:

> What subject can give sentence on his king?
> And who sits here that is not Richard's subject?
> (4.1.121–22)

Those who tried Charles were no less his subjects (as the King persisted in reminding them) but felt themselves qualified to pass judgment on the monarch. The trial was the final and obviously decisive step in a complex series of attacks on the royal prerogative and person. In spite of the protests of some Parliamentarians that their intentions were neither radical nor republican, the King all along knew exactly what was at stake. He knew that the Houses' desire to make law by majority vote was a program for

> The ruine . . . of Monarchy it Self (Which Wee may justly say, is more than ever was offered in any of Our Predecessours times; for though the person of the King hath been sometimes unjustly deposed, yet the Regall Power was never before this time stricken at) . . .[6]

In 1649, the court at Westminster Hall struck directly and powerfully at "the Regall Power"; it decreed Charles's treason and ordered his execution. Other English kings had been killed, of course, but, unlike Edward II or Richard II who were secretly murdered by subjects, Charles I was publicly tried and executed in the name of the "good people of this nation."[7]

I want to argue that the process that ended in the monarch's unwilling subjection to the authority of the "people" was encouraged by a subjection, that, like the courtier's jest, was verbal—or, more precisely, verbal and visual. The Elizabethan theater and especially the history play, which critics as different as E.M.W. Tillyard and Stephen Greenblatt agree effectively served the interests of royal power, seem to me to be at least as effective as a subversion of that authority, functioning as a significant cultural intervention in a process of political reformation.[8] In setting English kings before an audience of commoners, the theater nourished the cultural conditions that eventually permitted the nation to bring its king to trial, not because the theater approvingly represented subversive acts but rather because representation itself became subversive. Whatever their overt ideological content, history plays inevitably, if unconsciously, weakened the structure of authority: on stage the king became a subject—the subject of the author's imaginings and the subject of the attention and judgment of an audience of subjects. If, then, English history plays recollected and rehearsed the past, they also prophesied the future, as they placed the king on a scaffold before a judging public.

Though conceived of quite differently, the dangers of representation were a recurring theme of the antitheatrical sentiment that we conveniently if inaccurately label "Puritan."[9] This hostility to the theater obsessively focused on its threat to conventional moral and political authority. Plays, according to Phillip Stubbes in his *Anatomie of Abuses*, "are quite contrarie to the woorde of grace, and sucked out of the Deuilles teates, to nourishe us in Idolatrie, Heathenrie, and sinne."[10] But the antitheatrical argument is not merely that immoral behavior is acted on stage but that acting on stage is immoral. "The very forme of acting Playes," William Prynne declares, is "nought else but grosse hypocrisie." In the theater, he asserts, everything is "counterfeited, feined, dissembled; nothing really or sincerely acted."[11]

Though some of the theater's opponents, like Stubbes, would exempt religious drama from their denunciation,[12] most found that, rather than relaxing their concerns, the religious drama in fact intensified them. The problematic of representation becomes acute when what is counterfeited is the Godhead itself. First, of course, there is the practical problem of how to represent a God that is defined, according to the first of the Articles of Religion, as a being "without body, parts, or passion." One solution is revealed in the Late Banns to the Chester cycle. The organizers decided that God will be "a Voyce onlye to heare / And not god in shape or person to appeare."[13] But the problem is not merely mimetic; it is moral. It is not, as the Late Banns say, that "noe man can proportion that Godhead"; the crucial issue is whether any man should try. In 1576, when a Court of High Commission received "intelligence" that the Corpus Christi play was to be staged in Wakefield, it ordered

> that in the said playe no pageant be used or set further wherin the ma'ye of God the Father, God the Sonne, or God the Holie Ghoste or the administration of either the Sacramentes of baptisme or the Lordes Supper be counterfeited or represented, or anything plaied which tends to the maintenaunce of superstition and idolatrie or which be contrarie to the lawes of God or of the realme.

Revealingly the Commission's concern is as much with the play's aesthetic form as with its theological content. Having the sacred matter of the play "counterfeited and represented," the Commission feared, would "tende to the derogation of the Maiesty and glory of God . . . ."[14]

The York Commission holds that representation "derogates," that is, it diminishes and weakens the authority of what is represented. A similar consideration determines the decision of the Merchant Taylors' School in 1574 to suspend their playing. Here the issue is not sacred representation but secular: "our comon playes and such lyke exercises . . . bringeth the youthe to such an impudente famyliaritie with theire betters that often tymes greite contempte of maisters, parents, and magistrats foloweth thereof, as experience of late in this our comon hall hath sufficyently declared . . . ."[15]

Since the plays put on by the Merchant Taylors' School were not likely to be either scurrilous or subversive, it is clear that the problem lies not with the plays but with their playing. Merely by representing images of authority on stage, the Merchant Taylors' School's directive claims, plays induce in the audience "an impudent famyliaritie" with its "betters." Representation thus undermines rather than confirms authority, denying it its presumptive dignity by subjecting it to common view, as Sir Henry Wotton's account of a performance of *Henry VIII* reveals. The new play, he wrote, "which was set forth with many extraordinary circumstances of Pomp and Majesty, even to the matting of the stage" was "sufficient in truth within a while to make greatness very familiar, if not ridiculous."[16]

Artistic representation apparently leads "to the derogation," in the phrase of the York Commission, of secular majesty no less than of its sacred prototype, demystifying and diminishing its images of authority. Exactly this concern led Elizabeth to regulate royal portraiture. In 1563, a proclamation was drafted "that some special commission painter might be permitted, by access to her majesty to take the natural representation of her majesty, whereof she has always been very unwilling, but also to prohibit all manner of other persons to draw, paint, grave, or portray her majesty's personage or visage for a time until, by some perfect patron and example, the same may be by others followed."[17] In 1596, the Privy Council ordered "defaced" all "unseemly and improperly paintinge, gravinge and printing of her Majesty's person and vysage, to her Majesty's great offence and disgrace of that beautyfull and magnanimous Majesty wherwith God hathe blessed her."[18]

Elizabeth understood that it would not do to allow the queen to be subject to the artist's vision; always it must be subject to the queen's. Royal portraiture, as Roy Strong has shown,[19] effectively served the purposes of the monarchy, glorifying its power. Unregulated, however, the representation of the monarch was potentially dangerous; it might not enforce the desired distinction between ruler and ruled but might rather erode it, derogating majesty by subjecting it to the impudent gaze of its subjects. In 1603, just after James took the throne, Henry Crosse protested that in the theaters "there is no passion wherwith the king, the soueraigne maiestie of the Realme was possest, but is amplified, and openly sported with, and made a May-game to all the beholders."[20] It is no wonder, then, that English monarchs tried to ensure that they controlled the means of theatrical representation as well. As Charles happily recalled in 1624, in the face of the Spanish ambassador's bitter complaint about Middleton's *Game at Chess*, "there was a commandment and restraint given against the representing of any modern

Christian kings in those stage-plays."[21] Elizabeth could herself appear in plays like Peele's *Arraignment of Paris* or the court performance of Jonson's *Every Man Out of His Humour*, but, as Jonson discovered, an actor could not impersonate the queen. In spite of her enthusiasm for the theater, which led her in 1574 to issue a license to the Earl of Leicester's players to perform "for the recreacion of oure loving subiectes as for oure solace and pleasure when we shall thincke good to see them,"[22] Elizabeth was well aware of the dangers of unregulated playing. She understood that a license was necessary; that is, that actors' representations must be subject to statutory control no less than artists'.

Although she drew considerable "solace and pleasure" from the theater, Elizabeth was quick to smell a fault. She never would permit her passions openly to be sported with or made a May-game to the beholder—unless, of course, it was her May-game. "Sometimes Kings are content in Playes and Maskes to be admonished of divers things,"[23] wrote Thomas Scott in 1622; but rarely was Elizabeth so. She was always unusually sensitive to being subjected to her subject's representations. In 1565, Guzman de Silva, the Spanish ambassador, wrote to Philip that, at a dramatic debate between Juno and Diana on the virtues of marriage and chastity, Elizabeth angrily asserted, "This is all against me." However obscure the text, Elizabeth was able to find evidence of a personal application. At an entertainment put on by Essex in 1595, there was much discussion of the meaning of his devise. "The World makes many vntrue Constructions of these Speaches," wrote Rowland Whyte, but Elizabeth was sure of the proper one. Though from the description Whyte supplies, Elizabeth was not portrayed and was mentioned only flatteringly (as the source of "Vertue which made all his [Essex's] thoughts Deuine, whose Wisdom taught him all true Policy, whose Beauty and Worth, were at all Times able to make him fitt to comand armies"). Nonetheless, Whyte reports, "the Queen said, if she had thought their had bene so much said of her, she wold not haue bene their that Night, and soe went to Bed." Burghley's remark about a similar episode earlier that same year seems shrewd: "I thinke never a ladye besides her, nor a decipherer in the court, would have dissolved the figure to have found the sense as her Majestie hath done."[24]

Elizabeth was not merely being paranoid. As David Bevington has demonstrated, the theater did often engage sensitive political issues.[25] But perhaps more to the point is that the theater itself became a sensitive political issue, and its control a matter of contention between the Court and the City.

The theater's defenders and detractors each understood that dramatic representation has a powerful political effect. Defenders held that playing performed a valuable ideological function: "Playes are writ with this ayme, and carryed with this methode," wrote Thomas Heywood, "to teach the subiects obedience to their King, to show the people the untimely ends of such as have moved tumults, commotions, and insurrections, to present them with the flourishing estate of such as live in obedience, exhorting them to allegiance, dehorting them from all trayterous and fellonious strategems."[26] The theater's opponents argued exactly the reverse: plays were irreligious and seditious, and the playhouses themselves were at best nuisances and at worst serious threats to the public weal. As the Lord Mayor and the Aldermen of London wrote to the Privy Council in 1597, "They give opportunity to the refuze sort of euill disposed & vngodly people, that are within and abowte this Cytie, to assemble themselves & to make their matches for all their lewd and vngodly practices."[27] In general, it is the opponents of the theater, however obsessive their hostility appears, who seem to have the best of the argument. The defenders offer only a narrowly homiletic conception of drama that is belied by virtually every play of the period. The detractors come closer to understanding how the plays actually function; their fears respond to the subversive threat the theater potentially posed.

What underlies their anxieties about playing is the awareness that representation offers an inherent challenge to the fundamental categories of a culture that would organize itself hierarchically and present that organization as inevitable and permanent. Certainly, that is Gosson's objection to a theater which makes it necessary "for a boy to put one the attyre, the gesture, the passions of a woman; for a meane person to take vpon him the title of a Prince with counterfeit porte, and traine."[28] The "lye" of the theater demystifies the idealization of the social order that the ideology of degree demanded. The author of the character "Of an Excellent Actor" (1615) writes that "all men haue beene of his occupation: and indeed, what hee doth fainedly that doe others essentially: this day one plaies a Monarch, the next a priuate person. Heere one Acts a Tyrant, on the morrow an Exile: A Parasite this man to night, to morow a Precisian, and so of diuers others."[29] The actor's ability to represent the full range of social roles disturbingly identifies them as "roles"–"actions," as Hamlet says, "that a man might play"–rather than essential and immutable identities.

The theater thus works to expose the mystifications of power. Its counterfeit of royalty raises the possibility that royalty is a counterfeit. Erasmus, in his *Education of a Christian Prince*, had asked:

> if a necklace, a scepter, royal purple robes, a train of attendants are all that make a king, what is to prevent the actors who come on stage decked with all the pomp of state from being called king?[30]

The answer, in the highly theatricalized world of Renaissance politics and the highly politicized world of the Renaissance stage, is perhaps not quite as obvious as Erasmus presumes. Certainly "the actors who come on stage with all the pomp of state" are "*called* king," at least within the play, and in a play like Ford's *Perkin Warbeck* this becomes precisely the point, as the difficulty of enforcing a distinction between an actor playing the king and an actor playing an actor playing a king is turned into the "strange truth" of the drama. "The player's on the stage still, 'tis his part; / 'A does but act" (5.2.68–69), says Henry VII scornfully of Perkin; but, of course, exactly the same could be said of Henry as he stands before an audience in the theater.[31]

As represented on stage, true royalty is not always self-evident, and not merely because all there do "but act." In *The Merchant of Venice*, Portia confidently asserts that "A substitute shines as brightly as a king/ Until a king be by" (5.1.94–95), but in *1 Henry IV*, when Douglas has efficiently dispatched the various nobles wearing the King's coat and does at last come face to face with the King himself, Henry's majesty shines no more brightly than any of the substitutes Douglas has killed:

> What art thou
> That counterfeit'st the person of a king?
> Henry: The King himself . . .
> Douglas: I fear thou art another counterfeit.[32]
> (5.4.26–34)

On the battlefield at Shrewsbury at the end of *1 Henry IV*, the King is indistinguishable from his counterfeits; his majesty can be easily and effectively mimed. But even with real rather than represented kings the distinction that Erasmus would sharply draw between king and actor is blurred, though not by actors successfully playing the monarch but by the monarch successfully playing the monarch. This was the dangerous recognition of George Buchanan, who as Richard Bancroft complained, "gybeth at the state which

Princes take vppon them, when they shewe themselues to the people, comparinge *them to Childrens puppets, which are garishly attyred.*"[33] If the tone was demeaning, the insight was astute, and for Elizabeth, would have been less criticism than a fact of statecraft. She obviously was a brilliant actor, as perhaps she had to be in the absence of effective instruments of coercion. In his *Fragmenta Regalia* (1641), Sir Robert Naunton wrote that he knew

> no prince living that was so tender of honor and so exactly stood for the preservation of sovereignty, that was so great a courter of her people, yea, of the commons, and that stooped and descended lower in presenting her person to the public view as she passed in her progresses and perambulations. . . .[34]

From the moment her accession to the throne was announced, she was almost compulsively concerned with "presenting her person to the public view," recognizing that her rule could be—and in her case, perhaps, could *only* be—celebrated and confirmed theatrically.

On 14 January 1559, the day before her coronation, Elizabeth, dressed in cloth of gold and wearing her princess's crown, was carried through London in an open litter trimmed with gold brocade, accompanied by 1,000 attendants on horseback. The procession, beginning at the Tower and ending at Westminster, spectacularly demonstrated her mastery of the dramaturgy of royal power. "If a man should say well," wrote the author of *The Quene's Majestie's Passage*, "he could not better tearme the citie of London that time, than a stage wherin was shewed the wonderfull spectacle, of a noble hearted princesse toward her most loving people, and the people's exceeding comfort in beholding so worthy a sovereign, and hearing so princelike a voice. . . ."[35] Here and throughout her reign Elizabeth's use of pageant and progress enabled her to transform her country into a theater, and, in the absence of a standing army, create an audience, troops of loyal admirers, to guarantee her rule.

Renaissance rulers, as we know from the work of Stephen Orgel and Roy Strong, habitually expressed their power theatrically.[36] A spectacular sovereignty works to subject its audience to—and through—the royal power on display, captivating, in several senses, its onlookers. But this theatrical strategy of what Greenblatt has called "privileged visibility"[37] carries with it considerable risks. Significantly, it makes power contingent upon the spectators' assent (even if that assent is already assumed as an aspect of the royal script). However much it insists upon its audience's admiration and respect, sovereignty's visible presence demands and authorizes an audience of commoners as a condition of its authority (and it is precisely the anxieties produced by this, rather than any delight in theatricality, that generates the now familiar comments by Elizabeth and James that they are on "stage").

In addition, the effectiveness of the strategy depends on the effective control of the theatrical space. As early as May 1559, Elizabeth had ordered that no plays be permitted

> wherein either matters of religion or of the gouernaunce of the estate of the common weale shalbe handled or treated vpon, beyng no meete matters to be wrytten or treated vpon, but by menne of aucthoritie, learning and wisedome, nor to be handled before any audience, but of graue and discreete persons.

"Matters of religion or of the gouernaunce of the estate of the common weale" can be played only before an audience of "graue and discreete persons"; before an audience of commoners the representation of such matters is dangerous and "not conuenient," as the Proclamation states, "in any good ordred Christian common weale to be suffred."[38] What makes it "not conuenient . . . to be suffred" is that in the theater images of authority become subject to the approval of an audience. The pageantry of state, however, would presume—even co-opt—that approval. Near the end of Elizabeth's 1559 progress, for example, the Queen observed "an auncient citizen which wepte, and turned his head backe." The report wonders, "How may it be interpreted that he so doth, for sorowe or for gladnes"; but Elizabeth, who "wold turne the doutefull to the best," is certain of the citizen's response: "I warrant you it is for gladnes." The ambiguous reaction of the citizen is appropriated and converted by Elizabeth into an opportunity to display, as the report terms it, the "gracious interpretation of a noble courage."[39]

On the other hand, in the theater the actors do not have the option of interpreting, and incorporating, the audience's response. The theater creates and authorizes a critical "public," as Stephen Gosson nervously observed:

> If the commen people which resorte to Theaters being but an assemblie of Tailers, Tinkers, Cordwayners, Saylers, olde Men, yong Men, Women, Boyes, Girles, and such like, be the iudges of faultes there painted out, the rebuking of manners in that place, is neyther lawfull nor conuenient, but to be held for a kinde of libelling, and defaming.[40]

In the theater the audience of commoners becomes "the iudges of faultes there painted out." Its assembly of marginal persons is established as an authoritative body, as Dekker, if less anxiously than Gosson, also recognizes. He explains to his Gull that, since the theater

> is so free in entertainment, allowing a stool as well to the farmer's son as to your Templar, that your stinkard has the selfsame liberty to be there in his tobacco fumes, which your sweet courtier hath; and that your carman and tinker claim as strong a voice in their suffrage, and sit to give judgment on the play's life and death, as the proudest Momus among the Tribe of Critic.[41]

In the Renaissance playhouses, the audience need not—and did not—keep a respectful distance (unlike in the spectacle of state or, for that matter, in the modern theater). The modes of representation in the Elizabethan popular theater refuse to privilege what is represented. Renaissance staging practices, as Robert Weimann has shown, in shifting the action between an upstage *locus* and the downstage *platea*, literally displace the dominant aristocratic ideology.[42] But this dislocating perspective, which submits aristocratic postures and assumptions to the interrogation of clowns and commoners, is enacted on a larger scale in the theater itself—as the action is thrust into the space of the audience. There farmer's son and Templar, stinkard and courtier, carman and tinker, democratically come together, transcending, if only temporarily, the stratified social structure of Jacobean England, and are empowered, by the anti-aristocratic, commercial logic of the theater, to "give judgment on the play's life and death."

Reading history backward, it is tempting to see only a narrow gap between this kind of judgment on the life and death of plays in 1606 and the judgment on the King's life and death in 1649, but even without the imposed teleology and the misleading foreshortening of such a perspective, we cannot be surprised that the authorities found it "neyther lawfull nor conuenient" for an audience of commoners to begin to think of itself as a competent judge— whether of manners, plays, or matters of state. And when the theatrical space is the city itself rather than the playhouse, the immediate danger of unregulated representation increases. Elizabeth, like the Lord Mayors, had used the city streets to stage pageants of authority, but the streets were not to serve as public-access theaters. Elizabeth bitterly remarked to William Lambarde, when she was reminded of Essex's use of (what was presumably Shakespeare's) *Richard II* as prologue to his abortive rebellion: "this tragedy was played 40tie times in open streets and houses."[43] Obviously, the play itself, as the story of the deposition of a lawful (and self-dramatizing) monarch, all too clearly served Essex's political purposes, but, as Stephen Orgel has suggested, perhaps as serious to Elizabeth's mind is that Essex had appropriated her own political strategy, turning the city, as she claimed, into a stage on which her character and fate in the figure of Richard was represented—and some "40tie times" re-presented—in the open streets.[44]

Essex's appropriation of Elizabeth's politics of pageantry reveals an inherent weakness of the strategy: it is appropriable. Essex can play to the city and might well have stolen Elizabeth's audience. Camden reports that Essex and his "most intimate Friends" discussed "whether it were better forthwith to seize on the Court; or to try first the Affections of the *Londoners,* and with their Assistance to set upon the Court by force; or to save themselves by Flight."

> Whilst they were arguing concerning the Affection and Love of the *Londoners,* and the uncertain Disposition of the Vulgar, one came in of set purpose, who, as if he had been sent from the Citizens, made large Promises of Assistance from them against all his Adversaries. Herewith the Earl being somewhat animated, he began to discourse how much he was favoured throughout the City; and persuaded himself, by the former Acclamations of the People, and their Mutterings and Murmurings against his Adversaries, that many of them were devoted to him, to maintain his Credit and Fortune. . . . He resolved therefore . . . to enter the next day, which was Sunday, into the city with 200 Gentlemen . . . there to inform the Aldermen and people of the Reasons of his coming, and to crave their Aid against his Enemies. And if the Citizens showed themselves hard to be won, he determined to withdraw presently to some other part of the Kingdom: but if they showed themselves pliable, then to make himself a Way to the Queen by their Assistance.[45]

In the event, of course, his efforts failed: the city did not respond. He called "upon the citizens to arm but all in vain." The citizens remained "unshaken in their untainted Fidelity to their Prince," but clearly Elizabeth's rule depended on her ability to maintain the loyalty of the audience she had wooed and won rather than on any power or authority vested in the office. Had Essex been able to command "the Affection and Love of the *Londoners,*" he would have succeeded in his design to "alter the Form of the Commonwealth."[46]

What, then, to reverse the terms of Erasmus's question, is to prevent the king who comes on stage decked with all the pomp of state from being called an actor? This, I take it, is the central—and potentially subversive—question posed by Shakespeare's histories. In play after play we are confronted not with order but with turbulence, with the instability of rule and relationship. Yet, if in the almost continuous contention for the crown we see a dispiriting drama of human motives, we see also the power of the symbolic structures erected against anarchy and decay—and kingship itself stands chief among these. "King is a name of continuance,"[47] wrote Plowden, and the histories declare at once the lie of the jurist's assertion and the need. The ruler becomes an icon of immortality, and the struggle to establish and ensure "fair sequence and succession" (*Richard II*, 2.1.199) takes urgency from the necessity of the commonwealth to conceive of itself as permanent. In the "hapless time" of the history plays the fictions of stability insistently assert themselves, but the plays may be read virtually as the discovery that they are fictions, as England moves, in Kernan's phrase, "from ceremony and ritual to history."[48]

The plays reveal that the pageantry and props of rule are largely factitious, that their value is strategic rather than sacramental. Neither custom nor Grace preserves the crown, though their ceremonies often dress it gaudily. Henry V, Shakespeare's most successful—perhaps his only successful—king, knows that "ceremony"—"the balm, the scepter, and the ball, / The sword, the mace, the crown imperial, / The intertissued robe of gold and pearl" (4.1.256–58)—are props for the mystification of power:

> Art thou aught else but place, degree, and form,
> Creating awe and fear in other men[?] (4.1.242–43)

The histories expose the idealizations of political power by presenting rule as role, by revealing that power passes to him who can best control and manipulate the visual and verbal symbols of authority. At their most radical, their theatricality reveals that ceremony is, as Sir Henry Wotton understood, an instrumental "solemnity to contain the people still in good order with superstition, the foolish band of obedience."[49] But the recognition of people who need to be contained "in good order" simultaneously acknowledges their power of resistance and dissent. Even Henry's "greatness" is, as he understands (and resents), "subject to the breath / Of every fool" (4.1.230–31). The king must continually play to his subjects, subjecting himself to their admiration and awe that they may be subjected to his power.

Thus Bolingbroke triumphs over the anointed King Richard. York describes Henry's triumphant entrance into London (which Charles Kean spectacularly staged in his 1857 production of the play):

                                      Bolingbroke,
          Mounted upon a hot and fiery steed
          Which his aspiring rider seem'd to know,
          With slow but stately pace kept on his course,
          Whilst all tongues cried "God save thee, Bolingbroke!"
          You would have thought the very windows spake,
          So many greedy looks of young and old
          Through casements darted their desiring eyes
          Upon his visage; and that all the walls
          With painted imagery had said at once
          "Jesu preserve thee! Welcome, Bolingbroke!"
          Whilst he, from one side to the other turning,
          Bare headed, lower than his proud steed's neck,
          Bespake them thus, "I thank you, countrymen."
          And thus still doing, thus he pass'd along.   (5.2.7–21)

Bolingbroke satisfies the "desiring eyes" of the city; he agrees to be the subject of their gaze and they become the subjects of his rule. When the duchess
asks about Richard, York replies:

          As in a theater the eyes of men,
          After a well-grac'd actor leaves the stage,
          Are idly bent on him that enters next,
          Thinking his prattle to be tedious;
          Even so, or with much more contempt, men's eyes
          Did scowl on Richard. No man cried "God save him!"
          No joyful tongue gave him his welcome home,
          But dust was thrown upon his sacred head. . . .   (5.2.23–30)

     It is not only Richard's theatricality, as is often claimed, that the play
explores, but, as York's simile makes clear, Bolingbroke's as well. His
progress through the city is, if more consciously restrained, much like
Elizabeth's in 1559, a pageant which at once confers, clarifies, and celebrates
rule. Richard's mystified notions of numinous authority leave him quiescent,
unwilling to act—in any sense of the word—to preserve his title, and conse-
quently his "sacred head" becomes the object not of reverence but defile-
ment—of "dust" thrown down by the spectators who line the streets of the
royal progress.
     Richard takes refuge in concepts of charismatic majesty that even the
Bishop of Carlisle seeks to animate and direct more practically:

> That power that made you king
> Hath power to keep you king in spite of all.
> The means that Heavens yield must be imbrac'd
> And not neglected; else, heaven would,
> And we not. (3.2.27–31)

And Aumerle, impatient with Richard's passivity (and with the sacramental language that sustains it), translates the Bishop's prompting into even more explicitly pragmatic terms:

> He means, my lord, that we are too remiss;
> While Bolingbroke, through our security,
> Grows strong and great in substance and in power. (3.2.33–35)

In the face of Bolingbroke's substance and power, Richard holds to the efficacy of insubstantial assertions of sacred authority, assertions that are powerless before "the rage of Bolingbroke" which now covers Richard's "fearful land / With hard bright steel, and hearts harder than steel" (3.2.109–11). As Northumberland prophesies, Bolingbroke does successfully

> Redeem from broking pawn the blemish'd crown,
> Wipe off the dust that hides our sceptre's gilt,
> And make high majesty look like itself. (2.1.293–95)

The homonymic pun on "gilt" signals that the symbols of rule in Bolingbroke's usurping hand have been "derogated," we might say, tainted and diminished by the process of their attainment. "Gilt" has been tarnished by Henry's guilt, and if "high majesty" now looks "like itself" it may well be because Henry's presence on—and progress to—the throne effectively demystifies the character of domination. Richard is "unkinged" essentially because he understands far less than Henry about what "in this new world" (4.1.78), to use Fitzwater's phrase, it means to be a king.

Knowledge here is power, or at least power depends on the knowledge that power is power. When Richard finally learns the lesson of this brutal tautology it is too late to translate it into action. All he can do is force Henry publicly to enact the reality of their exchange of power rather than the privileged Lancastrian version that Henry wishes to have staged before Parliament. Though Richard can affect the formalization of the exchange, he cannot prevent the exchange itself. "For do we must what force would have us do" (3.3.207), he admits; yet when he resigns he will stage the event not as the abdication that Henry expects ("I thought you had been willing to resign" [4.1.190], Henry irritably remarks) but as a deposition. "Here, cousin, seize the crown" (4.1.181), Richard taunts, holding it, I assume, just out of Henry's comfortable reach.

Belatedly, Richard has come to understand something about the drama of public power; but even though he is successful in exposing the reality that Henry would disguise in the formal "resignation of . . . state and crown" (4.1.179) he cannot avoid staging his own defeat. Whether he is deposed or is resigned, he is, in either case, no longer king. He bids to become the subject of his audience's understanding and sympathy by enacting his subjection to Henry's power; and well may he ask, "subjected thus, / how can you say to me I am a king?" (3.2.176–77).

"Subjected," he is no longer king. Richard will be Henry's subject—for at least as long as he stays alive (though ex-kings unlike ex-presidents should not expect long and prosperous retirements). But Richard comes to see that in agreeing to make his political subjection the subject of his dramatizing he has become complicit in the political act:

> I find myself a traitor with the rest.
> For I have given here my soul's consent
> T'undeck the pompous body of a king;
> Made glory base and sovereignty a slave;
> Proud majesty a subject. . . .   (4.1.248–52)

I am not worrying the word "subject" here merely because the pun is available and attractive but because, as the jest of Louis XV's courtier shows, the pun focuses and clarifies certain significant structures of authority. When Spenser in *The Faerie Queene* writes about—and for—his "dred sovereign" Elizabeth, his own complex relationship to her power, his need for her approval and patronage, releases anxieties, even resentments, that he contains by turning her into his subject, thereby at least temporarily neutralizing the asymmetry of power that exists between a monarch and a would-be laureate.[50]

Representation is powerful and dangerous, and its subversions are not I think as easily contained or co-opted as the New Historicists would suggest. Stephen Greenblatt argues ingeniously that "actions that should have the effect of radically undermining authority turn out to be the props of that authority." But the argument is suspect on historical grounds alone: if subversion, as Greenblatt writes, is "the very condition of power,"[51] then how can we account for social change? If the mechanisms of Renaissance absolutism for dealing with cultural contradiction and challenge are as efficient as the new historicists would show them, then how is it that Charles I, that "Royal Actor," as Marvell terms him in the "Horatian Ode upon Cromwell's Return from Ireland," is put to death on 30 January 1649, on "the tragic scaffold" erected at Whitehall?

It is not that Greenblatt is wrong, only that his argument is unnecessarily totalized. He idealizes the operations of a culture that are more various, complex, even contradictory than he allows. Stephen Orgel suggests, more persuasively I think, that "To mime the monarch was a potentially revolutionary act—as both Essex and Elizabeth were well aware."[52] Certainly both Essex and Elizabeth understood the playing of *Richard II* on the eve of the rebellion as part of the treasonous imagining, as an invitation to the populace to participate—either in the fiction or in fact—in the deposition of an anointed king. Indeed, imagining the death of a king was literally treasonous. In response to Elizabeth's notorious recognition of herself in the figure of Richard II, William Lambarde condemned the "wicked imagination"[53] of Essex's rebellion, and the word "imagination," in his phrase, is a technical legal term. Treason, in the language of the Tudor law derived from a statute of 1352, is in part defined as "imagining and compassing the death of a king." (And Essex was formally charged with "conspiring and imagining at London . . . to depose and then slay the Queen and to subvert the Government."[54]) While in practice this section of the law was the source of juridical confusion and debate, the letter of the law itself acknowledges that imagining—that is, plotting (itself a word with both a political and literary sense) the deposition and death of a king was to be guilty of treason.[55]

Richard II, of course, does imagine—and invites its audience to imagine—the deposition and death of a king; and this is obviously the exact reason Essex and his followers paid forty shillings to have it played. We must, however, be careful not to idealize, in turn, the subversive power of theatrical representation. In the playhouse, divorced from any specific political intent, such imaginings are not treasonous (a similar argument was the basis of Sir John Hayward's defense when he was tried for treason for his history of *The Life and Raigne of King Henrie IIII*; and Bacon claimed in court, noting Hayward's extensive borrowings from Tacitus, that, in any case, it was for plagiarism not treason that he should justly be charged[56]); though the sensitivity of *Richard II*'s subject matter is acknowledged in the fact that none of the quartos of the play published during Elizabeth's lifetime includes the deposition scene. Under Elizabeth, in an atmosphere of growing cultural conflict, the theater's subversive potential came under ever greater governmental scrutiny and control, as the authorities sought ways of limiting and containing the actors' unnerving freedoms: the Master of the Revels began to license—and censor— plays; players were permitted to act only as members of licensed acting companies under noble patronage; and the theaters themselves were banished— by the city fathers—to the Liberties.

In the prologue to *Henry V*, the Chorus fantasizes about having "A kingdom for a stage, princes to act, / And monarchs to behold the swelling scene" (ll. 3–4). In such an idealized dramatic environment the contradictions of playing would disappear: representation would be simply presentation and history plays would be history itself—and significantly a history from which all social inequality is gone, though not through the democratization of the kingdom but through the complete erasure of the lower classes from it. The reality of Shakespeare's "wooden O" was, of course, quite different: a platform stage in Southwark, bourgeois actors, and an audience, not "gentles all," but fully reflective of the social stratification of the kingdom.[57]

As much as recent scholarship on the institution of the Elizabethan theater has demonstrated, Shakespeare's theater was oddly liminal—geographically, socially, and politically.[58] Located in the Liberties it was both part and not part of the City, which no doubt was appropriate for the home of a commerical acting company that was both dependent and not dependent upon its aristocratic patron; and the actors themselves, deemed to be rogues, vagabonds, and beggars by the 1572 *Acte for the punishement of Vacabondes and for Releif of the Poore & Impotent* (14 Eliz. c. 5), formally became members of aristocratic households, even in the case of the King's men entitled to call themselves gentlemen.

These contradictions of the Elizabethan theater are inescapable and irreconcilable—the essential conditions of its functioning—and are exactly what the Chorus in *Henry V* wishes to avoid. He wants a unified, aristocratic world (similar perhaps to what Richard Venner's *England's Joy* promised—a play about the monarch to be performed, as Venner's playbill advertised, "only by certain gentlemen and gentlewomen of account"[59]). If one could produce such theatrical conditions—and Venner tried to run off with the receipts without ever presenting his play—the problematics of representation if not resolved are at least reduced.

Ideally, in such a theater we could have "the warlike Harry, like himself"—not an actor looking like Harry or acting like Harry, but Harry looking and acting "like himself." This would be a theater in which we know not seems, but such a theater is impossible. It is not theater (and as Hamlet learns it is not life either). The theater is and tells us about a world of seeming. It sets before us images of authority that depend upon our cooperation to "piece out" the necessary "imperfections" of their representation. What must "deck our kings" is *our* "thoughts" rather than *their* inherent majesty. The theater, then, it could be said, enacts, not necessarily on stage but in its fundamental transaction with the audience, the exact shift in the conception of authority that brings a king to trial and ultimately locates sovereignty in the common will of its subjects. The audience becomes, as the political discourse of the seventeenth century increasingly maintained of the community, the ultimate source of authority in its willingness to credit and approve the representation of rule.

> The king's a beggar, now the play is done;
> All is well ended if this suit be won,
> That you express content; which we will pay
> With strife to please you, day exceeding day.
> Ours be your patience then and yours our parts;
> Your gentle hands lend us and take our hearts.
> (*All's Well That Ends Well*, epilogue)

This defines almost exactly the relation between subject and sovereign that was held to exist in 1649 at the trial of Charles I—but instead of taking his heart they took his head.

> Out of many, one: a logical impossibility; a piece of poetry, or symbolism; an enacted or incarnate metaphor; a poetic creation.
>
> –Norman O. Brown

Chapter 7

"The King hath many marching in his Coats," or, What did you do in the War, Daddy?

If *1 Henry IV* can be said to be "about" anything, it is about the production of power, an issue as acute in the early years of the reign of Henry IV as in the final years of the aging Elizabeth when the play was written. Henry has, of course, the problem of how to consolidate and maintain his authority, having deposed Richard who ruled by lineal succession. Elizabeth inherited her crown, but, in the complex religio-political world of post-Reformation England, her ability to succeed her Catholic half-sister was in some considerable doubt until the day before her accession, and, like Henry, she would rule over a divided country and similarly face a rebellion of Northern nobility led by the Percy family.[1]

Understandably "shaken" and "wan with care" (1.1.1), Henry recognizes the fragility of his delegitimized political position. In deposing Richard, exposing the insubstantiality of the assertions of sacred majesty, Henry's own claims of rightful authority ring hollow. His access to the powerful ideology of order is necessarily limited, as his presence on the throne reveals its tendentiousness. "Thus ever did rebellion find rebuke" (5.5.1), Henry chides Worcester, asserting the inevitability of the victory of legitimacy, but certainly Henry's own rebellion found no such "rebuke," as he successfully opposed Richard's legitimate kingship.

Henry rules over a nation whose boundaries are insecure and whose integrity is under attack from within. He is at war with the Scots in the North, the Welsh in the West, and the very nobles that helped him to power now oppose his rule. Henry's discussion of his intended crusade is then both an understandable fantasy of national unity and a strategy for its production. The national identity torn by civil war would be reformed in common purpose. The unitary state, "All of one nature, of one substance bred" (1.1.11), would be produced in opposition to an alien and barbaric "other"; almost precisely the way an idea of an orderly and coherent English nation was fashioned in Elizabethan England largely by reference to the alterity and inferiority of the Irish.[2] Henry promises

> To chase these pagans in those holy fields
> Over whose acres walked those blessed feet
> Which fourteen hundred years ago were nail'd
> For our advantage on the bitter cross. (1.1.24–27)

Henry would construct through the agency of the holy war the national unity he desperately seeks. The nation that

> Did lately meet in the intestine shock
> And furious close of civil butchery,
> Shall now, in mutual well-beseeming ranks,
> March all one way. . . . (1.1.12–15)

Henry knows, of course, that in fact his nation does not "march all one way," but is sharply divided by class loyalties, ethnic conflicts, and regional concerns, differences purposefully organized in hierarchies of inequality. The reality of his kingdom–of any kingdom–is that it is multiple and heterogeneous, a loose aggregation of individuals, families, counties, and so on, all with local and sectarian interests and commitments. The desire to undertake the crusade articulates a familiar fantasy of political incorporation, a utopian solution to the problems of difference; but Henry must acknowledge it as a fantasy denied by present circumstance:

> But this our purpose now is twelve month old,
> And bootless 'tis to tell you we will go. (1.1.28–29)

A similar insistence upon an imaginary unity marked the production of power in Elizabethan England. The familiar political metaphors of the well-ordered body or the patriarchal family articulate the would-be absolutist state's desire for an integral wholeness, and the multiple historical and mythological typologies of Elizabeth did the same. Elizabeth, the Tudor Rose, representing the unification of aristocratic factions, was also Deborah, uniting secular and divine authority, and Diana, expressing in her chastity the inviolability of the Queen's body and the body politic.[3] A nation that in sixty years had experienced five forms of official religion, endured four changes of monarch, the reign of each marked by a significant rebellion, that which now faced further instability as Elizabeth ruled without an heir and over a country whose traditional social and economic structures were changing with the pressures and possibilities of a nascent capitalism, no doubt demanded the various tropes of the integrity of the virgin Queen and the sovereign nation for which she stood. In the prologue of Dekker's *Old Fortunatus* (1599), an old man speaks of Eliza: "Some call her Pandora, some Gloriana, some Cynthia, some Belphoebe, some Astraea, all by several names to express several loves. Yet all those names make but one celestial body, as all those loves meet to create but one soul." And, if almost hysterically, Nicholas Breton, in his "Character of Queen Elizabeth," similarly finds a radical unity in the representations of the Queen:

> was shee not as she wrote herself *semper eadem* alwaies one? zealous in one religion, believinge in one god, constant in one truth, absolute vnder god in her self, one Queene, and but one Queene; for in her dayes was no such Queene; one Phoenix for her spiritt, one Angell for her person, and one Goddesse for her wisedome; one alwayes in her word, one alwayes of her word, and one alwaies, in one word ELIZABETHA βασιλεθ'εα, a princelie goddesse,

Elizabeth a deliverer of godes people from their spirituall thraldome and a provider for their rest: one chosen by one god to be then the one and onlie Queene of this one kingdome, of one Isle. . . .[4]

Not least of the inadequacies of this is that the "one isle" contained *two* kingdoms: England and Scotland, as well as the conquered principality of Wales; but such fantasies of imperial unity, however attractive, always occlude the reality that their unity is constructed only through acts of exclusion and homogenization. In Elizabethan England this was achieved by ideological configuration and political repression that either violently eliminated marginal subgroups—gypsies, witches, vagabonds, the Irish—from the articulation of the English nation or discursively arranged them into stable and stabilizing hierarchies. In *1 Henry IV*, with the rebels routed, Henry orders his forces to follow up their advantage and extinguish the remaining pockets of resistance:

> Rebellion in this land shall lose his sway,
> Meeting the check of such another day,
> And since this business so fair is done,
> Let us not leave till all our own be won. (5.5.41–45)

The homonymic pun (inexact but recognizable in late-sixteenth-century London English) between "won" and "one" exactly enacts the political process of unification, verbally reconciling what can only be coerced. "Winning" is "one-ing," we might say, but the processes of incorporation involves always a more violent repression of difference than can be admitted. In complex society, only what is "won" is "one."

The play registers its unreconciled social disjunctions generically. The comic plot voices what the unitary state would repress, indeed, exactly what the unitary *plot* would repress. Criticism has delighted in demonstrating the play's aesthetic unity by showing how the comic plot "serves" the historical plot, functions as a *sub*plot clarifying the "main" plot. But the play seems to me less coherent—not therefore less interesting or good, but less willing to organize its disparate voices into hierarchies—than such demonstrations of its putative unity would allow. The formal coherence that critics have demanded from the play can be achieved only by subordinating subplot to main plot, commoners to aristocrats, comedy to history, by imposing, that is, the same hierarchies of privilege and power that exist in the state upon the play. But the play does not so readily subordinate its comedy. Though Thomas Fuller in 1662 objected that Falstaff was merely "the property of pleasure" for Hal "to abuse,"[5] the fat knight resists all efforts completely to subjugate him to the prince's desires or designs. "The humorous conceits of Sir John Falstaff" in fact share the title-page of the 1598 quarto with "the battell at Shrewsburie" as the most notable aspects of *The History of Henrie the Fovrth.* As we have seen in chapter 5, throughout the seventeenth century the play as likely to be known as *Falstaff* as it was as *Henry IV.*

If this striking inversion of the traditional relationship of history and comedy perhaps overestimates the domination of Falstaff, it does reveal the inadequacy of the familiar critical demonstrations of the play's unity. Certainly, the comic plot gives voice to what is silent in the historical plot. I don't mean by this merely that the comic plot includes social elements absent from the "main" plot or even that the comic plot speaks the reality of class differentiation and domination that the aristocratic historical plot ignores or idealizes (though no doubt Hal's arrogant joking at the expense of Francis, for example, does do this). I mean something more radical: that the very existence of a comic plot serves to counter the totalizing fantasies of power, to expose and disrupt the hierarchies upon which they depend. History is displayed as something other—something more extensive, however less stable—than merely the history of what Renaissance historians characteristically called "matters of state."

To find in the play the ready subordination of comedy to history that has become the norm of formalist accounts of *1 Henry IV* is to accept Hal's version of events for Shakespeare's, or rather, it is to *behave* as Hal, to presume that the tavern world exists only for the production of aristocratic pleasure and value. Yet most accounts of the unity of the play's two plots do exactly this. They analyze the comic plot's thematic relation to the "main" plot, finding that it parallels or parodies the historical action. In either case, the analysis reproduces the priority and privilege of aristocratic history. The comedy is seen to exist primarily to clarify the meaning of the serious plot, thus unwittingly performing a formalist version of Stephen Greenblatt's elegant demonstration of the containment of subversion in the play and in Renaissance England.

For Greenblatt, as he argues in his influential article, "Invisible Bullets," the play, like the culture of Renaissance England, contains, in both senses of the word, the potential subversions of its countercultures. The play's comic energies are never able to challenge effectively the claims and claimants of power: "the subversiveness which is genuine and radical . . . is at the same time contained by the power it would appear to threaten. Indeed the subversiveness is the very product of that power and furthers its ends."[6] Thus, the actions and values of the tavern world are denied any disruptive effect; they serve to legitimate and consolidate political power rather than to contest it. Hal is seen as a master actor, merely playing at prodigality to achieve a purchase on rule. "The unyok'd humour of [his] idleness" (1.2.19), which seems a potential subversion of Hal's political destiny and desire, is revealed instead to be a "product" of that desire, designed to further "its ends," a carefully calculated intemperance designed to make his "reformation" the more extraordinary. Hal's insistent role-playing, that finds its essential form in the tavern, Greenblatt concludes, is then not opposed to power but rather "one of power's essential modes" (p. 46); and the comic plot is, therefore, not an alternative to the monological voice of aristocratic history but finally its justification.

This discussion of what could be called Hal's power play leads to Greenblatt's argument that the play enacts precisely the forms of power that dominated Elizabethan England. In the absence of the all too familiar forms of coercive power available to the modern state, authority in Elizabethan England was expressed and confirmed theatrically, in the public displays that bound the monarch to her nation. Spectacle was a fundamental *instrumentum regni*, a "theater of power," in Roy Strong's phrase, not merely celebrating sovereignty but actually producing the social relations upon which sovereignty depends.[7]

While, certainly, we need to recognize the relationship between Shakespeare's dramatic practices and Elizabethan political conditions if ever we are to historicize our understanding of his plays, it seems important and fortunately possible, to distinguish between the theatricalized world of Elizabethan politics and the politicized world of the Elizabethan theater. "Royal power" may be, as Greenblatt claims, "manifested to its subjects as in a theater" (p. 65) but the simile must not be quickly collapsed into an identity as it has often been by those who see the theater merely producing and legitimizing the ideology of royal power.[8] *Nullum simile est idem*, as was said proverbially. Royal power is not manifested to its subjects *in* the theater, only *as* in the theater. The simile would make the various modes of a culture's production homologies, occluding their uneven development that becomes a source of social contradiction, a space for the resistance to power that Greenblatt's argument precludes. The labile and unlegitimated representations of the popular theater prevent the drama, regardless of any overt political intentions of its play-wrights or patrons, from simply reproducing the dominant ideology, and clearly theatrical representation was never, as the insistent governmental efforts to supervise and control its production attest, merely a vehicle for the reproduction of royal authority.

The popular theater of Elizabethan England, as Robert Weimann has shown, does not simply endorse what is represented on its stage.[9] Characters and speeches are literally scrutinized from above and from below, from the galleries and from the yard, while on the stage aristocratic action is mimicked and criticized by commoner and clown. Both in its action and in its audience, the popular theater mixed linguistic and social consciousnesses. Artisan and courtier confronted one another in the theater as they confronted one anoth-er on the stage. Here "the toe of the peasant," as Hamlet says, or, at least the toe of the artisan, "comes so near the heel of the courtier he galls his kibe" (*Hamlet*, 5.1.139–40). The public theaters thus produced the situation that Bakhtin saw as characteristic of the Renaissance itself, in which the aristo-cratic and the common, the sacred and the vulgar, the elite and the popular "frankly and intensely peered into each other's faces."[10] Diverse accents and dialects, styles and values sounded, clashed, and sometimes blended, the polyphony challenging the homogenizing and unifying pressure of the theater of state: a drama that in presenting the spectacle of power reveals the fantasy of univocality that must be exposed and modified by the heterogeneity it anx-iously denies.

But in the public theater that heterogeneity found full expression, its diverse social and formal modalities expressed in the generic hybrids that came to dominate the stage. John Florio, in his *Second Frutes* (1591), includes a dialogue about the state of the English theater that holds that the plays are "neither right comedies, nor right tragedies," but "representations of histories, without any decorum" (sig. D4r). Florio, of course, is echoing Sidney, who had grumbled that the native drama contained

neither right tragedies, nor right comedies, mingling kings and clowns, not because the matter so carrieth it, but thrust in the clown by head and shoulders to play a part in majestical matters with neither decency nor discretion, so as neither the admiration and commiseration, nor the right sportfulness, is by their mongrel tragi-comedy achieved.[11]

Words like "mongrel," "mingle-mangle," and "gallimaufrey" appear again and again to describe, or at least to protest, these increasingly common miscegenated forms. In 1597, probably the year *1 Henry IV* was first performed, Joseph Hall, in his *Virgidemiarum*, complained about what he termed the "goodly *hoch-poch*" that results "when vile *Russetings* / Are match't with monarchs, & with mighty kings."[12] But in the popular theater, and certainly in *1 Henry IV*, kings and clowns did mingle; disparate languages and conventions regularly—or better, irregularly—shared the stage, competing for attention and control.

But this brings us back to Falstaff. It must be said of him, in Sidney's words, that he plays "his part in majestical matters with neither decency nor discretion." And Hal does say it, as he upbraids Falstaff on the battlefield for having a bottle of sack instead of his pistol: "What, is it a time to jest and dally now" (5.3.56). But Falstaff refuses to privilege "majestical matters" any more than the play does. Hal privileges them. They provide the telos of his prodigal son play, but not of Shakespeare's mingle-mangle. Falstaff's lack of decency and discretion is the sign of the play's resistance to the totalizations of power, massive evidence of the heterogeneity that will not be made one. His exuberance and excess will not be incorporated into the stabilizing hierarchies of the body politic.

Revealingly, when he imagines his life in the impending reign of Henry V, he thinks in terms of his social role:

> let us be Diana's foresters, gentlemen of the shade, minions of the moon; and
> let men say we be men of good government, being governed as the sea is, by
> our noble and chaste mistress the moon. . . ." (1.2.25–29)

This is the exact fantasy of social order in the England of Elizabeth, the virgin Queen. She, of course, was Diana in one of the familiar political mythologies that surrounded her, and her loyal subjects would be "men of good government, being governed . . . by our noble and chaste mistress." But for Falstaff this is not a submission to authority but an authorization of transgression; he serves not the monarch whose motto, as Nicholas Breton insisted, was "*semper eadem* alwaies one," but only the changeable moon, "under whose countenance we steal" (1.2.29).

Falstaff, then, is one of "the moon's men" (1.2.39), endlessly ebbing and flowing instead of filling a fixed place in a stable social hierarchy. He resists incorporation either into the hierarchical logic of the unitary state or that of the unified play. Nonetheless, Hal attempts to fix him. However much the Prince enjoys his banter with Falstaff, it is clear that Hal is using the fat knight to construct his own political identity. Hal is only a temporary inhabitant of the underworld of Eastcheap, and that only to make his inevitable assumption of responsibility the more remarkable and desired:

> I . . . will awhile uphold
> The unyok'd humour of your idleness.
> Yet herein will I imitate the sun,
> Who doth permit the base contagious clouds
> To smother up his beauty from the world,
> That, when he please again to be himself,
> Being wanted he be more wondered at . . . . (1.2.190–96)

This is exactly the political strategy of King Henry, though the King mistakes his son's behavior for a real rather than a carefully managed prodigality. In act three, scene two, when he rebukes Hal for his "inordinate and low desires," the King worries that Hal has put his authority at risk. Henry is not worried about the state of Hal's soul but about Hal as the soul of the state. Clearly, the issues are political not moral; what is at stake is the production of power.

> Had I so lavish of my presence been,
> So common-hackney'd in the eyes of men,
> So stale and cheap to vulgar company,
> Opinion, that did help me to the crown,
> Had still kept loyal to possession . . . . (3.2.39–43)

Henry would turn his aristocratic aloofness into a political asset: "By being seldom seen, I could not stir / But like a comet I was wonder'd at. . ." (3.2.46–47). Henry anticipates Edward Forset's assertion in 1606 that "seeing that both God and the Soule, working so vnlimitably, be yet vndiscerned, in their essence, as hidden and concealed from the eyes of men; it may seeme to stand more with maieste, and to work more regarding, more admiring, and more adoring if (howsoeuer their power doth shew it selfe) yet their presence be more sparing & lesse familiarly vouchsafed."[13] No doubt Forset here reflects King James's particular imperial style, his distaste for, as opposed to Elizabeth's apparent delight in, the theatricalizations of power by which it is constituted. But James, no less than Elizabeth, knew that it was precisely in the ability of the monarch to "work more regarding, more admiring, and more adoring" that sovereign authority resides. The spectacular presence of rule is the very condition of its power.

Certainly, it is Henry's understanding that power is not merely confirmed but actually constituted theatrically that leads him to fear that Hal has alienated opinion with his "rude society" (3.2.14). Hal seems to Henry too much like Richard, who

> Grew a companion to the common streets,
> Enfeoff'd himself to popularity . . .
> So, when he had occasion to be seen,
> He was but as the cuckoo is in June,
> Heard, not regarded; seen, but with such eyes
> As, sick and blunted with community,
> Afford no extraordinary gaze,
> Such as is bent on sun-like majesty
> When it shines seldom in admiring eyes. (3.2.68–80)

In his carousing, Hal has become similarly familiar, a "common sight" (3.2.88), affording no "extraordinary gaze" to the people and so apparently derogating his authority as Richard had his own: "thou hast lost thy princely privilege / With vile participation" (3.2.86–87).

Though obviously his father misrecognizes Hal's behavior, what is interesting is that for Henry, "participation" is "vile," "community" sickens, "popularity" enslaves. The familiar watchwords of modern democracy sound dangerously to the King who in deposing Richard has brought power into range of popular contestation or control. Nonetheless, in spite of the distinction Henry draws between a "common sight" and an "extraordinary gaze," his conception of majesty as what Hobbes resonantly termed "visible Power,"[14] silently demands and authorizes an audience of commoners as a condition of its authority. If a spectacular sovereignty would construct power in what Stephen Greenblatt calls its "privileged visibility" (p. 64), it risks, as Christopher Pye has written, reducing "the sovereign to the object of the spectator's unseen and masterfully panoptic gaze."[15] However reluctantly, a spectacular sovereignty must acknowledge the people's constitutive role even as it seeks to constrain, if not deny it. "Opinion did help [him] to the crown," Henry knows, but it is hypostatized "Opinion" that he acknowledges, erasing the agency of the people who must hold it.

Similarly, in his emphasis upon the "extraordinary gaze," Henry seeks to escape the destabilizing political implications of the subjection of the sovereign to the "admiring eyes" of his subjects. The unacknowledgeable power of the viewing subject is registered in Henry's disgust that Richard was "daily swallow'd by men's eyes" (3.2.70), and his own escape from the threat of this power is achieved through verbal magic: "My presence, like a robe pontifical, / [was] Ne'er seen but wonder'd at . . . (3.2.56–57). Most immediately, of course, this means that each time he was seen he was an object of wonder, but the lines must also mean that he was "ne'er seen" at all, only wondered at. This is the strategy by which spectacular sovereignty denies that its viewing subjects are the source of its power. The king is never seen, never subjected to the gaze of his subjects; he is only wondered at, subjecting them to his spectacular presence. The spectacle of the monarch must dazzle those it would captivate. Sidney calls Elizabeth "the only sun that dazzleth their eyes,"[16] and, with a similar understanding, in *Henry V*, Hal, now King, promises to unleash his power in France:

> I will rise there with so full a glory
> That I will dazzle all the eyes of France,
> Yea, strike the dauphin blind to look on us. (1.2.279–81)

But the English monarch must first "dazzle all the eyes of" England, eyes that are at once constitutive of and captivated by his spectacular sovereignty, and strike them "blind" that they not recognize their productive power; and it is this fundamental contradiction, unacknowledged and unresolved, underwriting the notion of spectacular authority that leads Henry IV to identify the legitimate Richard with the apparent political liabilities of Hal, and his own course with the rebel Hotspur.

> As thou art to this hour was Richard then
> When I from France set foot at Ravenspurgh,
> And even as I was then is Percy now. (3.2.94–96)

No doubt, in part this represents a residual class loyalty. Hotspur's aristocratic ambition would hold an inevitable appeal for the man who, in returning from exile to reclaim his ducal inheritance and achieving the crown, similarly asserted aristocratic privilege against the absolutist assertions of the King.

Henry has always been attracted to Hotspur, earlier admitting his envy of Northumberland and his hope that "some night-tripping fairy had exchang'd / In cradle-clothes our children where they lay, / And call'd mine Percy, his Plantagenet" (1.1.87–88). But however much Hotspur is the child of Henry's desire, clearly Hal is the child of his loins. Henry's hope is only a displacement of his knowledge of the illegitimacy of his rule. His identification with Hotspur is his unintended acknowledgment that his conception of sovereignty opens a space for resistance, empowering precisely those whom it would subject.

Henry's unnecessary advice to Hal is based on the idea that the destabilizing potential glimpsed in the conception of spectacular sovereignty can be kept under control by carefully managing its representations, by controlling what is made available to "admiring eyes" to ensure that it dazzles. But the play recognizes a similar instability lurking in the representations themselves, and nowhere more obviously than in act five, in scenes three and four. There the play explicitly becomes a representation *of* representation, as the rebels at Shrewsbury encounter various nobles "semblably furnish'd like the King himself" (5.3.21). Holinshed reports that Douglas "slew Sir Walter Blunt and three other appareled in the King's suit and clothing, saying, I marvell to see so many kings thus suddenlie arise one in the necke of an other." But Holinshed's narrative of the battle immediately goes on to emphasize the King's own actions: "The king in deed was raised, & did that daie manie a noble feat of armes, for as it is written, he slue that daie with his owne hands six and thirtie persons of his enimies."[17]

Shakespeare's dramatic account of Shrewsbury, however, erases the King's powerful and decisive intervention in the battle. Royal power appears in the play exclusively in represented form, and where the King is present on the battlefield, he must be saved in his confrontation with Douglas by the intervention of the Prince. In a sense, the multiple representations of the King at Shrewsbury (literally his lieu-tenants, his place-holders) can be seen not to weaken the idea of sovereign power but to literalize its operations; the state depends upon the authority of the sovereign being successfully communicated in acts of representation in various modalities. Power is both the effect of representation and its authorization. Nonetheless, the scene reveals the inevitable contradiction of representation. It is always an agent both of production and loss. If it communicates sovereign authority, it is necessary only in the absence of that authority; in standing as surrogate it cannot help calling attention to what is not there. Representation thus at once constructs and subverts authority, at once enables it and exposes its limitation.

This doubleness is what Derrida calls, in another context, the "risk of *mimesis*,"[18] the risk that any form of figuration will reveal the gap between the representing agent and what is represented, will admit their relation to be arbitrary and fragile, will expose the emptiness that it would fill. Representations mark the absence of a presence that is never fully available in and of itself, and they are, therefore, always more mobile, both less legitimate and legitimating, than theories of cultural dominance allow. Douglas, when he sees yet another representation of the King in the field at Shrewsbury, says with weary irritation: "they grow like Hydra's heads" (5.4.24), ironically using the familiar figure of rebellion to describe the replications of sovereignty he encounters, but thus articulating exactly the destabilizing potential, the possibility of a chaotic reproduction, that resides in the very notion of representation. At best, then, power might be understood as the effect of its representations; at worst, power might be seen actively to be undone by them.

Seeking the King, Douglas encounters a surplus of royal representations that he believes can be brutally dispatched to reveal their authorizing presence.

> Now, by my sword, I will kill all his coats;
> I'll murder all his wardrobe, piece by piece,
> Until I meet the King. (5.3.26–28)

Yet, although he works his way through the King's wardrobe with murderous efficiency, he is unable to recognize royalty when he finally confronts it. When Douglas does at last "meet the King," the monarch shines no more brightly than any of the substitutes Douglas has killed.

> What art thou
> That counterfeit'st the person of a king?
>
> Henry: The King himself, who, Douglas, grieves at heart
> So many of his shadows thou hast met,
> And not the very King. . . .
>
> Douglas: I fear thou art another counterfeit. (5.4.26–34)

The language of difference here, "shadows" and "counterfeit," clearly implies an authentic regal presence against which these imperfect representations can be measured; however, on the battlefield at Shrewsbury the King cannot be distinguished from his representations. Henry's majesty can be effectively mimed. Though Douglas admits to Henry that "thou bearest thee like a king" (5.4.35), royal bearing proves no guarantee of royalty. But the implications of the episode are not merely that Henry unheroically, if prudently, adopts a strategy in the interests of his safety, that appearances are manipulated to disguise the King. They are far more disturbing: that kingship itself is a disguise, a role, an action that a man might play. Even Henry can only bear himself "*like* the king"; he has no authentic royal identity prior to and untouched by representation. In dispossessing Richard from his throne, Henry, no less than Blunt, has only a "borrow'd title" (5.3.23), but he must manipulate the verbal and visual symbols of authority as if they were rightfully his own.

Yet the play perhaps registers an even deeper skepticism about the nature of authority: that Henry's inability to partake of an authentic majesty is not merely a result of his usurpation of Richard's crown but is indeed a condition of rule. To counterfeit "the person of the king" is always to counterfeit a counterfeit, for "person," as Hobbes observes, derives from the Latin *persona*, which "signifies the disguise or outward appearance of a man, counterfeited on the stage; and sometimes more particularly that part of it, which disguiseth the face, as a mask or vizard."[19] The "person of the king" is, then, always already a representation, unstable and ungrounded, and not the immanent presence of what Henry calls the "very King."

The language of Renaissance absolutism, responding to the same crisis of authority, attempted to resolve the regress of representation by locating authority finally in God. The king's title and dignity derive from divine source and sanction. However, it is not only that political power is "ordained of God," but, more radically, that it is itself God-like. If the monarch knew that to reign was to be "like the King," he (or she, in the case of Mary and Elizabeth) knew also that to be "like the king" was to be, in the system of hierarchical homologies that organized experience, like God; the monarch rules in God's name and in His manner. James, in his treatise on rule, *Basilikon Doron*, claimed that

> God giues not Kings the stile of *Gods* in vaine,
> For on his Throne his Scepter doe they swey.[20]

However, the appeal to divine authority is itself unsatisfying without a convincing account of how this sanction is transmitted and transferred. The King "by birth . . . commeth to his crowne,"[21] as James familiarly put it, but the principles of patrilineal inheritance providing for the succession of the eldest child, if they do provide for certain succession, the heir being always known, occlude the question of origin. Even in an unbroken line of rule somewhere there must be an initiating act that, except perhaps in the case of Saul in *1 Samuel*, is something other than an immediate ordination by God.

Sovereignty would construct itself upon a vertical axis of authorization, a synchronic principle of divine authority. But however much the state wishes to conceive of itself as timeless, permanently existing, the discontinuities of history must be acknowledged. The crown exists also upon a horizontal, diachronic axis of coercive power. Bodin held that "Reason, and the verie light of nature, leadeth vs to beleeue very force and violence to haue giuen course and beginning vnto Commonweals."[22] Even James had to admit the coercive origin of monarchical rule. In part to escape the dangerous implications of what has been recently called translation theory, the idea that monarchy begins with a transfer of power from the people, James acknowledged that the authority of the Scottish crown derived directly from the conquest of the Irish King, Fergus, though James attempted to defuse the potentially destabilizing implications of grounding authority in power by insisting that the "people willingly fell to him" and that, in any case, the country was "scantly inhabited."[23]

But once authority concedes these coercive origins, the distinction between, for example, Richard II's legitimate rule and Henry IV's usurpation soon begins to blur. Is there a significant difference in the legitimacy of a usurper and that of a usurper's heir? English monarchs habitually based their authority "on the goodness of the cause of William the Conqueror, and upon their lineal, and directest descent from him," as Hobbes notes, but, as he wryly continues, "whilst they needlessly think to justify themselves, they justify all the successful rebellions that ambition shall at any time raise against them, and their successors."[24] Deriving legitimacy from conquest risks, however, not merely authorizing rebellion but delegitimizing rule itself. William Segar in 1590 skeptically wrote that "Kings, Princes, and other soueraign commanders did (in the beginning) aspire vnto greatness by puissance and force: of which Cain was the first."[25] And once authority acknowledges its customary origins in "puissance and force," recognizing the mark of Cain upon the throne, the distinction between legitimate and usurped rule no longer can be made absolute. If authority is grounded only in power and sanctioned only by custom then all titles are merely "borrowed" rather than in any significant sense rightfully belonging to those who hold them.

Lacan notoriously asserted that the man who believes himself king is no more mad than the *king* who believes himself king[26]; that is, it is madness to believe that kingship resides magically in the person of the king rather than in the political relations that bind, even create, king and subject. But this is precisely Hal's enabling knowledge, the authorization of his impressive improvisations. He never confuses the charismatic claims of kingship with the political relations they would accomplish. In *2 Henry IV*, King Henry anxiously admits the "indirect, crooked ways" by which he achieved the crown, but for Hal the matter is almost comically simple, untouched by political irony or moral complexity:

> You won it, wore it, kept it, gave it me;
> Then plain and right must my possession be . . . . (4.5.221–22)

Hal knows that the crown is always illegitimate, that is, always an effect of social relations and not their cause, and therefore it must (and can) endlessly be legitimated by the improvisations of each wearer. Legitimacy is something forged, no less by kings in Westminster than by Falstaff in the Boar's Head. The king's state, scepter, and crown have no more intrinsic link to sovereignty than Falstaff's chair, dagger, and cushion. All are props in the representation of rule. If "the raised place of the stage" continuously refers to "the raised place of power," as Raymond Williams has said,[27] the reference works to materialize and thus demystify the gestures of authority, exposing their theatricality in its own. Puttenham speaks of "the great Emperour who had it usually in his mouth to say, *Qui nescit dissimulare nescit regnare.*"[28] But rather than an admission of the necessary tactics of rule, this is an acknowledgment of its inescapable nature. Certainly, Hal knows how to dissemble, is able and willing to "falsify men's hopes" (1.2.206). If Falstaff insists on the distinction between "a true piece of gold" and "a counterfeit" (2.4.485–86), Hal blurs the difference. He is always aware that kingship is only a role, however much a major one; and he is well prepared to play it, to "monarchize" (*Richard II,* 3.2.165), in Richard II's shocking word, with the same authority that Hal has played heir-apparent. He is what Henry terms him scornfully, "the shadow of succession" (3.2.99), not in the sense that Henry intends "shadow"–that, unlike Hotspur, Hal is a weak and unworthy successor–but in a more characteristic Renaissance colloquial sense of "actor." And Hal will successfully *act* his succession.

Indeed, he literally does act it, in the "play extempore" in act two, scene four. He deposes Falstaff from the "joint-stool" that is the throne, instantly capable of the language and gestures of sovereignty, and more, instantly aware that rule depends on the exclusion of what resists the incorporation of the unitary state. "Banish plump Jack, and banish all the world" (2.4.473–74), Falstaff warns, and the future is chillingly etched in Hal's "I do, I will."

But it really isn't that simple. Hal will, of course, banish Falstaff in *2 Henry IV*, but the popular energy of comic misrule is not so easily excluded or contained. At the end of *2 Henry IV*, the victory over misrule is announced as a linguistic purification, a triumph of the monoglot aristocratic hegemony: "all are banish'd till their conversations / Appear more wise and modest to the world" (5.5.101–102). But although, as Bakhtin says, the monological voice of authority always "pretends to be the *last word*,"[29] in *2 Henry IV* the "wise and modest" aristocratic voice does not have the final say; that, literally, belongs to the epilogue–and to the clown, I would argue, who has played Falstaff.[30] And *his* speech, like the dance that concludes it, exuberantly undermines both the unifying fantasies of charismatic kingship and the coherence and closure of the represented history that such kingship appropriates for its authorization.

Richard Helgerson sees similarly that "by including Falstaff, the play maintained its stake in a popular theater that mingled kings and clowns, a theater that could imagine a political nation comprising both high and low." But for Helgerson this political imagining is only temporary, indeed almost cynical, and he sees the play rejecting its fragile vision of inclusivity as Falstaff is carried to the Fleet: "in banishing him it awoke and despised that dream."[31] But "the play" doesn't banish Falstaff; Henry V does. The play literally brings him back, declaring Hal's victory to be limited and temporary, insisting on the social, ideological, linguistic, and aesthetic multiplicity that both the well-ordered play and the well-ordered state would deny, insisting, that is, precisely on an image of the political nation "comprising high and low," however more various and unruly than its charismatic king would have it.

If the historical action ends by confirming the neoclassic strictures against the mingling of kings and clowns with Hal's austere emergence as King

Henry and the banishment of fat Jack from the world of the court, the play itself counters this triumph of authority. The complete theatrical event challenges the victory of order as the aristocratic script of history gives way to the carnival energies of the clown. No doubt the historical action denies Falstaff's fond desire for prominence in the new reign of Henry V, but the epilogue confirms his hopes. "I shall be sent for soon at night" (5.5.90–91), he has assured Shallow, Bardolph, Pistol, and not least of all himself—and sent for soon indeed he is. Falstaff's reappearance in what is formally the jig, this play's version of his "resurrection" on the battlefield at Shrewsbury, announces the change of genre in which he will prevail with the help of the popular audience. Here his sentence can be commuted: "If my tongue cannot entreat you to acquit me, will you command me to use my legs? And yet that were light payment, to dance out of your debt" (Epi. ll. 18–20).

The epilogue is a scripted version of a largely forgotten convention of six-teenth-century drama (a convention that modern texts necessarily ignore): the jig that characteristically concluded the play. "Now adays," in Richard Knolles's phrase, "they put at the end of euerie tragedie (as poyson into meat) a comedie or jigge." The jig was so familiar an afterpiece to the drama in the popular play-houses around 1600 that it could serve Ben Jonson as the very sign of pre-dictability, when he refers to Puntarvolo's wooing as "a thing studied, and rehearst as ordinarily at his comming from hawking or hunting, as a jigge after a Play." These might indeed be thought, Jonson would later complain in his dedication of *Catiline*, "Jig-given times." As John Davies wrote in an epigram:

> For as we see at all the play house dores,
> When ended is the play, the daunce, and song:
> A thousand townsemen, gentlemen, and whores,
> Porters and serving-men togither throng.[32]

When "ended is the play," the day's entertainment was not yet done, and "the dance and the song" inevitably challenged and qualified the claims of the authorized script in the "throng" of popular energy that Davies, as well as Shakespeare, saw—and indeed that civic authorities similarly saw and feared. On 12 October 1612, "An Order for surpressinge of Jigges att the ende of Playes" was issued at Westminster, holding that "by reason of certayne lewde Jigges songes and dances . . . diuerse cutt-purses and other lewde and ill dis-posed persons in great multitude do resorte thither at the ende of euerye playe many tymes causinge tumultes and outrages"; and they ordered the

players to "utterlye abolishe all Jigges Rymes and Daunces after there playes
. . . vpon payne of ymprisonment and puttinge downe and suppressinge of
theire playes."[33] The authorities in 1612 were clearly trying to contain the
popular energies released in the theater, seeking to control precisely those elements that fat Jack Falstaff spoke both to and for. Here the democratic dream
is indeed despised, but in the theaters, as in the play, that dream proves
unnervingly difficult to banish.

> We be men and nat aungels, wherefore we know nothinge
> but by outward significations.
>
> > —Thomas Elyot
>
> Money changes everything.
>
> > —Cyndi Lauper

Chapter 8

Is There a Class in This (Shakespearean) Text?

At least two considerations may prevent a quick and confident "yes" to my titular question. The first is perhaps the more easily confronted. Historians have usefully reminded us that the language of class relations applied to the social formation of early modern England is an anachronism.[1] Indeed "class" is a nineteenth-century analytic category and as such was obviously conceptually unavailable to the people of Tudor and Stuart England.[2] But their own social vocabularies of "estate" or "degree," while insisting on social differentiation on the basis of status rather than on the basis of income and occupation, no less powerfully testify to a system of social inequality that the concept of class would help articulate and analyze. Classes, in the most precise economic definition, perhaps can be said to come into being only within the social conditions of bourgeois production, but classes, in their abstract social sense, can be seen to have existed as long as social organization has permitted an unequal distribution of property, privilege, and power.[3]

It may well be, then, that any anxiety about the deployment of the language of class in the discussion of Shakespeare's plays is an unnecessary scruple. Even if the culture did not experience its social relations overtly as class relations, certainly social stratification and the tensions resulting from the forms of inequality are evident in the plays and can be usefully examined. Hymen, at the end of *As You Like It*, announces the delight of the gods "when earthly things [are] made even" (5.4.106), but the plays again and again reveal that to be a delusive hope or a utopian dream, belied by social differentiation and conflict, that is, belied precisely by an *unevenness* that is reproduced both on stage and in the playhouse itself. Like the Chorus in *Henry V* who imagines the socially diverse Elizabethan audience as "gentles all" (1 Cho. 8), the King addresses his troops as "a band of brothers" (4.3.60), all "gentled" in their shared enterprise, but the resistant reality of social difference is made clear in the body count at Agincourt: "Where is the number of our English dead? / Edward the Duke of York; the Earl of Suffolk; / Sir Richard Keighley, Davy Gam, esquire: / None else of name, and of all other men / But five and twenty" (4.8.101–5). Even in the leveling of death, twenty-five of Henry's "brothers" retain their subaltern anonymity. In *Coriolanus*, Menenius's fable of the Belly idealizes the body politic as a harmoniously ordered whole, but Menenius immediately undermines his own corporate image: "Rome and her rats are at the point of battle" (1.1.161). The familiar fable here offers not a full articulation of the Roman polity but a tactical advantage for a privileged segment of it. Menenius buys time for Marcius's arrival to quell the uprising, and the tendentiousness of the elaborated analogy is revealed in the slide from imagining Rome as a unified, if differentiated, social body of patricians *and* plebs to seeing Rome only as its patricians and needing to defend itself from the "rats" that would feed upon it.

Yet even if "class" can be more or less happily accepted as an effective heuristic if not a properly historical category to describe and analyze the stratification of social relations in these plays (as well as in early modern England itself), a more problematic issue still remains to be addressed. The question "is there a class in this text?" cannot be answered merely by assessing the propriety of the analytic vocabulary. If the question were (to quote Mary Jacobus) "is there a woman in this text?"[4] the continuing difficulty emerges clearly. Certainly, women's roles are written into Shakespeare's plays, but boy actors were, of course, required to play the female parts; so the answer must be both "yes" and "no." Women are prescribed but were themselves not present on stage; they were *represented* in the transvestite acting tradition of the popular Elizabethan theater. To speak of the women in Shakespeare's plays is, then, to speak not of women as historical subjects but only of the heavily mediated representation of women that the commercial theater offered: male actors, speaking words written by a male writer, enacting female roles. Increasingly, therefore, we have come to see the need to analyze not simply "the women in Shakespeare" but their representation. In a significant sense, there are no women, only males playing "the woman's part." If these "parts" have something significant to say about women in early modern England, it is, then, not least because of the mediations that make them present.

But if a transvestite acting tradition determines the presentation of women on the stage, a similar fissure between the represented object and the representing agent affects the presentation of class. Plays may well present a variety of class locations (and locutions), but they are, of course, all themselves mediated by the modes of representation in the theater.[5] Though kings and clowns notoriously mingled on the English Renaissance stage, kings and clowns were not themselves present, only the actors who played them. In chapter 6 we saw the example of Richard Vennar of Lincoln's Inn, who in 1602 attempted to resolve, or at least reduce, the problematic of class representation by offering an aristocratic historical pageant, *England's Joy*, to be enacted at the Swan, as the playbill announced, "only by certain gentlemen and gentlewomen of account."[6] Vennar's promise of gentle instead of common players would not, of course, have fully closed the gap between those who are represented and those who represent, but it would at least have avoided any severe social dislocation between the two. But Vennar never produced his play, attempting to run off with the considerable receipts without ever performing it (and leaving the theater to be sacked by the outraged audience). In the commercial theater, however, aristocratic roles were not performed by "gentlemen and gentlewomen," nor were the actions of royalty represented, as the Chorus in *Henry V* desires, with "Princes to act." Actors of lower social rank, of course, mimed their social betters. Stephen Gosson, in his *Playes Confuted in Fiue Actions* (1582), says that the players were "either men of occupations . . . or common minstrals, or trained up from their childhood to this abominable exercise" (sig. G6v), though some of these "glorious vagabonds," as the academic authors of the *Parnassus* plays noted contemptuously, achieved an undeserved social eminence: "With mouthing words that better wits have framed, / They purchase lands, and now Esquiers are made" (*2 Return from Parnassus*, II. 1927–28). Class positions, then, appear on Shakespeare's stage exactly as women do, only in the mediations of a transvestite acting tradition. The oft-noted crossdressing of the Renaissance stage unnervingly crossed class as well as gender lines; not only did boy actors play women but commoners played kings.

In recent years, feminist scholarship has powerfully, if variously, considered the implications of crossdressing both in and outside of the theater for understanding the Renaissance sex-gender system,[7] but little attention has been paid to the implications of crossdressing for understanding the socioeconomic ordering of Elizabethan and Stuart England. "How many people crossdressed in early modern England?" Jean Howard has recently asked, and while she admits that the number must have been "limited," her estimate must be considerably revised upward if we include transgressions of class identity as well as of gender.[8]

If sexual crossdressing, like that of the notorious Mary Frith, was seen as scandalously bizarre, social crossdressing was seen as dangerously common. Protest was regularly heard against the "mingle-mangle," as Phillip Stubbes called it, produced by this social transvestism, "so that it is verie hard to knowe, who is noble, who is worshipful, who is a gentleman, who is not."[9] In addition to five "Acts of Apparel," at least nineteen proclamations to regulate dress were issued in Tudor England in order to preclude "the confusion . . . of degrees" that results "where the meanest are as richly appareled as their betters."[10] Though these sumptuary laws clearly were written for economic as well as political motives, being in part designed to cut down on imported luxuries and to protect the English wool trade by restricting the market for imported fabrics, the deep anxiety they voice about the "unmeasurable disorder" that crossdressing might bring about is unmistakable. The proclamation of 1559 laments "the wearing of such excessive and inordinate apparel as in no age hath been seen the like."[11] People did crossdress and in considerable numbers, and the state strove to prohibit it, acutely aware that such crossdressing threatened the carefully constructed hierarchical social order of early modern England. Regulation of dress was necessary to mark and secure social difference, in order to prevent, as William Perkins writes, "a confusion of such degrees and callings as God hath ordained, when as men of inferiour degree and calling, cannot be by their attire discerned from men of higher estate."[12] Or, as Gosson wrote in 1582, "if priuat men be suffered to forsake theire calling because they desire to walke gentlemanlike in sattine & velvet, with a buckler at theire heeles, proportion is so broken, unitie dissolued, harmony confounded & the whole body must be dismembered and the prince or the heade cannot chuse but sicken."[13] "Many good Lawes haue been made against this Babylonian confusion," remarked Fynes Moryson, "but either the Merchants buying out the penaltie, or the Magistrates not inflicting punishments, have made the multitude of Lawes hitherto unprofitable."[14]

But social crossdressing, legally prohibited on the streets of London, was, of course, the very essence of the London stage. Actors crossdressed with every performance, and although the early Tudor iterations of the sumptuary laws specifically exempted "players in enterludes" from its edict, none of the Elizabethan proclamations restating them mentions this exemption.[15] On stage, men of "inferior degree" unnervingly counterfeited their social betters, imitating not merely their language and gestures but their distinctive apparel. If there was no effort to produce historically accurate representations (recall Henry Peacham's drawing of the scene from *Titus Andronicus*), the stage did attempt to provide convincing representations of social rank. Philip Henslowe's wardrobe contained such gorgeous items as "a scarlett cloke wth ii brode gould Laces: wᵗ gould byttens of the same downe the sids," another in "scarlett wᵗ buttens of gould fact wᵗ blew velvett," and "a crimosin Robe strypt wᵗ gould fact wᵗ ermin."[16] Edward Alleyn apparently paid more than twenty pounds for a "black velvet cloak with sleeves embroidered all with silver and gold." But if such dress obviously permitted a lavish aristocratic display, its wearing was arguably criminal. The 1597 proclamation on apparel prohibited the wearing of "cloth of gold or silver . . . or cloth mixed or embroidered with pearl, gold or silver" to any "under the degree of a baron, except Knights of the Garter [and] Privy Councilors to the Queen's majesty" and denied the wearing of velvet "in gowns, cloaks, coats, or other uppermost garments" to all "under the degree of a knight, except gentlemen in ordinary office attending upon her majesty in her house or chamber, such as have been employed in embassage to foreign princes, the son and heir apparent of a knight, captains in her majesty's pay, and such as may dispend

£200 by the year for term of life in possession above all charges."[17]

Understandably, then, the theater, with its constitutive transgressions, was a politically charged arena in an age when social identities and relations seemed distressingly unstable, an instability in part constituted by the contradictory definition of status, as in the proclamation, both in terms of rank (a knight or baron) and in terms of wealth ("such as may dispend £200 by the year"). This contradiction reveals the vulnerability of the traditional culture based on hierarchy and deference to the transformative entrepreneurial energies of a nascent capitalism; and in the antitheatrical tracts that proliferated after the building of the Theatre in 1576 and the Curtain in 1577 the cultural anxiety about the fluidity of social role and identity found shrill voice. The oft-cited Deuteronomic prohibition (22.5) against males wearing female dress was regularly linked to a fear of social inferiors aping their betters. Gosson finds it equally objectionable that in the theater a boy would "put one the attyre, the gesture, the passions" of a woman and that "a meane person" would "take vpon him the title of a Prince with counterfeit port, and traine" (*Playes Confuted*, sig. E5ʳ). William Rankins, in his hysterical account of the monstrous contaminations of playing, insists that "Players ought not amidst their folly present the persons of Princes."[18] But anxiety was directed not merely at dressing "up," at the potential derogation of authority that its miming might effect; it was equally directed at dressing "down" (Rankins is as worried about the counterfeiting of rustics as he is of royalty). What was worrisome was that class positions could be mimed at all.

Though Stephen Greenblatt, following Thomas Laqueur's work on Renaissance anatomical knowledge, provocatively sees the transvestite acting tradition of the pre-Restoration stage as the inevitable result of a culture whose idea of gender was "teleologically male,"[19] viewed from the perspective of class rather than gender, a theater dependent upon crossdressing seems notably less inevitable or natural and perhaps more profoundly unsettling to the fundamental social categories of the culture. If the theater is not, as Jonas Barish enthusiastically claims, guilty of an "ontological subversiveness,"[20] at least in the context of the social anxieties of late-sixteenth-century England the theater, with its shape-shifting of professional actors, was a threat to the culture of degree. Acting threatened to reveal the artificial and arbitrary nature of social being. The constitutive role-playing of the theater demystifies the idealization of the social order that the ideology of degree would produce. The successful counterfeiting of social rank raises the unnerving possibility that social rank is a counterfeit, existing "but as the change of garments" in a play, in Walter Ralegh's telling phrase. In the theaters of London, if not in the *theatrum mundi*, class positions are exposed as something other than essential facts of human existence, revealed, rather, as changeable and constructed. When "every man wears but his own skin, the Players," as Ralegh writes, "are all alike."[21]

But if role-*playing* intellectually challenged the would-be stable and stabilizing social hierarchy, the role-*players* were themselves perhaps a greater social threat.[22] If the actors' ability to represent a full range of social roles disturbingly identified these *as* roles, the actors' conspicuous existence in society exposed the instability of the social categories themselves. Their success was perhaps the most visible of the contradictions that daily belied the fantasy of a stable social hierarchy. The actors' extravagant presence on the streets of London, no less than the substantial amphitheaters that they were able to erect, was an unmistakable sign of the vulnerability of the traditional culture of status to the transformative energies of capitalistic practice.

Though efforts were regularly made to fix players within the familiar terms of social organization, the actors and their companies conspicuously defied the prevailing social logic; if their "ouerlashing in apparel," in Gosson's phrase, and their "sumptuous Theatre houses," as Thomas White termed them, were, to such critics, alike "monument[s] of Londons prodigalitie and folly,"[23] they were also striking and unavoidable evidence of the considerable profits to be made in the burgeoning entertainment industry of Elizabethan London. "It is an evident token of a wicked time," wrote William Harrison, "when plaiers wexe so riche that they can build suche houses."[24] And while most of the players in fact remained poor, usually able only to counterfeit prosperity, the profits being limited to the sharers in the companies or the landlords of the playhouses themselves, a few, like Burbage or Shakespeare himself, did indeed "wexe . . . riche." Some "there are," wrote the author of *Ratseis Ghost*, glancing wryly at the affluence of Edward Alleyn, "whom Fortune hath so wel favored, that what by penny-sparing and long practise of playing, are growne so wealthy they have expected to be knighted, or at least to be conjunct in authority, and to sit with men of great worship, on the Bench of Justice."[25] While Alleyn never did attain his desired knighthood, he did become Master of the Royal Game and amass a fortune considerable enough to found Dulwich College in 1619. And Shakespeare, of course, was also able to turn his "share" into significant wealth and property, even purchasing a coat of arms for his father and "his posterite," apparently adorned with the resonant motto, *non sanz droict*.[26] The extraordinary claim of the parvenu was perhaps the immediate object of Jonson's gibe in *Every Man Out of His Humor*, when Puntarvolo suggests "*Not without mustard*" as the motto for the arms, with a crest of "a boar without a head *Rampant*," that the rustic Sogliardo purchased for £30 (3.4.86); and certainly in *The Poetaster*, Jonson unmistakably does condemn the social pretensions of the actors: "They forget they are i' the Statute, the Rascals; they are blazoned there; there they are tricked, they and their Pedigrees: they need no other Heralds, Iwisse" (1.2.53–55).

The "Statute" that Jonson invokes is one of the iterations of the 1572 act for the relief of the poor (14 Eliz. c. 5) that notoriously linked players to rogues and beggars. The social aspirations of the actors are belied by their juridical status: "Proud Statute Rogues," as the aspiring actors are termed in Marston's *Histriomastix* (3.1.241). Itinerant players were masterless men, their unauthorized presence disturbing to the social order and liable to harsh penalty. Convicted, they could "bee grevouslye whipped, and burnte through the gristle of the right Eare with a hot Yron of the compasse of an Ynche about"; and with a third conviction they were to "suffer paynes of death."[27]

But, of course, players were regularly licensed and legitimated, lawfully performing, by the terms of the legislation, in the service of a "Baron of this Realme" or "any other honorable Personage of greater Degree," or by permission of "two Justices of the Peace." In 1598, legislation removed the licensing authority from the magistrates, and then in 1603, when James assumed the throne, licensing rights passed even from the nobles of the realm into the hands of the royal family itself. Nonetheless, the licensing provision provided opportunities for companies of players to form and to perform. Players were freed from liability to prosecution, provided with the patronage that supposedly fixed them within the social order and legally subjected them to the statutes on retainers. Players were bound into a reciprocal relationship of control and responsibility.

If, however, the ability of actors legally to play depended upon this structure of service, it was a structure that existed more as legal fiction than social fact. The companies of players that nominally existed in the household of some great lord in fact functioned on a clear commercial basis, dependent on their patron only for the right to function professionally. When, for example, in 1572, a Statute of Retainers was executed that, like the Act for the Relief of the Poor enacted later that year, attempted to restrict the activities of various "masterless men," including "common players in interludes and minstrels, not belonging to any Baron or honourable person of greater degree," the six actors that made up Leicester's men petitioned their Lord not for any "stipend or benefit at your lordship's hands" but only for his "licence to certify that we are your household servants."[28] Service, then, was merely the protective coloring under which the commercial theater formed and flourished. In 1615, one critic protested that however much the actor "pretends to have a royall Master or Mistresse, his wages and dependance prove him to be the servant of the people."[29]

The commercial realities of playing could not successfully be hidden under the cover of livery. In 1584, the Queen's men appealed to the Privy Council for the right to perform publicly, first on the grounds that their public playing was merely rehearsal time for their court performances and, second, for "helpe and relief in our poore lyvinge."[30] The Corporation of London, however, filed a brief opposing the request on both grounds. They argued, first, that although the actors "pretend that they must haue exercise to enable them in their seruice before her maiestie . . . it is not convenient that they present before her maiestie such playes as haue ben before commonly played in open stages before all the basest assemblies in London and Middlesex" and, second, they insisted that in any case it was not appropriate "that players haue or shold make their lyuing on the art of playeng" when they might make their "lyuings vsing other honest and lawfull artes, or [be] reteyned in honest seruices."[31]

The players were, in spite of the insistent fictions of service, easily identified as professional actors, and their acting provoked continuous opposition precisely on the grounds of its professionalization. In 1591, Samuel Cox, condemning theaters as "dangerous schools of licentious liberty," focuses his disgust not on the plays but on the players, wishing that they "would use themselves nowadays, as in ancient former times they have done" when they either played for the king but "had other trades to live of and seldom or never played abroad," or were "ordinary servants" in the houses of noblemen "without making profession to be players to go abroad for gain," or were, like Shakespeare's mechanicals, "certain artisans . . . as shoemakers, tailors, and such like" that would play in the town halls "or some time in churches" only "to make the people merry."[32] Cox produces a fantasy of theatrical innocence when playing was uncontaminated by commerce. The reality, of course, was that playing was a profession and that players played for profit. Though in

1574 the London Common Council ordered that players act only "withowte publique or Commen Collection of money of the Auditorie or beholders theareof,"[33] this was a belated and ineffective effort to counter the patent granted by the crown earlier that year to James Burbage, John Perkin, John Laneham, William Johnson, and Robert Wilson for the first acting company licensed to play commercially throughout the country.

The professional theater, commercially organized and buoyed by royal support (a commitment of a piece with an economic policy that characteristically sought to establish monopolies to organize and restrict trade), provoked an increasingly impassioned antitheatricality, and, appropriately, one that often came to recognize professionalism itself as the proper object of attack. John Stockwood, in a sermon preached at Paul's Cross in 1578, speaks out against the "flocking and thronging to baudie playes by thousandes," and disgustedly observes that, "reckening with the leaste," theatrical profits "amounteth to 2000 pounds by the yeare."[34] Anthony Munday ends his diatribe against the stage by combining the familiar attack on the immorality of what is represented with an attack on the immorality of the motives for the representation: "To conclude, the principal end of all their interludes is to feede the worlde with sights, & fond pastimes; to juggle in good earnest the monie out of other mens purses into their owne handes."[35] Stubbes objects to the profane content of plays but equally to playing itself and players "making an occupation of it" (*Anatomie of Abuses*, sig. M1ᵛ); and Gosson similarly attacks the actors' professionalism: "let them not look to liue by playes" (*Playes Confuted*, sig. G7ʳ).

In 1618, a Catholic archpriest, William Harison, issued a general proclamation forbidding priests to attend plays, but under challenge he agreed that the order "doth not forbid to go to any stage plays, but to go to play or plays, acted by common players on common stages," defining "a common player [as] one that professeth himself a player and lives by the gain thereof, as by his trade or occupation."[36] Plays, argued William Prynne, "are but recreations, which must not be turned into professions."[37] Enacted privately and not for profit, however, plays may seem less noxious: John Northbrooke echoes a familiar position in holding that plays are tolerable so long as they "be not made a common exercise, publickly, for profit and gaine of money, but for learning and exercise sake." But, of course, playing did move out of the schools and into the theaters, the drama becoming, in "those places . . . whiche are made vppe and builded for such playes and enterludes, as the

Theatre and the Curtaine is," unmistakably "a common exercise" played primarily "for profit."[38]

In the new professional environment, when playing established itself literally as show business, actors achieved a remarkable measure of affluence and respect. The playhouses themselves were the most obvious indication of their success. Johannes de Witt commented in 1596, "There are four amphitheatres in London of notable beauty"; and by 1629, as Edmund Howes reports in his revision of John Stow's *Annales,* seventeen playhouses had been built in and around London, though not all still were standing.[39] And in these purpose-built playing spaces the drama flourished, both artistically and commercially. In 1617, Fynes Moryson remarked that not only were there "more Playes in London then in all the partes of the worlde I haue seene," but also that "these players or Comedians excell all other in the worlde."[40] The actors," according to Robert Greene in *Never Too Late,* "by continuall vse grewe not onely excellent but [he added bitterly] rich and insolent."[41] In 1603, King James's patent to the King's men permitted them "to shewe and exercise publiquely to theire best Commoditie" at "theire nowe vsual howse called the Globe within our County of Surrey, as alsoe within anie towne halls or Moute halls or other conveniente places within the liberties and freedome of anie other Cittie, vniversitie, towne, or Boroughe" and requested that the actors be allowed "such former Curtesies as hath bene given to men of their place and quallitie."[42] And by this patent, the actors became formally members of the Royal Household, Grooms of the Chamber, entitled to call themselves gentlemen.

And yet in spite of—or rather, precisely because of—the actors' new dignity, the old anxieties and familiar terms of abuse resurfaced. "The Statute hath done wisely to acknowledg him a Rogue errant," wrote an essayist in 1615, "for his chiefe essence is, *A daily Counterfeit:* He hath beene familiar so long with out-sides, that he professes himselfe (being unknowne) to be an apparant Gentleman."[43] Not merely a counterfeiter of roles *in* the theater, the actor is a "daily Counterfeit" *outside,* able to assume a social status not rightfully his own. Both "errant" and "unknowne," he unsettlingly moves up and down the countryside and the social scale—again a rogue in the anxious, antitheatrical imagination. The masterless actor, unnervingly mobile both socially and geographically and unmoored from the traditional, hierarchical culture of deference and dependency by the commercial practices of his profession, provoked widespread concern if not contempt.

"Hee is politic also to perceive the common-wealth doubts of his licence," continued the essayist, and within a generation the "common-wealth" would brutally rescind it. In 1648, when Parliament passed the third of its orders to close the theaters, it held that "all Stage-players and Players of interludes and common Playes . . . whether they be wanderers or no, and not withstanding any License whatsoever from the King or any person or persons to that purpose" are "declared to be, and are, and shall be taken to be Rogues" and "liable unto the pains and penalties" of the law.[44] An acting profession that achieved its most impressive aesthetic and economic successes in the face of a law that deemed it rogue and beggar, forcing commercial consolidation around the fiction of aristocratic patronage, was dissolved, if only until the Restoration, by a law that made the same judgment but closed the loophole that had served the profession virtually as its charter.

This is not the place to consider at any length the politics of the theaters' closing in the 1640s,[45] but clearly the parliamentary injunctions against playing cannot be understood primarily as an effort to dismantle a royalist institution. The theaters were always unreliable agents of cultural production, as the recurring governmental efforts at control and censorship bear witness. Indeed, the order to close the theaters in September 1642 may best be understood less as part of a parliamentary offensive against the monarch than as a defensive tactic, demanded by parliament's awareness of its own increasing vulnerability to the unruliness that the theater allowed, both on stage and in the audience. For parliament in the late summer of 1642 the theater's disorderly voices, precisely its errancy, became too troubling to endure.

The professional theater of Renaissance England, I've been arguing, by its constitutive masquerade as well as its commercial organization, contains in its materializations of an unnerving exchange a threat to social order, a threat the parliament of the 1640s instinctively recognized and articulated by reinscribing the actor within the demonized category of the masterless man. The commercial theater made it obvious that the actor had no master, whatever the juridical assertion, other than the audiences that he needed to please, and that he held no fixed position within the social formation, flaunting his mobility in the face of an increasingly defensive traditional culture. The autobiographical Roberto, in Greene's *Groats-worth of Witte*, meets up with a well-dressed stranger and is amazed to discover that he is an actor: "A player, quoth *Roberto*, I tooke you rather for a Gentleman of great liuing; if by outward habit men shuld be censured, I tell you, you would bee taken for a substantiall man.

So I am where I dwell (quoth the player) . . . . What though the world once went hard with me when I was fain to carry my Fardle a footeback . . . its otherwise now; for my share in playing apparell will not be solde for two hundred pounds."[46] Even the "hyerlings of some of our plaiers," Gosson wrote, "which stand at reversion of vi.s by the weeke" are able to "iet under gentlemens noses in sutes of silke," looking "askance ouer the shoulder at euery man of whom the Sunday before they begged an almes."[47]

Either by virtue of his own money or his access to the company's properties, the actor was able, even off stage, to mime social positions, calling into question the traditional culture of status that depends precisely on the fact that its attributes can neither be imitated nor purchased. But the exchanges that defined the theater relentlessly undermined the stability of that culture, insisting on the permeability of its social boundaries. Visible distinction cannot be maintained. Thomas Platter reports that "it is the English usage for eminent lords or knights at their decease to bequeath and leave almost the best of their clothes to their serving men, which it is unseemly for the latter to wear, so they offer them for sale for a small sum to the actors."[48] Thus, the silk suit that permitted the hireling to look askance at his social betters no doubt belonged to one when new.

But lest this fact be used to secure rather than disrupt the social hierarchy, we should note the complaint of Thomas Giles in 1572 against John Arnold, Yeoman of the Revels, protesting the policy to "lett to hyer" the gowns of the Revels' office. Giles's complaint lists twenty-one occasions in the previous year when gowns were rented out. Clearly the Revels' office regularly let or sold its costumes to professional players once they were too worn for court performance.[49] But Giles protested that Arnold was renting clothing to the citizens of London as formal wear: gowns were lent to the various Inns of Court; a gown was lent to the Lord Mayor; another for "the maryage of the dowter of my lord montague"; and, most scandalously, red cloth of gold gowns were lent to a "taylor" marrying in the Blackfriars. Giles complains about the "grett hurt spoylle & dyscredyt" that the garments suffer on account of their "comen usage," being worn by those "who for the most part be of the meanest sort of mene."[50] If clothes make the man, so apparently does the man make—or mar—the clothes. Giles's complaint is no doubt somewhat disingenuous, as he had a business with "apparell to lett" competing with the entrepreneurial Arnold; nonetheless, it is clear that clothing regularly circulated into and out of the playing spaces (Henslowe's contracts with actors often specified penalties for leaving the theater wearing the company's costumes[51]), endlessly producing and dissolving difference between inside and out, between surface and substance, between playing and being, producing and dissolving difference in the very social categories that the elite would have clothing make both legible and secure. If it isn't quite accurate to say that the theater, with its imitative disruption of the traditional culture of status, brought that culture to an end, certainly the theater's conspicuous presence signaled its vulnerability to dissolution in the transformative energies of the nascent capitalism of early modern England; and if it isn't quite accurate to say that the entrepreneurial successes of the acting companies actually brought "class" into being, certainly in the visible signs of their abundant energies and aspirations they brought class into view.

* * *

To explore, however tentatively, the politics of the transvestite playing I have been tracing, I want to end with a brief look at an example of cross-dressing in *King Lear*, though one not of dressing up but of dressing down: at Edgar and his assumption of the role of Poor Tom. Though no one seems to have explicitly related Edgar's disguise as a sturdy beggar to the dominant and demonized term of the antitheatrical discourse that surrounded the theater, a number of critics have shown that Edgar's disguise finds a source in the rogue literature that proliferated in the second half of the sixteenth century.[52] John Awdeley begins his *Fraternity of Vagabonds* (1561) with a description of the "abram-man" as "he that walketh bare-armed and bare-legged, and feigneth himself mad, and carryeth a pack of wool, or a stick with bacon on it, or such childlike toy, and nameth himself Poor Tom."[53] But the rogue literature functions ideologically to justify repression rather than compassion as a political response to the growing numbers of poor and homeless that actually were present in England, presenting their vulnerability as a tactic of a carefully crafted con-game. They become clever exploiters of a country's Christian charity instead of the pitiful victims of the early capitalistic state's social and economic dislocations.

If, however, the rogue literature, with its accounts of abram-men and other counterfeit poor, must be acknowledged as one source of Edgar's disguise, and the antitheatrical discourse another, each symptomatic of a potential for fraud, as Jean-Christophe Agnew has seen, in the emerging impersonal capitalistic market,[54] Shakespeare, as well as his audience, must also have found "proof and precedent / Of Bedlam beggars" (2.2.187–88) in the raw social realities of English life. One of the reiterated proclamations against vagrancy protested the increased presence in 1598 of "idle people and vagabonds" who were "in many parts of the realm and specially about the city of London and her majesty's court manifestly seen wandering in the common highways."[55] King James was disgusted enough by the vagrancy he saw at Newmarket to write the Virginia Company suggesting that the vagrant youths be transported to the new world. Edgar's "roaring," then, must sound as the all-too-familiar, alienated—and also alienating—voice of the homeless poor, loudly protesting their impoverished condition.

But Edgar's role-playing is, of course, fraudulent. Lear thinks he has discovered "the thing itself," "unaccommodated man" (3.4.105–6), but we know that he has found only an aristocrat playing a Bedlam beggar, or, more accurately, only an actor playing an aristocrat playing a Bedlam beggar, or, rather, as the antitheatrical voice would have it, only one sturdy beggar playing another. No doubt it could be argued that Edgar's spectacular counterfeiting, like that of the abram-men, similarly serves merely to manage anxieties about London's poor and to reinforce the very social boundaries that have been transgressed. But, at least within the play, his disguise pointedly does not work either to justify or confirm the existing social order. Poor Tom's poverty indeed becomes for Lear one mark of "how this world goes" (4.6.143–44), and if it is but mimed it is nonetheless part of the process that leads Lear to understand that disparities of wealth and power are not signs of an immutable hierarchical order but of an intolerable social injustice. "[C]ivill policies," Pierre de La Primaudaye cynically observed in *The French Academy*, "cannot well be preserved but by a certaine inequalitie,"[56] but Lear comes to see that the "inequalitie" in his kingdom, the world of "houseless heads and unfed sides" (3.4.30), is unacceptable and his own responsibility. The means of social amelioration rest not with Heaven but with sympathetic human action, with a redistribution of wealth, a shaking of "the superflux" to those in need that will alone "show the heavens more just" (3.4.35–36). "Distribution," as Gloucester says, "should undo excess, / And each man have enough" (4.1.73–74).

No doubt the play's utopian politics are undercut precisely by the gap *King Lear* insists upon between rich and poor.[57] The sympathy Lear discovers to animate his leveling depends upon an experience that the play insists is unique ("we that are young / Shall never see so much . . ."). As Jonathan Dollimore writes, "in a world where pity is the prerequisite for compassionate action, where a king has to share the suffering of his subjects in order to 'care,' the majority will remain poor, naked and wretched."[58] Still, the play itself, its representation, produces "pity," allows an audience "to share the suffering" not just of the fond and foolish king but of the "houseless poverty" he has "ta'en / Too little care of" (3.4.32–33). It is difficult, of course, to gauge the politics *of* the play (as opposed to the politics *in* the play) apart from an analysis of its playing in a particular place at a particular time; but certainly, as "houseless poverty" is again visible both as a social fact and a political issue, Edgar's counterfeiting may well remind even the bourgeois audience of our modern theater of the reality of human misery that waits outside and remind us as well that perhaps it need not be so.

> The political dimension of tragedy does not consist in illuminating the displacements of power, as happens in the long procession of sovereigns in the histories and even in *Julius Caesar*; it lies rather in posing the question of whether a *cultural foundation* of power is still possible, and in answering in the negative.
>
> —Franco Moretti

Chapter 9

Macbeth and the "Name of King"

Macbeth is at once the most violent of the major tragedies and the one whose violence has been most securely recuperated by criticism, if not by the text itself. Macbeth's savage tyranny is powerfully envisioned by the play but is seen to exist, in De Quincey's phrase, as "an awful parenthesis" in nature, a hideous aberration that at once opposes and legitimizes the moral order. Duncan's gracious sovereignty is shattered and replaced by Macbeth's increasingly gratuitous brutality, but Scotland is eventually released from the nightmare of Macbeth's rule by an army of English troops and disaffected Scottish nobles who come "to dew the sovereign flower, and drown the weeds" (5.2.30). With Malcolm's restoration of the line of Duncan, the forms of power are returned to legitimate hands and legitimate uses, the royal house and sovereignty itself successfully renewed. After a monstrous interregnum, authority is again natural and benign. Thus, critics characteristically hold that "the form of the play triumphantly asserts its thematic, moral resolution,"[1] reestablishing "the natural relationship between sovereign and subject,"[2] and, in affirming "the moral and natural legitimacy of rule through primogeniture,"[3] healing the breach in nature rent by Macbeth's violent usurpation and complimenting the absolutism of King James.

What, however, prevents this now familiar account of the moral reflex traced by the plot from being an entirely adequate description of the action of *Macbeth* is that it reduces the play to its confident moral assertions, reproducing rather than analyzing the construction of difference that underwrites them. It accepts as both normative and unassailable the moral oppositions produced (and dissolved) in the densities of the text. Legitimate is, of course, set against illegitimate, loyal against rebellious, natural against unnatural, good against evil. Indeed, Hazlitt observed that the play "is done upon a stronger and more systematic principle of contrast than any other of Shakespear's plays."[4] But the play is more disturbing than this would suggest. This insistent principle of moral contrast, wonderfully unconditional and reassuring, is not stable but is unnervingly unsettled by the text's compelling strategies of repetition and resemblance.

Like Lady Macbeth's hospitality, the play itself appears, with its two invasions, its two thanes of Cawdor, its two feasts, two doctors, two kings, and two kingdoms, "in every point twice done, and then done double" (1.6.15). These mirroring effects, what Jonathan Goldberg has incisively called the play's "specular contamination,"[5] insist that the radical difference asserted by its fierce moral oppositions is both tendentious and insecure. As a recent group of critics has argued, apparent opposites are discovered to be dismayingly similar, and, more dismaying still, even implicated in one another.[6] If the play does produce the almost inescapable binaries of its criticism, it reveals as well that the moral hierarchy they define is achieved and sustained only by denying the radical dependence of the dominant term upon its demonized contrary.

Duncan's benign sovereignty is no doubt set in opposition to Macbeth's willful brutality, but Duncan's rule depends upon—indeed demands—

Macbeth's violence. The unexplained revolt that begins the play is put down by Macbeth's brutal defense of Duncan's authority. Violent disruption is violently repaired. Certainly we are to distinguish Macbeth's killing *for* the king from Macbeth's killing *of* the king: in the service of Duncan, killing marks Macbeth as "valiant," a "worthy gentleman" (1.2.24); in the service of his own ambitions, killing marks Macbeth as monstrous, an "abhorred tyrant" (5.7.11). But if from the first the play asserts the absolute difference between loyal and rebellious action, it no less resolutely disrupts if not denies that difference, not merely in Macbeth's merciless treatment of "the merciless Macdonwald" (1.2.9), but in the unanchored pronouns that literally confuse the two: Macbeth carves "out his passage"

> Till he fac'd the slave
> Which ne'er shook hands, nor bade farewell to him,
> Till he unseam'd him from the nave to th' chops,
> And fix'd his head upon our battlements. (1.2.20–23)

Only "*our* battlements" is clearly differentiated; the referents of the third person singular pronouns are as "doubtful" (1.2.7) as the battle itself that the captain reports. All that is "fixed" is the head of a rebel.

Macbeth's violent defense of the King at once confirms Duncan's rule and collapses the distinctions upon which it rests. Difference dissolves into disruptive similarity. Hero and villain, as Harry Berger has ingeniously demonstrated,[7] are disturbingly intertwined and indistinguishable, as in the captain's image of the rebel forces and Duncan's troops as "two spent swimmers, that do cling together" (1.2.8). In the battle Macbeth fights bravely, but textual density and syntactic ambiguity uncannily dislocate his loyalties. Duncan "reads / [Macbeth's] personal venture in the rebels' fight" (1.3.91); the Scottish King "finds [Macbeth] in the stout Norweyan ranks" (1.3.95). Macbeth confronts the invading King of Norway, who is "assisted by that most disloyal traitor, / The Thane of Cawdor" (1.2.53–54), not with Duncan's certain authority but, disturbingly, only with "self-comparisons, / Point against point, rebellious arm 'gainst arm" (1.2.56–57).

Yet it might well be objected that the subtle reading gives too much away, that the legitimacy of Duncan, "clear in his great office" (1.7.18), itself stands as an absolute value that locates and fixes moral positions, necessitating and validating precisely the stark moral and political contrasts that textually, or rather *only* textually, blur. Duncan's unambiguous right demands and legitimates Macbeth's violent service as it later repudiates and demonizes Macbeth's violent ambition. Perhaps such a reading would have been James's own, and the play has regularly been seen as a compliment to the King ("a topick the most likely to conciliate the favour of the court,"[8] as Malone said), not merely in the vivid "show" of the Stewart kings, with their "two-fold balls and treble scepters" (4.1.11sd, 121), envisioning precisely the imperial claim of James's monarchy,[9] but also in the play's reproduction of the absolutist logic of James's own political theorizing. In spite of the murderous violation of "the Lord's anointed temple" (2.3.68), sovereign authority is here wondrously compelling and resilient, both worthy and capable of being defended and restored. "Things . . . climb upward to what they were before" (4.2.24–5); the usurper is purged, and natural hierarchy and lineal descent are reestablished. Even in the face of Macbeth's savage criminality, "Shakespeare makes it seem," writes Leonard Tennenhouse, "as if nothing can disrupt the progress of the crown from Banquo to James; all the elements of nature, like those of the theater, join to put Malcolm on the throne."[10]

But if Tennenhouse correctly recognizes the genealogical telos of Shakespeare's *Macbeth*, his formulation unwittingly reveals the impossibility of appealing to an absolute notion of sovereignty to authorize the play's oppositions, for Tennenhouse has in fact identified *two* dynastic genealogies, an embarrassing surplus that must unsettle the claim to legitimacy of either. If the Stewart line is seen to derive from Banquo, then Malcolm's claim to the throne and James's own seem to conflict. The play offers two seemingly incompatible sources of legitimacy: it is Banquo who will plant the "seeds of kings" (3.1.69) that will flower into the Stewart dynasty, but the play asserts as well that Malcolm's restoration of the line of Duncan reestablishes legitimate rule in Scotland.

Macbeth thus makes evident that Stewart legitimacy rests on something less certain than patrilineal descent, though the play is oddly silent about the contradiction that it makes visible. Historically (and that may be the wrong word since "Fleance" seems to be an invention of Hector Boece in 1527[11]), the dynastic lines eventually merge some six generations after the events of the play, when Walter, putatively the descendant of Fleance, marries Marjory, the daughter of Robert I. Their son, Robert II, is the first of the Stewart kings, claiming, however, his throne from his mother (and, ironically, given the later Stuarts' commitment to the Union, succeeding only after an effort by David Bruce to have the king of England or his son "undertake the Kingdom"[12]).

The play's emphasis upon Banquo as "father to a line of kings" (3.1.59) rather than Duncan has, then, the effect of avoiding the vexed problem of inheritance through the female, comfortably locating authority in the male body. But if this is appropriate for a play, if not a culture, that consistently demonizes female power, a play in which to be not "of woman born" (4.1.80) is to be invulnerable and to be "unknown to woman" (4.3.126) is to be virtuous, it leaves unmistakable the fault line in the play's, if not the culture's, understanding of legitimacy—and not least because James inherits his Scottish crown through the female, a fact at issue in the Witches' "show of eight kings," as the eighth monarch of the Stewart line was in fact James's mother, Mary, whose presence in, no less than her absence from the pageant must necessarily trouble its putative assertion of patrilineal succession.[13]

The plot's strenuous efforts to reestabalish sovereign authority by restoring the line of Duncan always exists uncomfortably, that is, too obviously, with its parallel insistence that "Banquo's issue" will "ever / Reign in this kingdom" (4.1.102–3), making it impossible to see "the progress of the crown" as inevitable and undeviating. With Malcolm's investiture the crown is returned to legitimate hands, but the Stuart future, stretching "out to th'crack of doom" (4.1.117), clearly has its source elsewhere. Though James was proud of "the continued line of lawfull discent, as therin he exceedeth all the Kings that the world now knoweth," as Ellesmere wrote,[14] Shakespeare's play at once demonizes the disruption of "lawfull discent" and seemingly insists upon it, valorizes the concept of legitimacy and discloses its instability.

Renaissance absolutism,[15] of course, usually attempted to stabilize the concept theoretically, if not historically, by insisting upon sovereignty's divine authorization. Thus, Henry VIII strove to establish "the surety of both his title and succession" by appealing to the "grants of jurisdiction given by God immediately to Emperors, kings and princes in succession to their heirs."[16] James claimed his throne on similar grounds, Coke arguing on his behalf that "the kinges's matie, in his lawful, juste & lineall title to the Crowne of Englaunde, comes not by succession onelye, or by election, but from God onelye . . . by reason of lineall discente."[17] And James spectacularly extended the implications of occupying "the office giuen him by God": "For Kings are not onely GODS Lieutenants vpon earth, and sit vpon GODS throne, but euen by GOD himselfe they are called Gods."[18]

Scripture commanded the Israelites: "set him a king over thee, whom the Lord thy God shall choose" (Deut. 17:15), but exactly how God's choice was to be known and established in rule was uncertain. The crown may well insist upon its origins in an absolute and direct grant of authority from God, but it cannot escape the evidence of its heavily mediated existence in a world of historical agency. Though authority usually seeks to occlude the fact, imagining itself always both sanctified and permanent, it characteristically originates, and usually maintains itself, in violent action. Trotsky, of course, provocatively claimed that "every state is founded on force,"[19] but even conservative Renaissance political thinkers usually understood that what came to be known as "divine right" did not solve the question of authority: it mystified it. Even while insisting that kingship is divinely sanctioned, they saw that its origins were decidedly more mundane and compromised. In 1595, William Covell, in his *Polimanteia*, admitted that most "common wealths had their beginnings by violent Tyrannies."[20] In 1604, Sir Henry Saville concurred, holding that of the kingdoms now in existence "all of them and perhaps all that ever were . . . [were] first purchased by conquest."[21] As Marchamont Nedham would say in later years, when the complex issue of legitimating a regime founded on violence had become apparent to all, "the power of the sword is, and ever hath been, the foundation of all titles to government."[22]

On the other hand, though the identification of authority's origins in power was commonplace, many recognized the political danger in acknowledging the fact, a danger uncannily admitted, in the folio orthography, in Macbeth's somatic response to the mere thought of the murder of sovereignty: the "horrid Image doth unfixe my Heire" (1.3.135; TLN 246). Both hairs and heirs may well be unfixed by the knowledge of sovereignty's violent origins, as the Presbyterian divine, Richard Baxter understood. Writing in prison in 1686, he argued that monarchs must suppress such knowledge, not because the truth was otherwise but for fear it would "encourage Rebels" or invasion from without: "while France is stronger than England, Holland or other Kings, I dare not say that if that Kingdom conquer them he is their rightfull monarch, lest such doctrine entice him to attempt it."

What had provoked Baxter's consideration and rejection of conquest theory was "a little book written by a namelesse Scot 1603, called the Law of free Monarchies" that "foundeth the originall right of Monarchy uppon *strugle and Conquest* by which only Kings are made Kings."[23] Baxter's "namelesse Scot," however, was King James himself, and in his *True Law of Free Monarchies* (which was originally published in 1598 with the pseudonym "C. Philopatris"), even James admitted the inevitable coercion in "the first maner of establishing the Lawes and forme of gouernement among vs."[24] In part to escape the dangerous implications of the view that monarchy begins with a transfer of power from the people, James was forced to concede that Scottish monarchical authority derived directly from the conquest of Scotland by the Irish King Fergus, "making himself master of the countrey, by his owne friendship, and force," just as English monarchical authority derived from the conquest of England by "the Bastard of *Normandie*" who "made himselfe king . . . by force, and with a mighty army."[25]

But once authority admits its customary origins in force and violence the question of legitimacy becomes complex. What king is then not a usurper, or at least a usurper's heir? While King James assumed that "the trew difference betwixt a lawful good King and an vsurping Tyran"[26] was absolute and unassailable, the distinction cannot be rigidly maintained, logically collapsing in the discussion of authority's origin (a collapse interestingly enacted in an anxious sentence in Bodin's *Six Bookes of a Commonweale* deploring interpreters "ioyning these two incompatible words together, *a King a Tyrant*,"[27] where Bodin hysterically performs at the level of syntax the very "ioyning" he seeks to prevent). If the crown is claimed by right of conquest, even if carefully designating it a second cause animated and validated by providence, the difference between lawful authority and usurped power must blur if not be completely erased.

The problem was a crucial one for Renaissance political theorists who increasingly recognized the difficulty posed by coercive origination for the theory of absolutism. The Book of Homilies had confidently asserted that "we be taught by experience, how Almighty God never suffereth the third heir to enjoy his father's wrong possessions,"[28] but, in fact, experience often taught otherwise, history regularly testifying to the successful legitimation of usurped authority. Indeed, in 1643, Henry Ferne maintained that "If this Answerer should looke through all Christendomne, he would scarce find a Kingdom that descends by inheritance, but had a beginning in Armes, and yet I thinke he will not say the Titles of these Kings are no better then of Plunderers; for though it may be unjust at first in him that invades and Conquers, yet in the succession, which is from him, that providence which translates Kingdomes, manifests it selfe and the will of God; and there are *momenta temporum*, for the justnesse of such Titles, though we cannot fixe them."[29]

Though Pocock has claimed that "conquest struck few roots in royalist thought,"[30] obviously a conquest theory had developed and taken hold by the end of the sixteenth century and, perhaps surprisingly, precisely among those most committed to royalism. King James himself had articulated it in his appeal to Fergus's conquest to authorize Scottish kingship, though James attempted to defuse the potentially subversive implications of grounding authority in power by insisting, improbably, that the "people willingly fell to him" and that, in any case, the country was "scantly inhabited.[31] Others, who recognized the impossibility of escaping the contradiction James attempted to evade, worried more about forging a political distinction that could rationalize the process by which power is converted into authority, fixing the *momenta temporum* that Ferne had invoked. William Barret, chaplain of Cambridge's Gonville and Caius College, reversed the claim of the Elizabethan homilist, insisting that several generations (*nonnulla secula*) of possession would validate and legitimize a usurped crown;[32] Thomas Preston similarly argued that tyrants and usurpers "with their progenie doe by prescription get a lawfull right to the souereigntie by possessing it a hundred yeeres or more";[33] and the Canons passed by the clergy in 1606, which King James significantly refused to endorse, were even more liberal: "new forms of government," the clergy held, even those "begun by rebellion," became legitimate as soon as they are "thoroughly settled."[34]

For *Macbeth*, of course, the problem is further complicated by the fact that in Scotland, unlike England, patrilineal succession to the crown was itself a "new" form of government, an innovation introduced at the end of the tenth century by Kenneth III. The traditional mode of transferring sovereignty in Scotland had been a quasi-elective system of succession within an extended royal family, consciously devised to prevent both the succession of a minor and the perpetuation of tyrannical rule. But Kenneth III (grandfather of the play's Duncan), "greeuing not a little," as Holinshed reports following Boece, "for that thereby his sonnes should be kept from inioieng the crowne," poisoned the prince who "ought to have succeeded in the rule of the kingdom," appointing his own eldest son, Malcolm, as heir and persuading the nobles to abrogate the old law of tanistry. The nobility, "perceiuing it was in vaine to denie that which would be had by violence," reluctantly agreed to the designation of Kenneth's son as Prince of Cumberland and to the institution of a system whereby "the sonne should without anie contradiction succeed the father in the heritage of the crowne and kinglie estate."[35]

Though scholars have questioned how well Shakespeare actually knew or understood the intricacies of Scottish political history,[36] he could not but be aware of this aspect of Scotland's past, which, as republican historians like George Buchanan made clear, exposes the mutable, historical (and hence contestable) nature of hereditary kingship. For *Macbeth*, which combines materials from several reigns, Shakespeare obviously read widely in Holinshed's *Historie of Scotland*, and so would certainly have encountered evidence and discussion of Scotland's earlier dependence for the transfer of authority upon the traditional system of collateral inheritance. But even in Holinshed's account of Macbeth's reign the procedures and principles by which authority is transmitted are prominent; indeed they are precisely what provokes Macbeth to act to obtain the crown. The chronicle notes not only that Macbeth had many qualities necessary for rule but also that by "the old lawes of the realme" he had a credible claim to the throne. Following Duncan's nomination of his son Malcolm as his successor, Holinshed (or rather Francis Thynne) writes, Macbeth "began to take counsell how he might usurpe the kingdome by force, having a just quarell so to doo (as he took the matter) for that Duncane did what in him lay to defraude him of all maner of title and claime, which he might in time to come, pretend unto the crowne."[37]

Shakespeare's play, of course, does nothing to question Duncan's right or assert Macbeth's own, and many critics have noted how Shakespeare selects and shapes his source material in writing *Macbeth* to clarify if not produce its sharp oppositions. Among other changes, the history's account of "the feeble and slothful administration of Duncane"[38] is unmentioned in the play, along with Macbeth's ten years of humane and effective rule, as Shakespeare erases the equivocations of the source material, transforming, as Peter Stallybrass has said, "dialectic into antithesis."[39] What has less often been considered is why Shakespeare's attention should be drawn to a reign that demanded such substantial alteration and erasure. No doubt he was attracted to the story because the chronicle account includes an extended digression tracing the origins of the Stuart dynasty back to Fleance.[40] Nonetheless, if the subject was chosen because of its relation to King James, Shakespeare has chosen historical matter determinedly resistant to the story he apparently wants to tell—and certainly incompatible with the absolutist politics of his sovereign. The Scottish history not only complicates, if not contests, the right of Duncan but presents patrilineal succession itself, which the play idealizes and naturalizes, as an innovation brought about by an ambitious and murderous tyrant. That is, Shakespeare's sources disturbingly suggest that the hereditary kingship that

Macbeth assails—and that King James champions—originates with a king who is, in fact, Macbeth's double rather than his opposite.

But Shakespeare's own story is profoundly a story of doubles, doubles, as Jonathan Goldberg has said, that render "determinate difference indeterminate,"[41] reinstating, that is, the complexities of the source material apparently banished by the insistent antitheses of the Shakespearean plot. Everywhere the play palters "with us in a double sense" (5.8.20), offering both an orthodox version of events and one disturbingly heterodox: a moral play "that maketh Kings feare to be Tyrants,"[42] in Sidney's phrase, and a subversive one that uncannily collapses the distinction between them. The ending may be seen either to restore the legitimate line of Duncan, redeeming the murderous interlude of Macbeth's tyranny, or merely to repeat the pattern of violent action that Macbeth initiates. The play both begins and ends with an attack upon established rule, with a loyal nobility rewarded with new titles, and with the execution of a rebellious thane of Cawdor. Malcolm is three times hailed as king exactly as Macbeth has been by the witches, and Malcolm's coronation at Scone either returns the nation to health and order or provides the conditions for a new round of temptation and disorder (as in Roman Polanski's 1971 film of the play, which ends with Donalbain going off to seek the witches and his own crown, or, indeed, as in the chronicles themselves, where the historical Donald Bane turned rebel, allying himself with the King of Norway, killing Malcolm's son and successfully claiming the throne).

The play's insistent doubling, then, insures that it cannot simply be seen as an orthodox demonstration, designed to delight and praise King James, of the inevitable recoil of the moral world, successfully purging sin and reestabalishing right. But that *is*, however, exactly how the troops accompanying Malcolm understand the action. "March we on," says Caithness, "To give obedience where 'tis truly ow'd: / Meet we the med'cine of the sickly weal; / and with him pour we, in our country's purge, / Each drop of us" (5.2.25–29). Malcolm may well be the "med'cine of the sickly weal," but if the moral alignments are certain and secure the political ones are significantly less so. The play makes it difficult to discover exactly where obedience is "truly owed." Macduff calls Macbeth an "untitled tyrant bloody-scepter'd" (4.3.104), but in fact, however bloody his scepter, he certainly is, as Macduff well knows, *titled*. Although Macbeth is undeniably a murderer, he lawfully succeeds and is crowned. "'Tis most like / The sovereignty will fall upon Macbeth," observes Ross; and Macduff responds: "He is already nam'd, and gone to Scone / To be invested" (2.4.29–32). "Named" and legally enthroned, Macbeth is king and arguably truly owed the obedience of his countrymen.

The difficulty of maintaining the distinction between a "lawful" king and a "usurping" tyrant is not only articulated by Macduff's contradictory judgments but registered structurally by his role in the play. He is obviously a loyal version of the ambitious Macbeth. Macbeth kills both a rebel then a king, exactly as does Macduff, but, as Alan Sinfield has shrewdly noted, Macduff's rebel and king are the same man.[43] Macbeth's acts, of course, are clearly differentiated: one is a heroic defense of the nation and its king, the other a murderous attack upon them; but Macduff's single act at once defends and attacks sovereignty. It is a liberation and a regicide, one more thing that is "fair and foul" in the "hurly-burly" of the play. While apparently an unproblematic reassertion of right and reason, it should be perhaps only as "welcome and unwelcome" (4.3.138) as his first impression of Malcolm.

If Macduff has rescued Scotland, freeing the time from the tyrant, avenging "crimes against the family and against the state,"[44] in David Norbrook's phrase, we should note also that Macduff is himself charged with "crimes against the family and the state," charged, that is, with being the "traitor" (4.2.81, 45) that both the first murderer and Lady Macduff term him. For the first murderer, Macduff is a "traitor" simply because he opposes the king of Scotland that has suborned the murderer's services. For Lady Macduff, of course, the charge is not that her husband has betrayed a political allegiance but that he betrayed his family precisely *in* his political allegiance: "He loves us not: / He wants the natural touch" (4.2.8–9). In a change from the source, where Macduff goes to England "to reuenge the slaughter so cruellie executed on his wife, his children, and other friends,"[45] Shakespeare's Macduff chooses the state over his family as his primary loyalty, in the process leaving his family vulnerable to the murderous "firstlings" (4.1.147) of Macbeth's heart as he seeks aid for his country.

Norbrook argues that "Shakespeare invents the scene of the murder of Lady Macduff and her son in order to bring home the 'natural' links between the public and the private."[46] But it seems to me possible to argue exactly the reverse: the episode reveals that the homology that absolutism characteristically posited between state and family is false. Kinship and kingship are not necessarily mutually reinforcing, as the ideological efforts to naturalize domination would insist, but here revealed as conflicting spheres of existence, distributing power and demanding service in ways that are incompatible and contradictory. "What is a traitor," innocently asks Macduff's young son, but the play prevents an easy answer; "Why, one that swears and lies" (4.2.46–47), bitterly answers Lady Macduff, resentful of her husband's betrayal of his familial obligations (and in words no doubt alluding to the equivocations of the Jesuit Henry Garnet in the Gunpowder trial in March of 1606). Yet in this play where it often seems that "nothing is, but what is not" (1.3.142), the first murderer's charge of treason is as true—and admittedly as false—as Lady Macduff's, and both charges speak the profound instability in the discourse of authority that was expected to rationalize and guarantee all social relations.

If considering Macduff a "traitor" seems hard justice for one who means so well and loses so much, it does reveal the difficulty of articulating persuasively and coherently a theory of resistence without at the same time admitting the conditional and contingent nature of political power. The Huguenot Theodore Beza, for example, attempted to discover a legitimate place for political opposition by distinguishing between tyranny by those who "by force or fraud" have "usurped a power that does not belong to them by law" (against whom "each private citizen" has the right to "exert all his strength to defend the legitimate institutions of his country") and a "sovereign magistrate" who is "otherwise legitimate" (against whom the people "have no other remedy" than "penitance and patience joined by prayers."[47] Macbeth's case, however, doesn't precisely fit either circumstance. Certainly he has proceeded by "force and fraud" but the crown may indeed be said "to belong to [him] by law." Not only has he right, but he achieves his kingship by proper election and investiture. And yet, although he is therefore a "sovereign magistrate," unquestionably he has compromised the "legitimate institutions of his country." Is he, then, owed obedience or not?

The conventional political answer was clear; though ironically it is not the one conventional readings of the play presume. William Sclater, a Protestant clergyman, asserted that neither the means by which a king assumed power nor his behavior in office affected his authority as king: "the persons are sometimes intruders, as in the case of vsurpation; sometimes abusers of their authoritie, as when they tyrannize: but the powers themselues haue God as their author."[48] Similarly, King James argued that a lawfully enthroned king no matter how monstrous must not be opposed. Determined to resist both Catholic and Calvinist resistance theories, King James insisted that even a murderous tyrant was to be patiently suffered, for the king was to be judged by God alone. "It is casten vp by diuers that employ their pennes vpon Apologies for rebellions and treasons," wrote James, "that euery man is borne to carry such a naturall zeale and duety to his common-wealth, as to his mother; that seeing it so rent and deadlie wounded, as whiles it will be by wicked and tyrannous Kings, good Citizens will be forced, for the naturall zeale and duety they owe to their owne natiue countrey, to put their hand to worke for freeing their common-wealth from such a pest."[49]

But this apparently natural and patriotic course, which exactly anticipates the moral claims and rhetorical strategies of the avenging Scots in the play, is, in fact, condemned by James, held to be both blasphemous and ineffective: first, it violates, he says, "a sure Axiome in *Theologie*, that evil should not be done, that good may come of it: The wickednesse therefore of the King shall never make them that are ordained to be iudged by him, to become his Iudges." Rebellion is "evil" in every circumstance; the behavior of the king in no way affects the fact that those "that are ordained to be iudged" must always stay so and support the status quo. And, second, James is certain that "in place of relieuing the common-wealth out of distresse (which is their onely excuse and colour) they shall heape double distresse and desolation vpon it; and so their rebellion should procure the contrary effercts they pretend it for."[50] Instead of improving the situation, their principled opposition only makes it worse.

Neither pragmatically nor theologically can any effort to oppose the "wickednesse . . . of the King" be justified. Indeed, writes James, a ruler might be "a Tyrant, and vsurper of their liberties; yet in respect that they had once received and acknowledged him for their king, he not only commandeth them to obey him, but euen to pray for his prosperitie. . . ."[51] Thus, strangely, in the play the orthodox moral position is at odds with the orthodox political position; the inevitable moral revulsion at Macbeth's brutal criminality produces a political reflex that must itself be condemned. As Macbeth's rule is lawful (having been "received and acknowleged"), the English troops and Scottish nobles that arrive as saviors of Scotland become exact doubles of the Norwegian troops and rebellious nobles that distress Duncan's lawful reign at the play's beginning.

In each case an indigenous force combines with a foreign power to assail the security of a Scottish monarch, the very neatness of the parallel undoing the overdetermined difference the play asserts. The repair of violated patrilineal succession (though it is perhaps worth noting that the play has not very clearly established the principle of patrilineal succession, "the due of birth," since Malcolm's right to the Scottish crown seems to originate in Duncan's nomination of his son), as well as the insistent Englishness of the resources that repair it, works, of course, to differentiate the recoil against Macbeth from the Norwegian-supported revolt against Duncan. Macbeth's savagery demands and legitimates any and all savagery in the campaign to dethrone him, and the English invasion is not merely *English* but is endowed with a unique spiritual authority, evident in Edward's "most pious" kingship (3.6.27), which, remarkably, keeps itself discretely aloof from the military action necessary to activate its moral charge.[52] Yet, for all the efforts to insure the sanctity of the restorative violence, it is nonetheless and inescapably violence, and almost uniquely visible on stage. Though the play would see Macbeth's violence as aberrative and blasphemous, as that which assails sovereign authority and must be repudiated, it offers no obvious alternative to that violence as that which is necessary to construct and defend sovereignty.

The spectacular sight of Macbeth's head fixed upon a pole, which might be seen as evidence of the inevitable triumph of moral order and political right, cannot, then, be easily used to stabilize the play's politics. Though the traitor's fate may be intended to signal "the terrible magnificence of sovereign power," like virtually all signs in the play it is equivocal, providing, as Karin Coddon argues, testimony only to "the inefficacy of symbolic closure."[53] "Behold, where stands / Th'usurper's cursed head" (5.9.20–21), proudly proclaims Macduff, but the visual image that in its spectacular assertion of legitimate power would resolve the political instability produced by the play's violence in fact reanimates the problematic. If it marks the end of Macbeth's savage tyranny, it marks as well the vulnerability of sacred kingship.

The image of the severed head certainly recalls the heads of traitors fixed on Tower Bridge, but, alternatively, it resonates as well with the crucial term of James's absolutism, characteristically articulated in the anthropomorphizing metaphor of the body politic. James, of course, conceived of the king as "the head of a body composed of diuers members,"[54] and the similitude produces a clear, if predictable, political logic. Quoting Gerson, James wrote that the people have no right to resist "the head" of the civil body even if the "deadlie poyson of tyrannie" infect it, and James finds that Gerson's arguments "doe make very strongly and expresly against butchering euen of Tyrannical Kings."[55] The head cut off, the body must wither. "It may very well fall out that the head will be forced to garre cut off some rotten members . . .

to keep the rest of the body in integritie," James wrote, "but what state the body can be in, if the head, for any infirmitie that can fall to it, be cut off, I leaue to the readers iudgement."[56] Strictly within the context of James's own political thought, then, Macduff's entrance with "the usurper's cursed head" can only be seen less as a "tribute to James"[57] than as a challenge to his "iudgement," the image of unlawful resistance rather than of lawful rule. The severed head of Macbeth would, at least for James, mark not the restoration of legitimate authority but its violation: the unwarranted and blasphemous "butchery" of a "tyrannical King." It could not be a sign of renewed sovereignty but must appear as a "breach in nature" (2.3.111) no less awful than the "gashed stabs" in Duncan's sacred body, a breach that within a generation would find its form in the severed head of James's son shockingly displayed upon another "bloody stage" (2.4.6).

My point, however, is obviously not that the play demands to be read in the context of James's own political thought or ambitions, though this has been a familiar critical assertion; it is more to show the impossibility of any such reading, to see the way the play inscribes not merely the contradictions present in the source material but in the absolutist logic itself. One could, of course, find in the English invasion that frees Scotland from Macbeth's murderousness tactful reference to James's profound hopes for the union of England and Scotland, and, indeed, George Buc had in 1605 used the alliance of Malcolm and the English Edward as an anticipation of and argument for ("a slight shadow of") the Union.[58] But if *Macbeth*'s emphasis on Englishness is designed to legitimize the Union of the Kingdoms (and one might wonder how neatly a view of England as physician to a diseased Scotland would fit with James's understanding of the Union project), ironically it was, as Holinshed reports, precisely this Englishness that left Scotland vulnerable to the depredations of Malcolm's rebellious brother:

> manie of the people abhorring the riotous maners and superfluous gormandizing brought in among them by the Englishmen were willing inough to recieve this Donald for their King, trusting (bicause he had beene broght up in the Iles with the old customes and maners of their ancient nation, without tast of the English likerous delicats) they should by his severe order in gouernement recouer againe the former temperance of their old progenitors.[59]

Shakespeare's play is silent about Donalbain's revolt, its possibility only dimly suggested by Lennox's reply to Caithness's question, "Who knows if

Donalbain be with his brother?": "For certain, sir, he is not" (5.2.7–8). And Macbeth alone articulates the "severe" Scottish view of the English, in his bitter response to his disloyal nobles: "fly, false Thanes / And mingle with the English epicures" (5.3.7–8).

Shakespeare, unsurprisingly, writes Englishness differently. His English are hardly rioters and epicures, though their social practices, perhaps ominously, do indeed influence Scottish custom, in Malcolm's introduction of English titles for his nobility: "Earls, the first that ever Scotland / In such an honour nam'd" (5.9.29–30). These new forms of honor are obviously, like those titles Duncan gave his followers, at once generous and instrumental, rewards for loyal service and opportunities to articulate the social order that would create and reflect the monarch's power. But the innovative English titles can also be read, as the English manners adopted by Malcolm's court were by both Boece and Buchanan, less benignly within this royal economy: not as "signs of nobleness" designed to "shine / On all deservers" (1.4.41–42) but as marks of corruption and catalysts for decline, less an argument for the Union than a motive for revolt.[60]

English-Scottish relations in the play do not, then, seem to promise or promote the joyful Union that James imagined. The corporate fantasy of "One King, one people, one law, and, as it was in the beginning, one land of Albion"[61] that underwrote the Union project is belied by *Macbeth*'s insistent doubles and inescapable double-talk. The very "name of king" is neither univocal nor fixed but is dislocated and destabilized in the recursive plot of the play no less than it was in the volatile political thought that the play engages. And "the name of king" was not merely an abstractly controversial focus for the ongoing Renaissance discussions about the nature and limits of sovereignty but was explicitly a contested term in the Union debates, as the English Commons in 1604 worried the effects of conceiving of Britain as a single geopolitical entity. James's desire to "discontinue the divided names of England and Scotland" and unite the two kingdoms "under one Imperiall Crown,"[62] was anxiously discussed, and the Commons expressed their discomfort with this new "imperial theme" (1.3.129) that seemed to threaten England and Englishness. "The Name of Emperour is impossible," they declared; "The name of King a sweet name:– Plenitude of Power in it:– A Name, which God taketh upon him."[63]

Certainly, in *Macbeth* "the name of King" has a "Plenitude of Power in it," though not a power inhering in the word itself but in the social relations its speaking defines. Acknowledged "king," the monarch can effectively mobilize the institutions and agencies of power that define and defend his sovereignty. For Malcolm, Edward the Confessor, the English king, is the type of sacred and efficacious majesty: "sundry blessings hang about his throne, / That speak him full of grace" (4.3.158–59). But what "speaks" his plenitude are less the "blessings" that "hang about his throne" than the loyalty of the "ten thousand warlike men" (4.3.134) who will fight to uphold it. And if the name of king activates the power of the state that constitutes and maintains the crown, it also works to naturalize that power, sanctioning violence, converting it into valor. Thus Malcolm and the avenging nobles insistently deny the name to Macbeth. He is always the "tyrant," whose violent acts make him unworthy of loyalty; Duncan and Malcolm alone are called "King of Scotland" (1.2.28; 5.9.25), a name that turns the acts of violence done on their behalf into loyal and heroic action.

Indeed, though Macbeth enters "*as King*" at the beginning of act three, and is lawfully "named" before he goes "to Scone / To be invested" (2.4.31–32), the word "King" seems to stick even in his own mouth. He speaks it only five times, on three occasions referring to the witches' prophecy (1.3.73; 1.3.144; 3.1.57), once to the apparition of a "child crowned" (4.1.87), and once to Duncan: "Let us toward the King" (1.3.153). Many critics have remarked on the euphemisms Macbeth uses to describe the murders he plans and commits, but "the name of king" is subject to exactly the same verbal displacements. "When 'tis, / It shall make honor for you," he says to Banquo (2.1.25–26), exactly like the pronomial evasions of "If it were done, when 'tis done, then 'twere well / It were done quickly" (1.7.1–2). Even Lady Macbeth cannot fully articulate his prophesied progress to the throne: "Glamis thou art, and Cawdor; and shalt be / What thou art promis'd" (1.5.14–15), not "King," as the witches' three-fold prophecy demands, but merely the paraphrastic "What thou art promised." The name of king, with its plenitude of power, is not so easily spoken, not quite so "sweet," when one admits the fearsome agency necessary to achieve and defend it.

I hope it is clear that my purpose here is neither to set the play in the context of Jacobean absolutist fantasies, nor to find in its doublings and dislocations mere indeterminacy, a hall of mirrors, endlessly reflecting and ultimately "signifying nothing" (5.5.28). "The name of king" that the witches first "put . . . upon" (3.1.57) Macbeth, like all their imperfect speaking, is, of course, equivocal, but it is, in fact, no more stable when Macbeth is "named" (2.4.31)

by the nobles, or as it functions in the diverse political discourses that circulate around and through the play. In all its iterations, the name of king is
unnervingly labile, but no less potent for being so. It would define itself as the
opposite of the blasphemous savagery the play calls "Macbeth," imagining
itself, stable and singular, as a benign principle of plenitude; but, in the play's
doublings and dislocations, it is revealed instead to be the name of the agency
able to command and legitimate the very savagery it demonizes—not, then,
the opposite of Macbeth but at least potentially, and unnervingly so, Macbeth
himself.[64] It is he who most thoroughly reveals the plenitude in "the name of
king," reveals it to be neither an empty signifier nor a transcendental signified,
but a name assuming meaning always and only in history and demanding to
be understood in historical terms, not least of which are our own.

> Every image of the past that is not recognized by the present as one of its own concerns threatens to disappear irretrievably.
>
> —Walter Benjamin

Chapter 10

"The Duke of Milan / And his Brave Son": Old Histories and New in *The Tempest*

It is, of course, *The Comedy of Errors* that alone among Shakespeare's plays mentions "America" (which the Syracusan Dromio exuberantly locates "upon [Nell's] nose, all o'er embellished with rubies, carbuncles, sapphires, declining their rich aspect to the hot breath of Spain"[1]), but it is Shakespeare's other comedy observing the unities of time and place, *The Tempest,* that has almost inescapably become his play of Europe's engagement with the New World. Since Malone in 1808 first called attention to the play's relation to the Virginia Company pamphlets, offering the closest thing we have to something that might be thought of as a source for *The Tempest*, the experience of Thomas Gates and his men in Bermuda has been taken to give a local habitation and a name to the stereotypical narrative of shipwreck and deliverance articulating the play's romance form.[2]

Following Malone, critics have long claimed that the accounts of the miraculous escape of Gates's ship from "the most dreadful tempest," as Strachey's report terms it, that drove it from the Virginia coast provided the material that stimulated Shakespeare's dramatic imagination. The texts of the various reports from Virginia have come to seem the determining source and subtext of the play itself. In 1901, Morton Luce, editor of the first Arden edition, argued that the wreck of the *Sea-Venture* "must have suggested the leading incidents of *The Tempest*"; "indeed," he continues, "we may fairly say that fully nine-tenths of the subjects touched upon by Shakespeare in *The Tempest* are suggested by the new enterprise of colonisation."[3] And critics have continued to insist, as John Gillies has recently put it, that the play is "vitally rather than casually implicated in the discourses of America and the Virginia Company," whose directors included the Earl of Southampton, to whom Shakespeare dedicated *Venus and Adonis* and *The Rape of Lucrece*, and the Earl of Pembroke, one of the dedicatees of the First Folio, making such a connection to Shakespeare plausible if not absolutely compelling.[4]

Recently, of course, criticism of *The Tempest*, while reasserting the New World context, has effectively wrested the play from the idealizations of romance (as Gillies's word "implicated" no doubt signals). The experience of the Virginia colonists is no longer merely a timely reminder of the timeless structures of a romance mode in which the world of "mortal accident" is discovered to "suffer a sea-change / Into something rich and strange" (1.2.403–4), in which the hand of "great creating nature" can be felt organizing the turbulence of earthly existence, reestabalishing love and human continuance. No longer is *The Tempest* a play of social reconciliation and moral renewal, of benevolent artistry and providential design; it now appears as a telling document of the first phase of English imperialism, implicated in the will-to-power of the Jacobean court, even as an "instrument of empire" itself.[5]

Prospero is no longer an inspiring magus but an arrogant and ill-tempered magistrate (not even the "good, authoritarian Governor" that Geoffrey Bullough saw[6]); and the romance form is no longer a utopian spectacle of wonder but itself a participant in the ideological activity of imperialism—performing the necessary act of colonialist legitimation by naturalizing domination as the activity of a "Providence divine" (1.2.159). Coleridge found *The Tempest* to be one of those plays "where the ideal is predominant,"[7] but for us the "ideal" usually now seems only the name that the powerful give to their desire. In our anxious postcolonial moment, the power of Prospero's art, once confidently viewed as benevolently civilizing, has become the colonizer's technology of domination and control. Prospero's magic in the play now appears, in Stephen Greenblatt's phrase, as "the romance equivalent of martial law," or, in Peter Hulme's version, marking out "the space really inhabited in colonial history by gunpowder."[8] And Caliban and, if somewhat less truculently, Ariel are the natives of the new world who have been unwillingly subjected to the coercive power of European knowledge.

This is the current orthodoxy of *Tempest* criticism, but not, it should be said, of *Tempest* performance, which most often has chosen, for obvious reasons, to emphasize the theme and spectacle of artistry, even as it has come to recognize the contradictions and stresses of the text. Nonetheless, there have been memorable "colonial" interpretations, as Jonathan Miller's production of the play at the Mermaid in 1970, casting black actors as Caliban and Ariel and explicitly depending, as Miller wrote, on "the whole colonial theme as knowledge which the audience brought to bear on Shakespeare's play."[9] But though undoubtedly "colonial," this was not a "new world" *Tempest*. Miller was thinking explicitly of the then current political situation in Nigeria, and he based his characterizations upon Octave Mannoni's analysis in *La Psychologie de la colonisation* (1950) of the 1947 revolt in Madagascar. And, more recently, George Wolfe's 1995 *Tempest* in Central Park (and then on Broadway), starring Patrick Stewart, did stage the play as a third-world fantasy and made its colonial theme explicit, if uncertainly located both temporally and geographically. But these productions are, in any case, more the exception than the rule.

If on stage *The Tempest*'s relation to the new world is still optional, the critical assertion of the play's relation to the colonial enterprise in the Americas is now seemingly inescapable, even historically extendable, as in Leslie Fiedler's claim that in the play "the whole history of imperialist America has been prophetically revealed to us."[10] Fiedler at least has the good grace not to see the play as solely a document of *English* imperialism; but clearly for Fiedler, as for most of us who have read it in his wake, the play unsettlingly defines the encounter of the old world with the new, of the powerful with the powerless, its bad faith evident in Prospero's bitter denunciation of Antonio's usurpation of his dukedom but his complete blindness to his own usurpation of the sovereignty of the island. "This island's mine," protests Caliban, "by Sycorax my mother, / Which thou tak'st from me . . . I am all the subjects that you have, / Which first was mine own King: and here you sty me / In this hard rock, whiles you do keep from me the rest o'th' island" (1.2.333–46). Prospero responds angrily: "thou most lying slave," not, however, angry about Caliban's claim of alienated sovereignty but at his assertion of undeserved hard-treatment: "I have us'd thee, / Filth thou art, with human care; / and lodg'd thee / In mine own cell, till thou didst seek to violate / The honour of my child" (1.2.346–50). What Prospero calls a lie is only the claim that he is an oppressor; Caliban's claim that he is a usurper is not contested, indeed, not even heard, so fully does Prospero feel his own right to rule to be beyond any question.

No doubt Prospero's bad faith (a bad faith not canceled out by the fact that Caliban's sovereign claim is itself based upon his Algerian mother's parallel domination of a native "spirit" population) is relevant to any understanding of the encounter with the new world, whose native inhabitants could have said to their putative "discoverers," no less tellingly than Prospero to Miranda, "'Tis new to thee" (5.1.184). But it is worth reminding ourselves how thin is the thread on which the play's relation to the new world hangs.

The play is obviously set in the old world; the tempest is called up as the Italian nobles are returning from Africa to Italy, and those who have escaped the storm are said to return "sadly" to Naples "upon the Mediterranean flote" (1.2.234). Ariel does refer to Bermuda, but pointedly as the place they are not: the Italian's ship, he tells Prospero, is safe in the harbor "where once / Thou call'dst me up at midnight to fetch dew / From the still-vex'd Bermoothes" (1.2.227–29). The only other explicit textual connections are the two references to "Setebos," whom Caliban identifies as "my dam's god" (1.2.375) and editors have identified in accounts of Magellan's voyages as a "great devil" of the Patagonian religion. Trinculo observes that the English who "will not give a doit to relieve a lame beggar . . . will lay out ten to see a dead Indian" (2.2.31–33), but Trinculo never takes the creature hiding beneath the cloak for an Indian; it is some kind of "monster" that "smells like a fish." That's it.

Some would add Gonzalo's use of the word "plantation," its only appearance in Shakespeare, though "plantation" is a word apparently coined for *old* world domination, to describe the English colonial project in Ireland, and even when applied to the new world is used to describe an exclusively English enclave: "a plantation of the people of your owne English nation," as John Hooker writes to Raleigh.[11] And, of course, Gonzalo's utopian fantasy is based on a passage in Montaigne's essay on the cannibals of Brazil. But its primitivist vision has little relevance to the dreams and desires of the Italian courtiers, as is revealed by its self-contradiction, where Gonzalo's imaginings of a world with "no sovereignty" (2.1.158) originate in its opposite, in a fantasy of power: "Had I plantation of this isle, my lord . . . And were the king on't. . ." (2.1.145, 147).

In all there is very little to go on, especially to validate the now common-place insistence that new world colonialism provides the play's "dominant discursive con-texts."[12] Though Prospero does locate Caliban in anthropolog-ical, social, moral, even theological discourses—"beast," "slave," "demi-devil"—that sanction and support his own hierarchical superiority, we might note that Caliban is described as "freckled" and of a "blue-ey'd" dam (1.2.283, 269; and though editors regularly remind us that "blue-eyed may well refer to the dark blue of the eyelid understood as a mark of pregnancy or even be an error for "blear-eyed," to an English audience for whom blue eyes were not at all unusual the term must inevitably have been heard, if not necessari-ly intended, conventionally, as an indication of the color of the iris). Caliban is not, therefore, easily imagined either as an indigenous American or African slave. Indeed, as long ago as 1927, E. E. Stoll would emphatically deny that the play had any relation to the new world at all. "There is not a word in *The Tempest*," he writes, "about America or Virginia, colonies or colonizing, Indians or tomahawks, maize, mocking-birds, or tobacco. Nothing but the Bermudas, once barely mentioned as faraway places, like Tokio or Mandalay."[13] And more recently Geoffrey Bullough stated bluntly: "*The Tempest* is not a play about colonization."[14]

Stoll and Bullough are, of course, too absolute, but if the play has a rela-tion to the new world colonial activity it is not writ deep into its texture; the relation is allusive and elusive, existing primarily in the negations, like Ariel's or Trinculo's, that deny that the experience on the island is the experience of the Americas. The negations, of course, make the new world present, in a sense, but we may wonder why, if colonialism is, as Francis Barker and Peter Hulme put it, "the articulatory principle of the play," the principle is almost completely effaced and when present is established negatively rather than by a direct engagement with the material of Virginia.[15]

Possibly this is evidence of the play's uneasy conscience about the colonial project, or possibly our hypersensitivity to it is evidence merely of our own

uneasy conscience in the postcolonial world we inhabit. In any case, part of
the desire to locate the play within the discourses of early colonialism, to
return the play to a historical moment, is evidence of the degree to which the
imagination of the past now enthralls us as once we were enthralled by the
imagination of the future, and seems worthily motivated by the felt need to
rescue the play from the banality of the moral claims made for it in the name
of its putative timelessness and transcendence. Yet one might ask about the
specific historicizing gesture: why this moment, why these discourses that are
arguably no less eccentric in the play than they were in the culture of
Jacobean England? Certainly, it is possible to suggest other and more obvious
contexts, and then perhaps to wonder about why they do not appear to us the
play's "articulatory principle," if only to suggest that the Americanization of
The Tempest may be itself an act of cultural imperialism.

The play is much more obviously a play about European dynastic concerns than European colonial activities, but this has largely slipped from
view—or at least from critical comment. The Italian courtiers have no interest
in colonizing the island on which they find themselves, no desire to "plant a
nation / Where none before had stood," as Rich's *Newes From Virginia* (1610,
sig. B2ʳ) defines the goals of the first English settlers. The Italians' journey was
not to explore or settle a new world but was intended as a return home, a
return from a royal wedding of Alonso's daughter Claribel to the King of
Tunis. And only Trinculo and Stephano worry about sovereignty on the
island: "the King and all our company else being drowned," says Stephano,
"we will inherit *here*" (2.2.173); Antonio and Sebastian, on the contrary, think
only about crowns in Europe: "As thou got'st Milan, / I'll come by Naples"
(2.1.292–93), Sebastian eagerly declares, urging Antonio to draw his sword
and murder the Neapolitan king. Even Ferdinand immediately understands
and articulates his situation in the explicitly dynastic terms of the world he has
come from. When he hears Miranda speak, he responds with amazement:
"My language! heavens! / I am the best of them that speak this speech"
(1.2.431–32), instantly locating his sorrow in a set of political relations:
"myself am Naples, / Who with mine eyes, never since at ebb, beheld / The
King my father wrack'd" (1.2.437–39), just as he, with the same alacrity, finds
political measure for his love for Miranda: "I'll make you / The Queen of
Naples" (1.2.451–52). And Alonso at the end, hearing that Prospero has "lost"
his daughter, thinks of her and his own lost son as a royal couple to provide
the terms of loss for the tragic cutting off of their children's too brief lives: "O

heavens, that they were living both in Naples, / The King and Queen there"
(5.1.149–50).

Indeed, the critical emphasis upon the new world not only obscures the
play's more prominent discourses of dynastic politics but also blinds us to disturbances in the text that should alert us to this aspect of the play's engagement with its own historical moment. When Alonso mourns the apparent
death of his son, he, perhaps predictably, identifies him not by name but by
his dynastic position: "O thou mine heir / Of Naples and Milan" (2.1.113–14).
No edition of the play feels the line worthy of comment, but it seemingly
poses a problem. As son of the Neapolitan King, Ferdinand is obviously heir
to the crown of Naples, but why is he heir of "Milan"? Antonio has replaced
Prospero as duke—and Antonio has a son who presumably would be his successor: reporting on his experience of the tempest, Ferdinand reports his dismay at seeing Antonio "and his brave son being twain" (1.2.441), a line that
editors usually gloss by predicating some earlier and then abandoned conception of the play in which this dynastic relation would have been developed. Thus Dover Wilson writes in his note in the New Cambridge edition
(now, of course, the "old" New Cambridge) that "he must be one of the
Alonso group in an earlier version" of the play, as if a prior, and differing, version of *The Tempest* is certain to have existed. Stephen Orgel in his Oxford edition more cautiously writes that "possibly a parallel to Ferdinand was originally contemplated by Shakespeare, and then abandoned as the drama took
shape." And Frank Kermode, in his Arden edition, somewhat despairingly
concludes that "Shakespeare began writing with a somewhat hazy understanding of the dynastic relationships he was to deal with."

But the "dynastic relations" are adequately, indeed tellingly, developed
here. Antonio's arrangement with Naples, in which, in return, as Prospero
says, for "homage and I know not how much tribute" (1.2.124), Alonso has
conferred "fair Milan, / With all the honours, on my brother" (1.2.126–27),
clearly reserves Milanese sovereignty for Naples, alienating Antonio's son
from the succession. Indeed, when Alonso at the end begs Prospero to "par-
don" his wrongs, it is he, not Antonio, who offers: "Thy dukedom I resign"
(5.1.118), another line that has generally escaped critical comment. The
romance action is to rescue Milan from vassalage to Naples and yet still allow
the merging of national interests that James's fantasy of European peace and
coherence would demand. As the truth of the strange events of the play
emerges fully, leading those who will to "rejoice / Beyond a common joy"

(5.1.206–7), even the utopian Gonzalo recognizes that the true source of wonder is the political miracle that has been performed: "Was Milan thrust from
Milan, that his issue / Should become Kings of Naples?" (5.1.205–6). It is this
happy dynastic resolution that he would see set down "With gold on lasting
pillars" (5.1.208), invoking the imperial iconography of Charles V, which was
soon adopted by other European monarchies.[16] Ariel's terms for the success
of Prospero's tempest are thus homonymically apt; in the play's magical
rewriting of history there is "not so much perdition as an hair" (1.2.30).
Indeed the only thing that apparently is lost in the tempest is the usurper
Antonio's disinherited son, the one "hair"–or heir–that can be cut from the
restorative action of the play.

Certainly, for the audience of *The Tempest* at Court in 1613, when the play
was performed as one of fourteen plays selected for the festivities leading up
to the marriage of the King's daughter, Elizabeth, to Frederick, the Elector
Palatine (this was, it should be noted, the second recorded performance of the
play, the first on Hallowmas night of 1611 at Whitehall before "ye kinges
Maiestie"[17]), the play's events were more likely to resonate with political
issues in Europe rather than in the Americas. Alonso's sadness at having
apparently lost his son and married his daughter to a foreign prince might
well have seemed a virtual mirror of the situation of their King, whose son,
Henry, had died the previous year, and who now was marrying his daughter,
Elizabeth, to a foreign prince (and who would, exactly as Alonso feared for
himself, never see his daughter again).

The marriage of the Princess Elizabeth was, like all royal weddings, politics by other means, designed primarily to serve the political interests of the
nation or at least its king, rather than the emotional needs of the marrying
couple. The match had long been rumored, and negotiations for it had begun
as early as 1608, though there were always other prominent candidates for
Elizabeth's hand, most notably the Prince of Piedmont, heir of the Duke of
Savoy, and the recently widowed King of Spain, Philip III. A contemporary
discussion of "suitable alliances" for Elizabeth interestingly comments: "the
Prince of Piedmont an unequal match for the Princess, unless the King of
Spain will give him the Duchy of Milan on his marriage, which is not likely,
as that King is said to want her for himself. She could not marry him without
changing her religion, and such a marriage would be dangerous to the two
that are between her and the Crown. A match with Sweden or the Prince
Palatine suggested for her . . . ." (*CSPD* 1611–18, p. 97).

It was the match with the Prince Palatine to which James finally agreed. In many ways the "most suitable" (*CSPD* 1611–18, p. 97), the choice, of course, was designed not least to satisfy the interests of the Protestant nation and more immediately to tie James to the Union of Protestant Princes in the struggle against the Austrian Habsburgs and the states of the Catholic League. Though James's original hope had been to avoid sectarian alliance—or rather, while Henry lived, to pair sectarian alliances—Henry to the Spanish Infanta; Elizabeth to the Palatine prince—in order to play his planned role as mediator of Europe's religious conflicts, with Henry's death in 1612, that particular balancing act was impossible. While the Treaty of Antwerp in 1609, reconciling Spain to the United Provinces, seemed initially to promise peace in Europe, within a few weeks a dispute over succession in the Rhine principality of Cleves–Jülich divided the Protestant and Catholic States and again pushed Europe toward full-scale religious war, "a generall altercacion in Christendome," as Salisbury feared.[18] James had little choice then but to side with the Protestant princes—and, indeed, the marriage of Elizabeth to the Palatine Prince was finally agreed to as a result of the negotiations with the Evangelical Union for English support in their struggle against the Catholic League.[19]

England seemed now fully committed to the international Protestant cause. Dudley Carleton reported that "all well-affected people take great pleasure and contentment in this Match, as being a firm foundation and stablishing of religion . . . and the Roman Catholics malign it as much, as being the ruin of their hopes."[20] Though, in fact, as James's almost immediate search for a Spanish match for Prince Charles reveals, the King never abandoned his fantasy of being Rex Pacificus, to play the role of mediator between the rival religious blocs to secure a lasting peace. His willingness to side with the Evangelical Union was motivated less by his commitment to international Protestantism than by the desire to counterbalance the destabilizing aggressions of the Habsburg monarchy.

This all may seem to be taking us far from the island world of *The Tempest*, even farther than the new world narratives claimed as the play's source; but it may well bring us closer to the historical center of the play—and possibly to the heart of the interpretive problem it poses—than do the tracts of the Virginia Company. While southern Europe, including the Kingdom of Naples and the Dukedom of Milan, was largely at peace under the administration of the Spanish monarchy, the Holy Roman Empire was marked by a crisis of authority. In 1606, the Habsburg archdukes stripped administrative control from the Emperor, Rudolf II, conferring it upon his brother Matthias. In 1608, Rudolf was forced to surrender to his brother the crowns of Austria, Hungary, and Moravia, keeping only the imperial crown and the crown of Bohemia. In April 1611, Rudolf was deposed from the throne of Bohemia as his brother was proclaimed Emperor.[21]

Rudolf turned to the Evangelical Union for support, and to James. Envoys were sent to England from the Diet of Protestant Princes in November asking James to back the reinstatement of the deposed Habsburg and to agree to the marriage of Elizabeth with the Elector Palatine to secure his commitment. While James's respect for the authority of princes could perhaps alone be reasonably expected to produce support for the reinstatement—and James had dedicated his own 1609 *Apology for the Oath of Allegiance* to "the Most Sacred and invincible Prince, Rudolf the II"—the English King certainly knew that the Emperor had brought about his own troubles by being irascible, indecisive, and increasingly unavailable. As early as 1591, Sir Henry Wotton had observed that Rudolf seems "now rather to bear the title of Emperor for fashion sake, than authority to command by virtue of it."[22] Gradually the Emperor withdrew from the affairs of state, shutting himself up in his palace, dedicating himself to scientific and occult study. Indeed, in 1606 the archdukes justified the reassignment of authority to Matthias by commenting that "[h]is majesty is interested only in wizards, alkymists, Kabbalists, and the like, sparing no expense to find all kinds of treasure, learn secrets, and use scandalous ways of harming his enemies" and noted his "whole library of magic books."[23] The responsibilities of government of little interest and increasingly beyond his control, Rudolf took refuge in his books behind the walls of his palace, uncannily like another ruler "transported / And rapt in secret studies" (1.2.76–77) who would be deposed by his brother for "neglecting worldly ends" (1.2.89).

Part Two of John Barclay's popular *roman a clef, Euphormionis Lusinini Satyricon*, published in Paris in 1609 (but circulating widely in England, so much so that it is named as what any "Young Gentleman of the Universitie" would be reading in the character in John Earle's *MicroCosmographie*), has a readily identifiable portrait of Rudolf in the Theban ruler Aquilius who "abandons all thoughts of public matters, foreign and domestic" (sig. K2^r; translation mine) for "voluntary solitude" (sig,. I2^r) in his "beloved laboratory" (sig. K5^r) where he "searches into nature's secret places" (sig. K2^r). Similarly,

Jonson's *Alchemist*, performed in 1610, reveals the English knowledge of Rudolf's habits in its reference to the alchemist and medium Edward Kelly, who, along with John Dee, was, like Jonson's "divine instructor" Subtle, "courted" by "the Emp'ror" (4.1.90–92) in Prague with the extraordinary commitment to alchemy and magic.

Though Rudolf's interests and political fate would inevitably have been known to many, I certainly am not claiming that Rudolf II is the sole inspiration for Shakespeare's Duke.[24] Here I am primarily concerned with showing the relevance of an available and unquestionably urgent European courtly context for the concerns of the play, and one that accounts for more of its textual density than the colonial theme that has come to dominate our readings. This is perhaps merely the move of the old historicism, eurocentric and courtly; though James, of course, would never have approved of either Rudolf's or Prospero's interest in magic or neglect of the concerns of state. Though George Marcelline hailed James as "The king of wonders, or the wonder of Kings" (1610, sig. H3ᵛ), what "wonders" James achieved and his own appeal as an object of admiration were far more predictably worldly than the arcane interests and attractions of Rudolf's court in Prague or, more modestly, in Prospero's island cell.

In his *Daemonologie*, James explicitly condemns "diuerse Christian Princes" who allow magicians to live in their realms, and "euen some-times delight to see them prooue some of their practicques"; these princes, he says "sinne heavilie against their office in that poynt."[25] And in *Basilikon Doron* he instructs his son that "it is necessarie yee delight in reading and seeking the knowledge of all lawful things, but with these two restrictions. First, that yee choose idle houres for it, not interfering therewith the discharge of your office: and next, that yee studie not for knowledge nakedly, but that your principall ende be, to make you able thereby to vse your office."[26] The renunciation of magic to return to the reponsibilities of rule allows Prospero to redeem Rudolf's kingship—or rather allows him to escape the damning parallel with Rudolf and achieve a saving one with James himself. Prospero drowns his magic book, not, of course, the only reading matter with which Gonzalo had provided him, and returns to the teachings of the *speculum principiis*, like James's own *Basilikon Doron*, which always knows the priority of the arts of rule over the rules of magical art.

All interpretation is in a sense allegorical, offering a meaning other than the literal. But I am not suggesting here that we should substitute another allegory, not the biographical one of Prospero as Shakespeare, or the humanistic one of his magic as art, or in its recent, suspicious form as colonial domination, in order to see Prospero now as the Holy Roman Emperor; though certainly I am arguing that the world of European politics has receded too far from our view. In *The Winter's Tale*, Shakespeare, in following Greene's *Pandosto*, may well have mistakenly given Bohemia a seacoast, but the complex politics of Bohemia and the other Habsburg states were arguably more deeply connected to the hopes and anxieties of the Jacobean court than were the struggling settlements in the new world.

This shift in focus from the new world to the old is not to evade or erase the history of colonialism as it has left its traces in the play but to individualize and clarify that history—perhaps indeed to motivate it. The colonial activity of seventeenth-century Europe must itself be understood in relation to the politics of the great European powers, to recognize at once England's deep involvements in Europe (a historical dimension that has worryingly dropped out of our recent attentions to the politics of early modern England) and the differing forms of colonial activity produced by its differing impulses and circumstances in England, Spain, and the Netherlands. If our attention to early modern colonialism is to be more than reflexive it must see its practices for what they were, as various and admittedly overdetermined activities within the conflicts of seventeenth-century European absolutism rather than as examples of a unified and transhistorical imperial desire and administration.[27]

Certainly, European expansionism is evident in the play, but more, it must be insisted, in the marriage of Claribel to the King of Tunis or Alonso's support of Antonio in exchange for Milan's vassalage than in Prospero's domination of the island. Or rather, the old world examples reveal the old technologies of expansion; the action on the island is symbolic of the new. And the two were always understood to support one another. Even as Europe looked west, it was mainly as it sought to thrive at home. Thinking about the incredible riches available in the new world, Hakluyt, that quintessential voice of English imperialism, observes enthusiastically (and in terms that uncannily explain something of the geopolitics of *The Tempest*): "with this great treasure, did not the emperor Charles get from the French king the kingdom of Naples, the dukedom of Milan, and all other his dominions in Italy, Lombardy, Piedmont, and Savoy."[28]

But though I would say (and have said) that the play clearly engages the social and political concerns of seventeenth-century Europe, concerns that the

insistent focus on the new world in recent criticism has largely obscured, I am
not now claiming that European court politics must replace new world colonialism as the "dominant discursive con-text" that reveals the meaning of *The
Tempest.* Indeed, I am as much interested in the process by which a historical
reading of a text is generated and grounded as I am in any particular reading,
especially given the familiar charge of the arbitrariness of New Historicism's
strategies of contextualization (in its most expansive form, evident in
Dominick LaCapra's laundry-list of disparaging epithets: "facile association-
ism, juxtaposition or pastiche . . . weak montage, or, if you prefer, cut-and-
paste bricolage"[29]).

Facile or not, New Historicism has often brilliantly connected apparently
disparate cultural moments and practices to reveal their common participation in a cultural system. In part, this has worked to erase the familiar opposition of text and context. Where the context once served as the flat backdrop
against which the text's verbal display showed brilliantly in all of its artistic
and intellectual complexity, now context and text are not so easily distinguished. Literary texts are no longer understood as repositories of meaning,
but are seen as places where meanings are being made—places no more necessarily efficacious or valuable in this construction of social meaning than any
other discursive form. It is this refusal to privilege automatically the literary
over other discursive activities that has produced much of the hostility to New
Historicism (and other poststructural critical modes). The literary text, however, is seen to be imbricated with a range of material and symbolic practices
that make its distinction, in both senses of the word, from what formerly was
understood as its context no longer sustainable.

The notion of context has thus been usefully problematized, understood
now not as the static ground external to the text and reflected by it, but as the
set of discourses that the literary text intersects and is intersected by. Texts and
contexts are thus related dynamically rather than hierarchically: the text
inevitably serves as a context for other texts, while the context is itself
revealed as a text demanding interpretation before it yields its meanings.
Many critics have therefore grown uncomfortable with the very term "context," fearing that its use reinstates the autonomy and presumptive value of
the literary text that has been pointedly called into question.

Yet clearly the notion of context cannot be dispensed with. Indeed, once
the meaning of the literary work is no longer sought in its aesthetic autonomy
and formal perfection, all that is left is context. The text as it is both written

and read is necessarily context-rich and context-dependent, and this is the source of its meaning. The written text takes meaning from the discourses that circulate through it; the text as read becomes meaningful through the contexts that structure the reader's engagement. That is, the text "means" only through the processes by which its particularities are seen to exist in relation to something outside it. Meaning may be of "different kinds," as Richard Palmer recognizes, "but it is always a kind of cohesion, relationship, or binding force; it is always in a context."[30]

But if meaning is necessarily context-bound, the number of meaningful contexts is apparently boundless.[31] By definition they can be neither singular nor inevitable. Certainly the frames in which one chooses to see a text, the horizons of interpretation, to use Gadamer's term, through which an interpreter engages it,[32] logically are virtually infinite (a single point can be intersected by an infinite number of lines), and they are valuable as they—and only as they—serve the interests and needs of the interpreter.

Once, this is granted, however, it must be worth asking more about the contexts that appear to us to be relevant. *The Tempest* can profitably be viewed in relation to various historical and non-historical (e.g., ethical, psychological, theological, even, may I say it, aesthetic) contexts, and no one is inevitable and determining. If, however, one's interpretive desire is to reinsert the play into its own historical moment, into the space of its own diegetic setting as well as the performative space of its own earliest productions (and this is a thoroughly reasonable and productive desire, though hardly the only useful interpretive desire we might have), it seems to me that we should look more closely at the old world than the new, at the wedding of Elizabeth and Frederick rather than of Pocahontas and John Rolfe, at James's own writings rather than the writings from Jamestown. This seems to me so both because old world history marks the play (context as discourse) more insistently than does the history of the new world that has dominated recent criticism—a history which, in fact, the play conspicuously avoids—and because the European history allows a reader to make sense of more in the text (context as frame) that would otherwise seem arbitrary or inexplicable. If, however, one's interpretive desire is to locate the play in *our* historical moment—also a reasonable and productive desire—then the colonial reading has more purchase; plays absorb history as much as they are marked by it at their inception.[33]

In either case, the critical attention to the new world is not, of course, merely willful; the play does find its source in the narrative accounts of a ship-

wreck of would-be colonists bound for Jamestown. But Shakespeare's relocation of the narrative from the new world to the old is not the unconscious displacement of this imperial theme as much as it is its deliberate erasure. In *The
Tempest*, Shakespeare actively chooses *not* to tell the new world story that was
before him. And if a later history has insisted that we restore the tale of colonial adventurism to the play, it is at least as much because we know we can
use Shakespeare's cultural authority to claim a hearing for our political interests as because Shakespeare's political interests demand it from us. Certainly,
such readings tell us something important, but arguably more about our
world than about Shakespeare's. But if the shift in focus from Bermuda to
Bohemia, from Harriot to Habsburg, removes the play from the colonial
encounter of Europe with the Americas, it is not to evade or dull its political
edges. Indeed, arguably it is to sharpen them, but it is to find them less in the
conquest of the new world than in the killing religious conflicts and territori-
al ambitions of the old, where tragically they can still be found.[34]

The Tempest effectively stages and manages these anxieties about European
politics and England's role within them, harmonizing and securing absolutist
desire through the marriage of Miranda and Ferdinand. The play drives purposefully to fulfill Gonzalo's prayer: "look down, you gods, / And on this
couple drop a blessed crown" (5.1.201–2). But this utopian solution to the
problem of political conflict—a solution that by temperament, ideology, and
financial limitation appealed to James and led him to conduct his foreign policy through marriage negotiation—is vulnerable, if only to irony. If the crown
is "blessed," we should remember that the impending marriage will accomplish precisely what the "inveterate" (1.2.122) hatred of Alonso for Prospero
attempted: the dissolution of Milanese sovereignty into Neapolitan dynastic
rule. However, in the reparative fantasy of the *The Tempest*, nothing—nothing,
that is, except the brave son of Antonio, who has no place in its ambitious
political relations—is finally lost.

FIVE

Coda:
The Closing
of the Theaters

> It was in this intrinsically mixed and mobile cultural situation, at a broad but heterogeneous level of popular participation, that, still under the risk and under pressure of received authorities, new kinds of speech, which were also new forms of what could now be publicly spoken, were intensively explored and often intensely achieved.
>
> —Raymond Williams

Chapter 11

"Publike Sports" and "Publike Calamities": Plays, Playing, and Politics

No doubt the best-known date in the history of the professional theater of the English Renaissance is that of what is conventionally taken to be its end. On 2 September 1642, Parliament ordered the theaters closed:

whereas publike Sports doe not well agree with publike Calamities, nor publike Stage-plays with the Seasons of Humiliation, this being an Exercise of sad and pious solemnity, and the other being Spectacles of pleasure, too commonly expressing laciuious Mirth and

Levitie: It is therefore thought fit, and Ordeined by the Lords and Commons in this Parliament Assembled, that while these sad Causes and set times of Humiliation doe continue, publike Stage-playes shall cease, and bee forborne.[1]

Literary historians have usually seen the parliamentary action as the culmination of a twin-pronged campaign of so-called "Puritan" antitheatrical sentiment, and, though Margot Heinemann, for example, in her *Puritanism and Theatre*, has convincingly challenged that commonplace history,[2] clearly there was considerable hostility to the plays and players. A sermon by Thomas White, preached at Paul's Cross "on Sunday the thirde of November 1577 in the time of the Plague," indeed had argued that "the cause of plagues is sinne, if you look to it well: and the cause of sinne are playes: therefore the cause of plagues are playes."[3] White reduces the often hysterical opposition to the theater (Prynne, for example, excoriates the theater's immorality in a book of over eleven hundred pages) to a neat, if epidemiologically unconvincing, syllogism. Similar responses to the theater's supposedly dangerous immorality echo through the last quarter of the sixteenth century and the first third of the seventeenth, and until recently it had been convenient to see the reiterated antitheatricality as, what Brian Morris has called, "a perpetual war"[4] waged by opponents that ended only with the legislated closing in 1642 by a Parliament dominated by Puritan ethics and aesthetics.

The 1642 ban does, of course, register the oft-remarked antitheatrical sentiment in its obvious discomfort with the "lascivious Mirth and Levitie" produced by the theaters' "Spectacles of pleasure," but it is too simple to see this as the triumph of a precise puritanism over those who still enjoyed their cakes and ale. First of all, the term "Puritan" is notoriously slippery, as even contemporaries realized. "Concerning the name," Giles Widdowes observed in 1631, "it is ambiguous, and so it is fallacious."[5] Yet even where the term seems to apply reasonably comfortably, the work of Heinemann and others has persuasively demonstrated the need to rethink the familiar homology between puritanism and antitheatricality.

All Puritans were not opponents of the theater, nor were all opponents of the theater Puritans. "All men are not alike," as the author of *A Discourse Concerning Puritans* (1641) usefully reminds us, "which either affect or disaffect, either Puritans or Antipuritans."[6] Men who by most definitions must be thought Puritans, such as Milton or Marvell, or Leicester and Walsingham, for that matter, were obviously sympathetic to, even fascinated by, theatrical activity. William Herbert, the third Earl of Pembroke, whom the Venetian ambassador identified as the "head of the Puritans" in the government of James I,[7] annually gave Ben Jonson £20 to buy books and was, along with his brother, the dedicatee of Shakespeare's first folio. Henry Hastings, the fifth Earl of Huntingdon, of radical Protestant background and beliefs, was the patron of John Fletcher. Indeed, Cromwell himself patronized the theater in the 1650s, allowing Davenant's operas to be performed at court.[8] And conversely, though voices plausibly identified as "Puritan," like those of John Stockwood, William Perkins, and William Prynne, were indeed loudly heard among those hostile to the theater, equally strong antitheatrical attitudes were held by those, like Robert Anton or Richard Braithwaite, who were well known for their anti-Puritan sentiments. Archbishop Laud, the target of Puritan hostility, himself strove in 1637 to prevent the reopening of the theaters after they had been closed for fifteen months during a severe outbreak of the plague.

A further difficulty with the traditional explanation of the theaters' closing is that the antitheatrical tracts are far more numerous in the last part of the sixteenth century than, as the thesis would seem to demand, in the years immediately before the theater's closing in 1642. Though there were a number of antitheatrical writings in the 1620s, Prynne's vituperative *Histrio-mastix* was less the "culmination" of the attack on the stage, as Jonas Barish has it, than an anachronism at the time of its publication in 1633, and it had no immediate successors.[9] Prynne's antitheatricality echoes the anxieties of an earlier generation of Englishmen (though it, in fact, responds to a different theatrical environment: not the new commercial theaters but the court theatricals). John Northbrooke wrote against the theater in 1577, Stephen Gosson in 1579, Stubbes in 1583, William Rankins in 1587, John Rainolds in 1599. Sermons were preached against plays and play-going at Paul's Cross in each of the last four years of the 1570s (that is, in the years immediately following the erection of The Theatre in Shoreditch), but none of the published Paul's Cross sermons between 1630 and 1642 mentions the theater or theater-going among London's proliferating vices.

It seems impossible, then, to assent to the familiar notion that an evergrowing Puritan hostility to the theater resulted finally in the prohibition of playing. Indeed, the very timing of the order suggests that the considerations were at least as much pragmatic as doctrinal. Though Grierson confidently asserted that "when the Long Parliament meets, one of its earliest acts is to close the public theaters,"[10] the truth is far otherwise. The Long Parliament did immediately begin dismantling the royal bureaucracy when it first sat in November of 1640, but almost two years passed before it acted to prohibit stage plays. And, then, it did so not with the consolidation of the power of the parliamentary Puritans in January of 1642—when a bill for the theaters' closing was introduced by a moderate Puritan, Edward Partridge, the baron for Sandwich, but quickly defeated, opposed by, among others, Pym, on the grounds that playing was a "trade" that should not be inhibited[11]—but only much later in 1642, eleven days after the King's raising of his standard at Nottingham on August 22. What Milton said of Catholics was then perhaps more true of the theaters in 1642: "if they ought not to be tolerated, it is for just reason of state, more then of religion."[12]

Yet if the theaters' closing was at least as much politically as theologically inspired, it is perhaps not immediately obvious what tactical function the action served for Parliament. In spite of the reiterated critical assertions that "the players were the King's puppets,"[13] the popular stage, as Heinemann and Martin Butler have convincingly shown,[14] had increasingly come to serve an oppositional political function; and, with the King's departure from London in January of 1642, the elite theaters, in any case, had apparently lost much of their traditional audience. James Shirley observed bitterly: "*London* is gone to *York* . . . / . . . and a Play / Though n'er so new, will starve the second day."[15]

Nonetheless, if closing the theaters seems neither a necessary nor an effective strike against royal authority, the Parliamentary action clearly was not casually undertaken. The order forbidding playing was approved on the same day that Parliament debated military appropriations, considered "daily tumults in the Westerne Counties," and, significantly, ordered restitution made by those guilty of "disarming and rifling of Papists and other suspected houses," even though the ammunition, money, and goods were to "be sent to his Majesty."[16] That the theaters were even considered at this critical time indicates clearly that they were understood as an institution of some consequence, but, just as clearly, parliament in its consideration was motivated by practical concerns for security more than by religious zeal. The timing of the injunction suggests that the anxiety produced by the theaters was not least a function of their perceived potential for encouraging further disorder "during these troublesome and tumultuous times."[17]

Where the political issues have been examined, however, literary and political historians have generally focused on the parliamentary prohibition as an attack upon a royalist institution, unconsciously reproducing the royalist narrative of the mid-century culture wars. Philip Edwards, for example, argues that "the central motivation (in which religion had a share) was antagonism to the monarchy and all its works,"[18] and, certainly, some contemporaries did see the legislation against stage plays as a form of opposition to the King. "[N]ever rebel was to arts a friend," scornfully wrote Dryden in *Absolom and Achitophel*; and, pointedly, John Denham claimed: "They that would have no *KING*, would have no Play: / The *Laurel* and the *Crown* together went, / Had the same *Foes*, and the same *Banishment*."[19] More sardonic is the royalist pamphlet of 1642, *A Discourse between a Citizen and a Country-Gentleman*. The gentleman proclaims: "I thought the plays & play-houses had beene put downe." "Yes so they were in the Suburbes," the citizen replies, "but they were set up in the City, and Guild-hall is made a Play-house."

> Count.   But I pray, what Play was it that was Acted?
> Cit.   In troth, I cannot well tell, I saw it not I thank God; there were none but great ones there: the Marshall that kept the door would let no honest men come in.
> Count.   But could you by no meanes here the name of it?
> Cit.   Some say it was called A King or no King, or King Careo.20

As the common joke had it, Parliament had turned Westminster into the only playhouse. "We perceive at last why Plays went down," Samuel Butler later noted acidly, "to wit, that Murders might be acted in earnest. Stages must submit to Scaffolds, and personated Tragedies to real ones . . . No need of heightening Revels; these Herods can behead without the allurements of a Dance."[21]

Even before the ordinance prohibiting stage plays was passed, some saw the inevitability of the action and related it to parliamentary efforts to restrain the royal prerogative. In 1641, a dialogue called *The Stage-Players Complaint* was published in which Quick, an actor, notes apprehensively that various sites of royal authority have already been attacked by Parliament: "Monopolers are downe, Projectors are downe, the High Commission Court is downe, the Starre-Chamber is downe, & (some think) Bishops will downe, and why should we then that are farre inferior to any of those not justly feare, least we should be downe too." His colleague Light assures him that there is nothing to fear: "Pish, I can show thee many infallible reasons to the contrary we are very necessary and commodious to all people." But in spite of his confidence that "we [actors] are so needful for the Common good, that in some respect it were almost a sinne to put us downe,"[22] Parliament did indeed put the actors "downe." The players were, as the parliamentarian historian Thomas May said, "fitly silenc'd by the Lawes,"[23] their playhouses closed and a number of them later destroyed. According to a fourteen-leaved manuscript found bound in a copy of Stowe's *Annals*, the Globe was torn down in April 1644, by "S[r] Mathew Brand . . . to make tennements in the roome in it"; in March 1649, along with the Fortune, "the playhouse in Salsbury Court, in fleetstreete, was pulled downe by a company of Souldiers set on by the Sectuaries of these sad times"; and the Blackfriars playhouse, "which had stood many yeares, was pulled downe to the ground on Munday the 6 daye of August. 1655. and tennements built in the rome."[24] Though Herbert Berry has recently raised questions about the evidentiary value of the manuscript material,[25] there is no question that the theaters were systematically dismantled, as Edmund Gayton wrote, by the "severe correctors, who knowing not how to amend or repaire, have pluckt all downe, and left themselves the only spectacle of their times."[26]

It isn't obvious, however, as even Heinemann, for example, assumes, that this antitheatrical fervor should be understood as "primarily an anti-Royalist move."[27] Or, at very least, it isn't obvious that it can be understood as an *effective* "anti-Royalist move." As Heinemann herself and others have convincingly demonstrated, the theater, rather than being a cooperative agent of royalist ideology, often offered pointed and powerful criticism of royal policies and practices. As soon as Elizabeth took the throne in 1558, playing began to come under royal patronage and control, but the theater early proved itself a notably unreliable source of stable ideological production. In spite of the familiar claims that the Renaissance stage was essentially "a vehicle for disseminating court ideology,"[28] reproducing the official strategies of idealization, the commercial theater did not—and, as I have been arguing throughout, could not—passively re-present the figural logic involved in the reproduction of royal power but, rather, aggressively rewrote and displaced it into a far broader context of social representation.

Merely locating the forms of power in a commercial theater had the effect of rendering them vulnerable to judgment and challenge in ways that were unthinkable, at least until the 1640s, outside of the theater: proud majesty was disturbingly made a subject to an audience's gaze and an author's imagining.[29] In 1605, Samuel Calvert wrote to Ralph Winwood that the "play[er]s do not forbear to represent upon their Stage the whole Course of this present Time, not sparing either King, State, or Religion, in so great Absurdity, and with such Liberty, that any would be afraid to hear them."[30] In 1623, Henry Herbert became Master of the Revels and ordered that "all ould plays" be re-licensed, since they "may be full of offensive things against church and state, the rather that in former time the poetts tooke greater liberty than is allowed them by mee."[31] But Herbert himself, in the summer of 1624, licensed Middleton's *A Game at Chess*, a thinly veiled topical allegory in which not only was the English court clearly drawn but the Spanish ambassador Gondamor was "counterfeited . . . to the life," as John Chamberlain wrote Dudley Carleton: the players having "gotten (they say) a cast sute of his apparell for the purpose," as well as the "Lytter" on which Gondamor was customarily borne on account of a painful fistula.[32] Understandably, the play created extraordinary interest and drew huge crowds to the Globe ("more than 3000 there on the day that the audience was smallest,"[33] as Coloma complained) and infuriating the Spanish ambassador and the English King.

Even the plays of the fashionable "private houses" of Caroline London, though their topical comment was less overt and charged, were engaged with current social and political issues. Neither servile nor escapist, this drama, as Butler and others have demonstrated, regularly subjected royal policies to scrutiny and challenge.[34] In the period of the personal rule, willful and unpop-ular monarchs regularly blustered on the stage, and loyal subjects at least there were allowed to admit, like Suckling's Brennoralt, that they were "angry / With the King and State sometimes."[35] In Davenant's *Fair Favourite* (1638), the King's "dark prerogative" echoes through the play, and, if he comes finally to understand that "Monarchical sway" to be "beloved" requires less "a perfec-tion in skill / To rule" than a "perfect will,"[36] the perfection of the royal will is conceived of in terms that are emotional rather than political, personal rather than public. The King's worthiness to rule is established by his abandonment of his pursuit of Eumena and acceptance of the love of his queen, but it is unaf-fected by his contempt for the people he would govern, who remain distant and largely unconsidered, merely "that dull crowd, whom kings through cursed fate / Must please."

But "that dull crowd" would not long be disregarded and the king's abili-ty to "please" so easily assumed. Even a play performed at Court, like William Habington's *Queen of Aragon* (1640) could assert that "the supreame Law/ Of Princes is the peoples safety (sig. C4ᵛ). The appeal to the *salus populi* would soon become more insistent and disruptive, but even in the private theaters at the end of the period of the personal rule, the narrow self-interest of the court was displayed on stage, and its criticisms sometimes felt to be too pointed to ignore. In 1640, William Beeston was imprisoned and removed from the directorate of the King's and Queen's boys for performing Richard Brome's *The Court Beggar* which, in Henry Herbert's phrase, "had relation to the passages of the [King's] journey into the Northe," but was clearly a more general attack, as Martin Butler has argued, on "the bankruptcy of the personal rule."[37]

In spite of their royal patronage, then, the players had often proven ungrateful clients. The indoor playhouses with their audiences, as Brome writes in the epilogue to *The Court Beggar*, largely made up of "Ladyes," "Cavaliers," and "generous spirits of the City," as well as the amphitheaters like the Fortune and the Red Bull, which, as James Wright recalled in 1699, "were mostly frequented by Citizens, and the meaner sort of People,"[38] were as likely to serve oppositional interests, if only those of a disaffected gentry, as those of the crown. Why, then, should Parliament seek to close the playhouses late in the summer of 1642 when a critical theater might well prove a powerful weapon of propaganda in the war against the King?

Certainly, both sides understood full well that the war was as much a war of contesting representations as of contending armies. The abolition of the Star Chamber and the Court of High Commission in 1641 had left the government without effective means of controlling the presses, and royalists and radicals rushed to exploit the unprecedented freedom that resulted. But even two years earlier, Charles, feeling the sting of published criticism, had protested the use, and not merely the abuse, of the presses. It was the appropriation of the medium that concerned him more than the nature or even the existence of the opposition. "For whereas the Print is the King's in all Kingdoms, these seditious Men have taken upon them to print what they please, though we forbid it."[39] And, indeed, it was the printing and publishing, more than the substance, of the Grand Remonstrance in November of 1641, that divided the parliamentarians, leading many, like Edward Dering, to vote against the account of Charles's malfeasance and Parliament's radical recommendations for reform: "I did not dream that we should remonstrate downward, tell stories to the people, and talk of the King as of a third person."[40] But, especially between 1641 and 1643 in the absence of licensing provisions, "the Print" did not belong solely to the King, and "telling stories to the people" was in the civil war, as in most wars, a major tactic of the confrontation. Significantly, the King took a printing press with him as he left London for Oxford.

Much like "the Print," the theater was a popular medium where cultural images and values were constructed, contested, and changed. Its representations were similarly claimed by the King, but it was also, as the persistent efforts at control and censorship themselves attest, a potential source of criticism and social disturbance. This is not, however, merely to invert the familiar terms, replacing the idea of a royalist theater with a subversive one, but rather to challenge and transform the simplifying binary itself.

In the wake of Kett's Rebellion, a proclamation of 1549 suspended plays "in the English tongue" for two months, justifying the ban on the grounds that most "contain matter tendyng to sedicion and condempnyng of sundery good orders and laws."[41] A century later, Newcastle urged Charles II to encourage playing upon his restoration, since "these Devertismentes will amuse the peoples thoughts And keep them in harmless actions which will free your Majestie from Faction & Rebellion."[42] Somehow plays can "contain matter tendyng to sedicion" and yet also serve to free the monarch "from Faction & Rebellion." Plays apparently may both provoke rebellion and prevent it. If the contradiction reveals that the response of authority itself politicizes the theater, it also reveals the theater's unstable political constitution. Only in the specific historical circumstances of performance can the political meanings and effects of theatrical representation be determined—and even then, unless the audience is impossibly idealized, those meanings and effects are multiple and often contradictory.

The theater neither has nor grants an a priori or fixed political valence. In 1603, Henry Crosse, in *Vertues Common-Wealth*, had argued that plays encourage "execrable actio[n], commotions, mutinies, rebellio[n]s," but that same year Montaigne's *Essays* appeared in English, insisting on the contrary that "wel ordered commonwealths" should promote playing because the theater encourages "common societie and loving friendship" and serves "as a diverting of worse inconveniences, and secret actions."[43] The contradiction, however, may suggest more than merely that the culture is ambivalent about the theater; it suggests, rather, that the theater is itself constitutively ambivalent. Like the forms of carnival that Peter Stallybrass and Allon White have brilliantly explored,[44] the theater is itself always a contested arena of power and desire, never inherently *either* an agent of subversion *or* an apparatus of royal authority. In Caroline England, it belonged neither to the King nor to his critics. However, the theater could be, and was, claimed by both, for it was a significant site of voluble articulation, a locus of the production of meanings and images that could neither be stabilized nor controlled.

At least in part what motivates the parliamentary action against the theater seems precisely the recognition of this mobile and unlegitimated productivity. The theater generates unauthorized representations that are then available for contest and appropriation. Certainly, the parliamentary ordinance against playing cannot be understood solely or even primarily as an effort to neutralize a royalist institution, for the theaters were never simply that, as Parliament itself knew well. Rather, the theaters defined a public space that opened to view and judgment topics over which the authority of church or state previously had exerted a virtual monopoly of interpretation. The closing of the theaters must, therefore, be understood more as a defensive action, responsive to Parliament's awareness of its own vulnerability to the unauthorized voices, on stage and in the audience, that the theater empowered, than as some aspect of the parliamentary campaign against the monarch and royalist ideology.

In part, of course, the cessation order can be seen as of a kind with similar interruptions of playing at other times demanding "sad and pious solemnity," like those following the death of Henry, the Prince of Wales in 1612 or the death of King James in 1625 holding "that these tymes doe not suite with such playes and idle shewes."[45] But the ban on playing in 1642 was motivated at least as much by politics as by propriety. The prohibition claims to be a temporary measure designed to inhibit the unseemly display of "Publike Sports" at a time when fasts and prayers were ordered (the "set times of Humiliation") to "appease and avert the wrath of God," reflecting the godliness of its author, Francis Rous,[46] but for most of its supporters it was, as Martin Butler astutely writes, "an act of public safety rather than of puritan reform,"[47] a means to avert public disorder by limiting assembly and the circulation of radical ideas, by resisting, that is, the theaters' contribution to the construction of a public engaged in critical scrutiny of the state.

Indeed, in this respect it is not dissimilar from or, in fact, unrelated to Parliament's response to the unprecedented freedom of the presses that existed in the absence of any effective system of control. Initially buoyed by the support mobilized for its position by the radical press, Parliament quickly came to recognize the danger to its own position that existed in the absence of licensing provisions, and as early as February of 1641, a subcommittee was established "to examine all Abuses in Printing."[48] Little was done at that time, however, and over a year passed before Commons, on 7 April of 1642, irritably ordered the subcommittee to "bring in To-morrow, the Order they are appointed to prepare, to hinder this Liberty of Printing."[49] In August, as the polemics on all sides became more outrageous, both houses finally approved a bill to control the "great Disorders and Abuses by irregular Printing," designed to inhibit the publication of anything "false or scandalous to the Proceedings of the Houses of Parliament."[50]

It was less than a week later that the Commons sent the House of Lords a message desiring them "to join with this House in an Order that all Stage Plays may be put down, during this Time of Distractions, and of Fasting."[51] As with the unlicensed press, if the theater's unanchored and unlegitimated production permitted a critique of the authority of the court, it also enabled a challenge to the no less legitimated site that was Parliament, exposing and exacerbating the fragility and strain of the alliance between the parliamentarians and the common people, revealing it as temporary and transitional. (It is perhaps useful to say here that Parliament is not here imagined as a monolith but as itself marked by disagreement and division along economic, regional, and sectarian lines; nonetheless, Parliament, however much its coherence was compromised by the various allegiances of its membership, increasingly served as the focus for effective opposition to the monarch, if not to the monarchy.[52]) Though Parliament was dependent upon the support of commoners, the two groups had very different political interests and outlooks, ultimately insuring the fracturing of their common purpose and the dissipation of the revolutionary ethos.

In the event, the first phase of the civil war was fought not between the King and the commons but between competing elites, "two sovereign contending powers," as the Westminster Assembly said in 1643[53]; and the citizens who aligned themselves with the parliamentarians soon learned the limits of their association. Though the tradesmen of London massively rallied for the parliamentary cause—according to one pamphlet of 1642, 8,000 apprentices enlisted in Essex's army[54]—their presence was often (and perhaps with some justice) viewed warily. John Potts wrote to Simonds D'Ewes on August 19: "I concur with you in the fears of an ungovernable multitude, from whence my thoughts always apprehended the most remediless dangers, which God avert . . . . Whensoever necessity shall enforce us to make use of the multitude I do not promise myself safety."[55] As Wellington later commented about the troops fighting under him: "I don't know whether they frighten the enemy, but by

God, they frighten me,"[56] and Essex himself saw the danger of the parliamentary alliance with the far more radical commoners: "Our posterity will say that to deliver them from the yoke of the King we have subjected them to that of the common people. If we do this the finger of scorn will be pointed at us and so I am determined to devote my life to repressing the audacity of the people."[57]

If parliamentarians feared "the audacity of the people," the radicals themselves came to scorn the arrogance of their aristocratic allies and quickly recognized the limitations of Parliament's gentry constitutionalism for their own political ambitions. What was the difference if all that was accomplished was, as a radical pamphlet asked in 1649, "to take down Monarchical Tyranny, and set up an Aristocratical Tyranny"?[58] Many came to understand that the conflict was not about a fundamental reformation of society but merely about which of the competing elites would prevail. "The ground of the late war between the King and you," wrote one Leveller to Parliament, "was a contention whether he or you should exercise the supreame power over us,"[59] and John Lilburne, who began the war as second-in-command of Lord Brooke's regiment, by 1646 could tell the House of Lords: "All you intended when you set us a-fighting was merely to unhorse and dismount our old riders and tyrants, that so you might get up and ride us in their stead. And therefore my Lords . . . if you shall be so unworthy as to persevere . . . in the destruction of the fundamental laws and liberties of England . . . I will venture my life and heart's blood against you with as much zeal and courage as ever I did against any of the King's party."[60]

As early as 1640, the populace of London had begun to prove itself an effective political agent, willing, if not yet aggressively to contest oligarchical control, at least to insist that its desires and expectations be heard. After Burton and Prynne were released from prison, thousands of men and women accompanied them into the city, "the people flocking together to behold them, and receiving them with acclamations, and almost adoration, as if they had been let down from heaven."[61] This unprecedented popular response was correctly perceived as an attack upon the authority of the Star Chamber and the High Commission, indeed, as an assault on the King's authority itself. Clarendon called the orderly display of support an "insurrection (for it was no better) and frenzy of the people"[62]; but if royalist anxiety rather than reportorial accuracy shapes Clarendon's judgment of the event, the demonstration was, according to a newsbook, "generally esteemed the greatest affront that ever was given to the Courts of Justice in *England.*"[63] Clarendon believed that it was at this moment that the civil war was both begun and lost: "without doubt, if either the Privy Council, or the judges and the king's learned counsel, had assumed the courage to have questioned . . . the seditious riots upon the triumph of these . . . scandalous men . . . it had been no hard matter to have destroyed those seeds and pulled up the plants, which, neglected, grew up and prospered to a full harvest of rebellion and treason."[64] What was perceived as dangerous was precisely the expression of popular will, as even Thomas May recognized, lamenting "actions of that nature, where the people, of their own accords, in a seeming tumultuous manner, do express their liking or dislike of matters in government."[65]

Increasingly, however, the people did begin to "express their liking or dislike of matters in government." "The multitude" began to assemble and demonstrate, insisting upon the exercise of their voices. Fifteen thousand Londoners signed a petition for the abolition of episcopacy in November of 1640, and, when the petition was at last accepted, the intervention by the people was as much the issue as the reform of church government. Lord Digby was one of the many who objected to "the manner of bringing" the petition, considering it reason enough for its rejection: "what can there bee of greater presumption, then for Petitioners, not only to prescribe to a Parliament, what, and how it shall do; but for a multitude to teach a Parliament, what, and what is not, the government according to God's Word"?[66] But the popular will demanded to be heard ever more insistently ("impatiently demanded by the universal voice," in the words of the Venetian ambassador[67]). Sir John Coke reported that "there is a petition preparing in the City with 20,000 or 30,000 subscribed . . . to demand justice against the earl of Strafford."[68] On 3 May 1641, a huge crowd, estimated by Nehemiah Wallington at 15,000 people, assembled at Westminster in support of the petition, promising they would "never rest from petitioning, till not only the Lieutenant's matter, but also all things else that concern a Reformation, be fully perfected."[69] The next day a larger and more sullen crowd assembled which dispersed, according to the Venetian ambassador, only "upon the condition that inside this week the Lieutenant should be condemned to death, otherwise they promise the most violent action."[70] On May 12, Strafford was beheaded, and though the populace greeted the event with "the greatest demonstrations of joy, that could possibly be expressed,"[71] the King, the army, and even many members of Parliament who had opposed Strafford were obviously apprehensive at the evidence of the power of the multitude. Popular opinion had forced the King's hand to sacrifice Strafford, as the Venetian ambassador wrote, "at the alter of the public satisfaction."[72] "My Lord of Strafford had not died," wrote a troubled London citizen, "if the people had not pressed the Lords in a tumult as they did."[73]

In the ensuing years, popular demonstrations and disturbances increased, "the people . . . press[ing] . . . in a tumult," as did levels of anxiety among the gentry who observed them. Citizens, often armed with swords and staves, assembled ominously before Parliament, as on November 28, when Robert Slingsby reports that "the factious citizens begin to come again to the House with their swords by their sides, hundreds in companies."[74] The parliamentary cause was no doubt advanced by the demonstrations, which at once showed popular support for their policies and which could also be used to demonstrate the King's inability to rule and to justify the extension of legislative powers. If, however, Parliament learned successfully to exploit popular disruption (as the Venetian ambassador claimed, noting how "members of the lower house . . . encourage disturbance with all their might, in the assurance of raising their own estate upon the ruins of the sovereign's authority"[75]), it always remained aware of the danger to their own authority in releasing the radical potential latent within the volatile social and political environment.

By 1642, the threat posed by the focus and exercise of popular energy was every bit as unnerving to Parliament as it was to the court. A royalist, Sir Thomas Aston imagined the nobility and gentry "situate as the Low Countries, in a flat, under the banks and bounds of the Lawes, secured from that Ocean, the Vulgar, which by the breach of those bounds would quickly overwhelme us, and deface all distinctions of degrees and persons."[76] But even Pym, who in December of 1641 had declared the common people "our surest friends,"[77] was already worried in late January about the danger of "Tumults and Insurrections of the meaner sort of people": "what they cannot buy they will take, and from them the like necessity will quickly be derived to the farmers and husbandmen, and so grow higher, and involve all men in an equality of misery and distress, if it be not prevented."[78] Both contending parties had reason to fear being swept away in the turbulent "ocean" of the vulgar. Bulstrode Whitelock's moralizing about women petitioners in 1646 exactly articulated the parliamentarians' troubled awareness of the risk of encouraging "the beginning of any unfit thing, thought to promote your designs at that time, least the growth of those unfit things, become afterward a greater prejudice, than it was before an advantage to you."[79]

It is in the context of the spreading public discontent and disorder of the summer of 1642–or at least in the context of the *fear* of such public discontent and disorder–that the order to prohibit stage plays must be placed. Earlier, in January, a bill to close the theaters was introduced but, even with the ascendancy of the parliamentary Puritans, easily defeated; in late August, however, a similar bill was presented and approved by both houses on September 2. In the seven or so months between the legislation's first introduction and its eventual success, the King had abandoned the city, formally declared war, and left Parliament to control the popular pressures it had previously encouraged or at least exploited. In spite of their initial dependence upon the support of the "meaner sorts," parliamentarians increasingly realized that "prudent men," as John Corbet observed, should tolerate popular political intervention "no farther then themselves can over-rule and moderate,"[80] and actions were taken to assure that control, among them the ban on "publike Stage-Plays." Significantly, the parliamentary order to prohibit stage plays was formally published in tandem with a proclamation "for the appeasing and quietting of all unlawfull Tumults and Insurrections in the severall Counties of England."[81] Though a determined "Puritan" hostility to playing no doubt contributed to the desire to close the theaters, the bill to do so was finally passed in the summer of 1642 largely to prevent disorder, attempting to stabilize the political situation even as Parliament sought to replace the crown as the source of political stability.

From the time of its institutional origins in the reign of Elizabeth, the theater, of course, had been suspected of encouraging unrest. City fathers regularly protested, as the Lord Mayor wrote in 1592, that "the politique state & government of this Citie" is by nothing "so greatly annoyed and disquieted as by players & playes, & the disorders which follow thearvpon."[82] Earlier, in 1574, the Lord Mayor and Aldermen of London had written the Lord Chamberlain about the application of "one Holmes . . . that he might have the appointment of places for playes and enterludes within this citie." They objected to a license since it affected "the governance of this citie in one of the greatest matters therof, namely the assemblies of multitudes of the Queenes people, and regard to be had to sundry inconveniences, whereof the peril is continually, upon everie occasion, to be foreseen by the rulers of this citie . . . ."[83] In December of 1574, an act of the London Common Council proclaimed that "sondrye greate disorders and inconvenyences have benne

found to ensewe to this Cittie by the inordynate hauntyinge of great multitudes of people, speciallye youthe, to playes, enterludes, and shewes . . . ."[84]
Though this proclamation did maintain that the content of plays could be disruptive, insisting that plays be approved by the authorities before performance and warning against the addition of unlicensed materials, in general
City authorities were more concerned to control the theatrical spaces themselves, rather than the plays therein performed. The theaters were, according
to the anxious Lord Mayor in 1594, "the ordinary places of meeting for all
vagrant persones, & maisterles men that hang about the Citie, theeues, hors-
estealers, whoremoongers, coozeners, conycatching persones, practizers of
treason, & such other lyke."[85] More than moral or religious objections to playing, fears of social disorder along with anxieties about the spread of plague
combined to motivate the City's committed antitheatricality, as in 1583,
when the Lord Mayor wrote urging Walsingham to restrain playing in the
theaters in the liberties "to which doe resorte great multitudes of the basist
sort of people; and many enfected with sores runing on them."[86] Throughout
the century, theatrical activity came under increasing scrutiny and control,
the Crown mainly seeking to control the content of plays, the City the conditions of their playing.

In the late summer of 1642, it was primarily the fear of social disturbance
that seems to have motivated Parliament as it acted to prohibit stage plays.
The popular unrest that had previously aided the parliamentary cause now
had to be controlled, and the theaters, notorious "places of common assembly," came to be viewed as both sites and catalysts of disobedience. Yet what
made the theater threatening was not merely that crowds assembled. Other
places of public assembly continued to function unchallenged. Indeed, the
actors in January of 1644 recognized that they had been singled out: "Stage-
playes, only of all publike recreations are prohibited," they complained, while
"other publike recreations of farre more harmfull consequence [are] permitted still to stand in statu quo prius, namely that Nurse of barbarisme and
beastlinesse, the Beare-Garden."[87] But the theaters did represent a unique
threat. Unlike the bear-baiting houses, theaters were places not only where
private people came together but where they came together *as a public*. In the
theaters people assembled, were provided with a political vocabulary that
served to construct and clarify their interests, and were endowed, by the theaters' commercial logic, with an authority over its representations. The audience was thus not merely a public assembly but a public now constituted as

a domain of political significance, and it was largely this that made playing unacceptable to Parliament in 1642.

Plays continued to be published. The impressive Beaumont and Fletcher folio, for example, appeared in 1647. And other, smaller format collections were issued: some of Suckling's plays were included in *Fragmenta Aurea* (1646); Cartwright's *Comedies, Tragi-comedies, With other Poems*, appeared in 1651; a collection of Marston's *Comedies, Tragicomedies, and Tragedies* was published in 1652; a collection of Chapman's plays also appeared that year. *Six New Playes* by Shirley (1653), *Five New Playes* by Richard Brome (1653), *Three New Plays* by Massinger (1655), *Two New Plays* by Middleton (1657), and *Two New Playes* by Lodowick Carlell (1657) also all found an eager market.

And publishers brought forth numerous editions of individual plays, some clearly designed to be bound with the previously published collections, like Humphrey Moseley's publication of *The Wild-Goose Chase* in 1652, which, as he had lamented in his preface to the 1647 Beaumont and Fletcher folio, was the only previously unprinted play he could not acquire, and which he now prints in folio to allow it to be bound with the earlier volume. Similarly, in 1655, Moseley published two plays by Shirley, *The Politician* and *The Gentleman of Venice*, issuing each simultaneously in quarto and octavo formats to allow owners of the octavo collection of 1653 to bind these in should they wish to.

With the theaters closed, the appetite for drama was met by a willing book trade. Richard Brome's prefatory poem to the 1647 Beaumont and Fletcher folio remarks how this situation works "*to th' Stationers gaines*," and so shall continue "*till some After-age / Shall put down* Printing, *as this doth the* Stage." But the government, at least, seemed uninterested in putting down the printing of playbooks. The prologue to *Craftie Cromwell* (1648), one of a number of political pamphlets adopting play form, sarcastically acknowledged the government's tolerance of printed drama, even as the attack on the theaters was intensified:

> An Ordinance from our pretended State,
> Sowes up the Players mouths, they must not prate
> Like Parrats what they're taught upon the Stage,
> Yet we may Print the Errors of the Age.[88]

Printed drama thrived.[89] Playbooks were readily available in the bookstalls, and readers were directed to them by the booksellers' catalogues that

often appeared in their published books. One appended to *The Old Law*
(1656) lists over six hundred and fifty plays ("all the Plaies that were ever
printed," according to the heading) that are available either "at the Signe of
the *Adam and Eve*, in Little Britain; or, at the *Ben Johnson's* Head in
Thredneedle-street, over against the Exchange" (sig. a1ʳ). Clearly, publishers
and booksellers felt no fear of governmental displeasure, advertisements for
playbooks appearing even in pamphlets published directly under parliamentary authority.[90] Parliament was not concerned about people reading plays,
even though it could not easily have mistaken the conspicuous royalism of
much of this production, most notably the Beaumont and Fletcher folio.[91] In
the forty-one pages of prefatory material, the dead Fletcher is repeatedly
remembered and mourned in a language of royalty: "King of Poets" (sig. f1ᵛ);
"abs'lute Sovereign"; "sole Monarch" of "Wits great Empire" (sig. f4ᵛ);
"Imperiall FLETCHER" (sig. e2ʳ). The volume itself a "Kingdome" (sig. a3ᵛ).
"FLETCHER the people cry! / Just so when kings approach" (sig. f1ᵛ). One
contributor worried that his praise of Fletcher "might raise a discontent/
Between the Muses and the _____ " (sig. a2ᵛ). The absent rhyme word would
not have been difficult to supply. And lest the overall point be missed, Shirley
ends his contribution, capping the collection of thirty four commendatory
poems: "A Balme unto the wounded Age I sing/ And nothing now is wanting
but the King" (sig. g1ᵛ).

Obviously, then, it wasn't plays that were thought to be dangerous; it was
their public playing. And this was what was controlled. A surreptitious performance after the ordered closing was stopped and the actors arrested,
according to *Mercurius Melancholius*, "to prevent such dangerous Assemblies,"[92] and, indeed, the Venetian ambassador later observed that the government has "absolutely forbidden plays suspecting that these gatherings of
the people might occasion some disadvantage to the present state of affairs."[93]

Members of Parliament, in their desire to control playing, were clearly
aiming at the popular energies they had nourished more than at the King. In
1646, the players formerly of Blackfriars, the King's men, petitioned
Parliament for the salary that was owed them, and on March 24, the House
of Lords "specially recommended to the House of Commons that they may
have their Monies paid them."[94] If the prohibition against playing were directed primarily at the King, this parliamentary scrupulousness becomes virtually inexplicable, especially if, as James Wright claimed, most of the actors
"went into the King's Army, and like good Men and true, Serv'd their Old

Master, tho' in a different, yet more honourable, Capacity."[95]

It was not, however, the King or even the King's men but the political aspirations of the populace as they came in conflict with the central dynamic of the civil war that was the primary object of the closing ordinance. The commercial theaters were places, in Hannah Arendt's phrase, "where freedom could appear,"[96] places where authority was contested—on stage, in the plays themselves that interrogated and challenged authority, not least by subjecting their images of rule to the judgment and censure of an audience of commoners, as well as in the democratic constitution of the audience, where "maisterles men & vagabond persons" were permitted to assemble, as the Lord Mayor had written nervously in 1595, "to recreate themselfes,"[97] or worse, as Parliament now feared, to re-create themselves, to multiply the heads on the already many-headed monster of the people. For Parliament in the late summer of 1642 the threat of the unauthorized and unruly voices—the threat of a public, however diverse in social identity and interest, increasingly independent of the control of government authority—was too great to bear.

Playing, of course, did not end with the ordinance of 1642 forbidding "publike Stage-playes." The players "persevering in their forbidden Art," as an issue of the *Weekly Account* in 1643 put it, led in November of 1644 to the inclusion of an article in the Treaty of Uxbridge demanding the King's assent to an act "for the supressing of interludes and stage plays" (a suppression that was to be "perpetual"), and, indeed, the continued inability to eliminate playing forced Parliament in 1647 and 1648 formally to renew its own prohibition.[98] Against Parliament's desires permanently to close the theaters, voices were increasingly heard urging their reopening. Interestingly, however, this pressure to resume playing was recognized to come not merely from royalists but from radicals as well. Certainly, many royalists had continuously from the moment of the theaters' closing argued for a resumption of playing, but the radical sectaries, at least according to Thomas Edwards, also began calling "for a Toleration of Stage-playes, and that the Players might be set up again."[99] In 1648, the republican John Hall of Durham advocated the immediate reopening of the theaters, a position seconded by John Streater, a former member of the New Model Army, who saw in public playing potential support for his popular republican values. The classical precedent at least was encouraging: "The Grecians in their plays delighted much to see the destruction of Tyrants acted."[100]

No less than Parliament, then, the radicals recognized that the theaters' unlegitimated production was available to serve their own purposes. A royalist newspaper, *Mercurius Pragmaticus*, commenting on the reiterated order to ban playing in 1648, saw the action as a move to restrict public discussion of sensitive matters: "for feare all in time should be publish't upon the *house-Tops*, the Houses have new vamp't an *old Ordinance* for abolishing Stage-Playes."[101] And the paper understood the prohibition to be not one more successful attack of the parliamentary Puritans upon a residual royalism but to be, in fact, a bill directed against the radical sects themselves, particularly John Lilburne and "his Party" of Levellers: "For, now to show that *Freedome* must downe, they [the houses of Parliament] begin to double their *Files* against them." The highly mobile articulation of the theater was a spur to a freedom that had to be "put down." "Publike Stage-playes" provided a disturbing and destabilizing echo of the voice of the radicals, not by re-presenting the content of their discourse but by reproducing the unlegitimated voice with which they spoke.

Notes

Introduction

1. Lisa Jardine has, of course, beaten me to the title; see her *Reading Shakespeare Historically* (London and New York: Routledge, 1996).

2. *Coleridge's Writings on Shakespeare*, ed. Terence Hawkes (New York: G.P. Putnam's Sons, 1959), p. 106.

3. For a fuller version of this argument, see my introduction to *A Companion to Shakespeare* (Oxford: Blackwell, 1999) from which some sentences have been borrowed.

4. *Aesthetics and Politics*, trans. Ronald Taylor (1977; rpt. London: Verso, 1980), p. 127.

5. Chartier, *Forms and Meanings: Texts, Performances, and Audiences from Codex to Computer* (Philadelphia: Univ. of Pennsylvania Press, 1995), p. 2.

Chapter 1

1. The phrase seems to be Harold Bloom's; at least it is claimed by him in his review of Robert Alter and Frank Kermode's *Literary Guide to the Bible*, in *The New York Review of Books*, March 31, 1988, p. 23.

2. Roger Kimball, "The Periphery v. the Center: The MLA in Chicago," in *Debating P.C.: The Controversy over Political Correctness on College Campuses*, ed. Paul Berman (New York: Dell, 1992), p. 65.

3. Dinesh D'Souza, "The Visigoths in Tweed," *Forbes*, April 1, 1991, p. 81.

4. *The Collected Letters of Thomas and Jane Welsh Carlyle*, ed. Charles Richard Sanders (Durham: Duke Univ. Press, 1977), pp. 7, 9.

5. Alexis de Tocqueville, *Democracy in America*, trans. Henry Reeve, rev. Francis Bowen, ed. Phillips Bradley (New York: Vintage, 1945), pp. 58, 64.

6. This point is cogently argued by Josephine M. Guy and Ian Small, *Politics and Value in English Studies: A Discipline in Crisis* (Cambridge: Cambridge Univ. Press, 1993), pp. 19–28.

7. "Discourse and Discos: Theory in the Space between Culture and Capitalism," *TLS*, July 15, 1994: p. 3.

8. The phrase belongs to Louis Montrose, who similarly seeing the "multiplicity of unstable, variously conjoined and conflicting discourses" that function under the totalizing name of "theory," finds their commonality in their mutual commitment to "a problematization" of these processes. See *The Purpose of Playing: Shakespeare and the Cultural Politics of the Elizabethan Theatre* (Chicago: Univ. of Chicago Press, 1996), p. 2.

9. "Morphology and the Book from an American Perspective," *Printing History* 17 (1987): 2.

10. Cohen, "Political Criticism in Shakespeare," in *Shakespeare Reproduced*, ed. Jean E. Howard and Marion F. O'Connor (London and New York: Methuen, 1988), pp. 33–34.

11. Louis Montrose acknowledges New Historicism's "affinities with formalist modes of analysis" (p. 401) in his excellent reconsideration of the various critical practices that bear the name. See his "New Historicisms," in *Redrawing the Boundaries: The Transformation of English and American Literary Studies,* ed. Stephen Greenblatt and Giles Gunn (New York: MLA, 1992). Carolyn Porter, in a provocative article that anticipates a number of my observations here, earlier criticized the New Historicism (which she pointedly terms "Colonialist Formalism") for merely "expanding the range of the various formalisms which it so manifestly wants to challenge" (p. 261). See her "History and Literature: 'After the New Historicism,'" *NLH* 21 (1990): 253–72.

12. For example, Stephen Greenblatt writes that "The relation I wish to establish between medical and theatrical practice is not one of cause and effect or source and literary realization. We are dealing rather with a shared code, a set of interlocking tropes and similitudes that function not only as objects but as the conditions of representation." See *Shakespearean Negotiations: The Circulation of Social Energy in Renaissance England* (Berkeley: Univ. of California Press, 1988), p. 86; or see Harold Veeser, who defines the practice as the ability to reveal "through the analysis of tiny particulars the behavioural codes, logics, and motive forces controlling a whole society" (*The New Historicism*, ed. Harold Aram Veeser [New York: Routledge, 1989], p. ix).

13. While under the pressure of this now familiar charge, some practitioners of New Historicism have attempted a rationale of its characteristic strategies of reading and writing, most would agree with Joel Fineman's witty insistence that the practice is marked by a "programmatic refusal to specify a methodological program for itself." See "The History of the

Anecdote: Fiction and Fiction," in *The New Historicism*, ed. Harold Aram Veeser, p. 52.

14. Harold Aram Veeser, *The New Historicism*, p. ix. The essays in this volume, however, especially Louis Montrose's "Professing the Renaissance: The Poetics and Politics of Culture," do valuably consider the "relationship between cultural practices and social, political, and economic processes" (p. 19).

15. "Consequences," in *Against Theory*, ed. W. J. T. Mitchell (Chicago: Univ. of Chicago Press, 1985), p. 128.

16. The oft-invoked phrase certainly owes its currency to Roland Barthes, "The Death of the Author," in *Image, Music, Text*, ed. and trans. Stephen Heath (London: Fontana, 1977), pp. 142–48.

17. *The Letters of Sir Thomas Bodley to Thomas James, First Keeper of the Bodleian Library*, ed. G. W. Wheeler (Oxford: Clarendon Press, 1926), pp. 219, 222.

18. Gerald E. Bentley, *The Profession of the Dramatist in Shakespeare's Time, 1590–1642* (Princeton: Princeton Univ. Press, 1971), pp. 198–99.

19. Apparently at the urging of the King's men, the Lord Chamberlain ordered that no plays of the company should be published without the "consent" of its sharers. This stopped the planned-for collection, but Pavier and Jaggard issued the play-texts individually with falsely dated title-pages, presumably so they would seem old stock that could be safely sold at Pavier's shop in Ivy Lane (not at the Cat and the Parrott near the Royal Exchange, as Greg has it) where Pavier had moved in 1614. See W. W. Greg, *The Shakespeare First Folio: Its Bibliographic and Textual History* (Oxford: Oxford Univ. Press, 1955), pp. 9–17, 24.

20. Peter W.M. Blayney, "The Publication of Playbooks," in *A New History of Early English Drama*, ed. John D. Cox and David Scott Kastan (New York: Columbia Univ. Press, 1997), p. 389.

21. James P. Saeger and Christopher J. Fassler, "The London Professional Theater, 1576–1642: A Catalogue and Analysis of Extant Printed Plays," *Research Opportunities in Renaissance Drama* 34 (1995): 106–8.

22. Not until 1633 is another playwright so identified, when the title-page of *The Bird in the Cage* names "The author Iames Shirley," and *A New Way to Pay Old Debts* specifies on its title-page "The Author. Philip Massinger." Although the usage then becomes more common as drama becomes more explicitly literary, still, from 1633 to 1640, only eleven other play quartos identify the playwright as an "author."

23. See, for example, Grace Ioppolo's *Revising Shakespeare* (Cambridge, Mass. and London: Harvard Univ. Press, 1991). Ioppolo's argument for revision in the variant texts of "individual" Shakespeare plays is usually compelling, but there is no convincing evidence that Shakespeare was himself the revisor.

24. This idea of the institutional and collaborative nature of textual production is identified most strongly with the work of Jerome J. McGann and D. F. McKenzie, each of whom has argued for the social nature of textual production. Authorship, as McGann writes in *The Textual Condition* (Princeton: Princeton Univ. Press, 1986), "is a special form of human communicative exchange, and it cannot be carried out without interactions, cooperative and otherwise, with various persons and audiences" (p. 64). See also McKenzie's seminal *Bibliography and the Sociology of Texts* (London: British Museum, 1986).

25. Pierre Macherey, *A Theory of Literary Production*, trans. Geoffrey Wall (London: Routledge and Kegan Paul, 1978), p. 53.

26. "The Materiality of the Shakespearean Text," *Shakespeare Quarterly* 44 (1993): 283. As should be apparent, I am everywhere indebted to this important essay that brilliantly questions the very identity of the literary object.

27. This is, of course, part of the influential argument of Michel Foucault in his "What Is an Author," in *Language, Counter-Memory, Practice*, trans. Donald Bouchard (Oxford: Basil Blackwell, 1977), p. 137.

28. See Alexander Nehamas, "Writer, Text, Work, Author," in *Literature and the Question of Philosophy*, ed. Anthony Cascardi (Baltimore: The Johns Hopkins Univ. Press, 1987), p. 278.

29. Michael Riffaterre, of course, has argued precisely for this self-sufficiency, most explicitly in his essay "The Self-sufficient Text," *Diacritics* 3 (1973): 39–45.

30. *The World, the Text, and the Critic* (Cambridge, Mass.: Harvard Univ. Press, 1983), p. 4.

Chapter 2

1. This was the NACBS meeting in Chicago in 1996. In 1998, a conference with the same title was held at Centre for English Studies at the University of London, but this, more predictably, was a meeting of literary scholars at which Stephen Greenblatt and Catherine Gallagher were plenary speakers. In 1990, Carolyn Porter used the phrase but noted that she was not claiming that New Historicism's time had passed; rather she found the need "to go 'after' the New Historicism" for being an insufficiently "historized critical practice" (p. 253). See her "History and Literature: 'After the New Historicism,'" *NLH* 21 (1990): 253–72.

2. It will, no doubt, be asserted by some that I, however, do precisely that in this book. See my discussions of New Historicism, especially in chapters 1 and 6. I am, however, much in sympathy with its goals and admiring of its achievements. In many ways still the best consideration of the assumptions of New Historicism is Jean Howard's elegant essay, "Historicism in Renaissance Studies," *ELR* 16 (1986): 13–43; among many other fine accounts, see also Brook Thomas, *The New Historicism and Other Old-fashioned Topics* (Princeton: Princeton Univ. Press, 1991).

3. See, for example, Stephen L. Collins, "Where's the History in the New Literary Historicism? The Case of the English Renaissance," *Annals of Scholarship* 6 (1989): 231–47. Nonetheless, I realize that I am guilty of generalizing throughout this chapter about the attitudes and practices of both historians and literary scholars. I am aware that there are exceptions to most of my generalizations here, but they represent, I believe, merely exceptions rather than any substantial refutation of the central assertions. No doubt most of the sentences about disciplinary practices should include the word "usually," and the reader is hereby authorized to introduce it into any sentence where its absence offends.

4. "Revisionist History and Shakespeare's Political Context," *Shakespeare Yearbook* 6 (1996): 5.

5. Fredric Jameson, *The Political Unconscious* (Ithaca: Cornell Univ. Press, 1981), p. 9.

6. "The Historical Text as Literary Artifact," in *The Writing of History: Literary Forms and Historical Understanding*, ed. Robert H. Canary and Henry Kozicki (Madison: Univ. of Wisconsin Press, 1978), pp. 41–62.

7. Louis O. Mink, "The Theory of Practice: Hexter's Historiography," *After the Reformation: Essays in Honor of J. H. Hexter*, ed. Barbara Malament (Philadelphia: Univ. of Pennsylvania Press, 1980), p. 19.

8. What is new is not the contextualism of literary works, which in fact was a staple of earlier historicist work like that of Lilian Winstanley, Edwin Greenlaw, or Lily Campbell. What is

arguably new is that the nature of the historical context is itself understood differently, not as a secure and static background setting off and clarifying the complexities of the literary work, but as part of the same discursive environment that the text exists in and no less in need of interpretation.

9. Brook Thomas, though to a somewhat different end, similarly remarks this tendency toward a "disciplinary imperialism, masquerading as interdisciplinary work," in *The New Historicism and Other Old-fashioned Topics*, p. 10.

10. Leslie A. Fiedler, "Toward an Amateur Criticism," *Kenyon Review* 12 (1950): 564.

11. This assertion has as a corollary my "Strand" theory of theory. The Strand is, of course, the enormous used-book store on Broadway in Manhattan. The Strand theory of theory is that literary scholars, loving books but needing bargains, regularly inhabit such shops and so usually encounter the theory of other disciplines only when that theory is no longer current and, thus, readily available on remainder tables and on second-hand shelves.

12. Geoffrey Hartman, "English as Something Else," in *English Inside and Out*, ed. Susan Gubar and Jonathan Kamholtz (New York and London: Routledge, 1993), p. 38.

13. Interestingly, the very few who are read and admired by historians almost all work on the seventeenth century (e.g., Annabel Patterson, David Norbrook, Nigel Smith, and Steven Zwicker) and are interested in the literary text as exemplary of certain political ideas.

14. E. D. Hirsch, *Validity in Interpretation* (New Haven: Yale Univ. Press, 1967), p. 8.

15. "Locutionary" and "illocutionary" are, of course, two of the key terms in J. L. Austin's *How to Do Things with Words*, ed. J. O. Urmson (Cambridge, Mass.: Harvard Univ. Press, 1962); for Skinner's use of Austin, see his "'Social Meaning' and the Explanation of Social Action," in *The Philosophy of History*, ed. Patrick Gardiner (Oxford: Oxford Univ. Press, 1974), esp. pp. 111–13.

16. See his "Meaning and Understanding in the History of Ideas," *History and Theory* 8 (1969): 3–53.

17. Skinner, *The Foundations of Modern Political Thought* (1978; rpt. Cambridge: Cambridge Univ. Press, 1988), pp. i, xi.

18. It is perhaps Roger Chartier whose work most powerfully has insisted that meaning is a product not only of a text's semantic order but also of the material forms that present it to its readers. See his *The Cultural Uses of Print in Early Modern France*, trans. Lydia G. Cochrane (Princeton: Princeton Univ. Press, 1987), *The Order of Books*, trans. Lydia G. Cochrane (Stanford: Stanford Univ. Press, 1994), and *Forms and Meanings: Texts, Performances, and Audiences from Codex to Computer* (Philadelphia: Univ. of Pennsylvania Press, 1995). See also D. F. McKenzie's Panizzi Lectures of 1985, published as *Bibliography and the Sociology of Texts: The Panizzi Lectures 1985* (London: The British Library, 1986).

19. The phrase, though not the commitment, is Brook Thomas's; see his *The New Historicism and Other Old-fashioned Topics*, p. 215.

Chapter 3

1. F. O. Matthiessen, *American Renaissance: Art and Experience in the Age of Emerson and Whitman* (New York: Oxford Univ. Press, 1941), pp. 390–95; the 1933 American edition of Yeats's *Collected Poems* reads "Soldier Aristotle," notoriously puzzling Delmore Schwartz in his "An

Unwritten Book," *The Southern Review* 7 (1942): 488–90. See Fredson Bowers, *Textual and Literary Criticism* (Cambridge: Cambridge Univ. Press, 1959), pp. 1–35.

2. *William Shakespeare: The Complete Works*, ed. Stanley Wells, Gary Taylor, John Jowett, and William Montgomery (Oxford: Clarendon Press, 1986), p. 1025.

3. Harley Granville Barker, *Prefaces to Shakespeare* (Princeton: Princeton Univ. Press, 1946), vol. 1, p. 332.

4. *The Text of "King Lear"* (Stanford: Stanford Univ. Press, 1931), but see her revised position in her review of W. W. Greg's *Variants in the First Quarto of "King Lear"* in *RES* 17 (1941): 468–74.

5. Alexander Pope, "The Preface of the Editor," in *The Works of Shakespeare in Six Volumes* (London: Jacob Tonson, 1725), vol. 1, p. xxii.

6. *The Division of the Kingdoms: Shakespeare's Two Versions of "King Lear,"* ed. Gary Taylor and Michael Warren (Oxford: Oxford Univ. Press, 1983).

7. Stanley Wells says that in the 1608 Quarto and the 1623 folio, we have "two versions of the play, each consciously and distinctly fashioned" ("The Once and Future *King Lear*," in *The Division of the Kingdoms*, pp. 10–11); though see R. A. Foakes's Arden edition of the play (London: Thomas Nelson, 1997), which conflates (but differentiates) the texts and argues powerfully for seeing the play as "a single work of which we have variant versions" (p. 118).

8. The most determined argument for Shakespeare as revisor is in Grace Ioppolo's *Revising Shakespeare* (Cambridge, Mass.: Harvard Univ. Press, 1991). See also Steven Urkowitz, *Shakespeare's Revision of "King Lear"* (Princeton: Princeton Univ. Press, 1980).

9. *The Pictorial Edition of the Works of William Shakespeare*, ed. Charles Knight (London: C. Knight and Co., 1843), vol. 6, p. 392.

10. *On Editing Shakespeare* (Charlottesville: The Univ. Press of Virginia, 1966) p. 87.

11. Stanley Wells and Gary Taylor, with John Jowett and William Montgomery, *William Shakespeare: A Textual Companion* (Oxford: Clarendon Press, 1987), p. 60.

12. Werstine, "Narratives about Printed Shakespeare Texts: 'Foul Papers' and 'Bad' Quartos," *Shakespeare Quarterly* 41 (1990): 81. It should, however, be noted that there is at least some evidence of the use of "foul papers" to indicate an author's working draft (though none to indicate that this was the play "substantially in its final form" as Greg assumed), as in Edward Knight's account of having had access to the "the fowle papers" of the text of *Bonduca*. See W. W. Greg, *Dramatic Documents from the Elizabethan Playhouse*. (Oxford: Clarendon Press, 1931), pp. 5–6n.

13. W. W. Greg, *The Editorial Problem in Shakespeare*, 3rd ed. (Oxford: Oxford Univ. Press, 1954), pp. viii–ix.

14. G. Thomas Tanselle, "The Editorial Problem of Final Authorial Intention," *Studies in Bibliography* 29 (1976): 167. My thinking about texts and editing is deeply indebted not only to this essay and his other important publications but to numerous conversations with Tom Tanselle, who, even when he finds it necessary to disagree with me, never fails to impress with the clarity of his thought, the precision of his expression, and his generosity of spirit.

15. "Proposals for Printing By Subscription Shakespeare's Plays," in *Samuel Johnson on Shakespeare*, ed. H. R. Woudhuysen (London: Penguin, 1989), p. 117. For example, editors have often followed Hanmer in emending the folio reading of *The Winter's Tale*, 4.4.244, TLN 2069, "whistle of these secrets" to "whistle off these secrets" ("whistle off" being a falconry term meaning "set loose"); nonetheless, "whistle" meaning "whisper" is a familiar early modern usage (OED 10), though it is nowhere else used by Shakespeare. Metrical irregularity provides a similar temptation for the critical editor. While metrical regulariza-

tion has now largely gone out of fashion, Stanley Wells has recently argued that "we should pay our poet the compliment of assuming that he cares for metrical values, and be willing to emend when the surviving text is demonstrably deficient" in his *Re-editing Shakespeare for the Modern Reader* (Oxford: Oxford Univ. Press, 1984), p. 50. For Wells, it is a dereliction of editorial responsibility to refuse to emend in these cases. It might be objected, however, that this may bring us disturbingly close to the intrusive practices of Pope and other eighteenth-century editors, insisting on metrical norms that "our poet" could easily choose to violate, and forcing us to invent and insert various expletive syllables to "complete" a line.

16. Peter Shillingsburg makes this distinction, although to a different end in his *Scholarly Editing in the Computer Age* (Athens: Univ. of Georgia Press, 1986), esp. pp. 27–29. What I am pointing to here is that authors necessarily have various competing intentions as they write–to be read, to be admired, to make money, etc. (i.e., the intention to *do*) which may not be coincident with their desire to achieve some specific artistic effect (the intention to *mean*). Thus, to assume that Shakespeare's intentions are best represented by a line that is his own rather than, say, one that shows evidence of theatrical revision or even censorship is to value artistic intentions over theatrical ones, or, it could be said, meaning over doing. Given the source of Shakespeare's income (not, in fact, as playwright but as sharer in the acting company), it is not clear that this priority would necessarily be his own. Arguably his most pressing intention was to get the play on stage and spectators into the theater. See also James McLaverty, "The Concept of Authorial Intention in Textual Criticism," *The Library*, 6th series, 6 (1984): 121–38.

17. *William Shakespeare: The Complete Works*, p. xxxix.

18. See his "Precious Few: The Surviving English Manuscript Playbooks," in *A Companion to Shakespeare*, ed. David Scott Kastan (Oxford: Blackwell, 1999), pp. 414–33.

19. Paul Werstine, "McKerrow's 'Suggestion' and Twentieth-Century Shakespeare Criticism," *Renaissance Drama* 19 (1988): 169.

20. See Stephen Orgel, "Acting Scripts, Performing Texts," in *Crisis in Editing: Texts of the English Renaissance*, ed. Randall McLeod (New York: AMS Press, 1994), pp. 272–91. Orgel, here and elsewhere, has brilliantly challenged the idea of the text as singular, finished, or autonomous. See especially his "The Authentic Shakespeare," *Representations* 21 (1988): 1–25.

21. James P. Saeger and Christopher J. Fassler, "The London Professional Theater, 1576–1642: A Catalogue and Analysis of the Extant Printed Plays," *Research Opportunities in Renaissance Drama* 34 (1995): 63–110.

22. Webster's *Duchess of Malfi* (1623) seems curiously schizophrenic in this regard, the title-page saying both that the text is presented "As it was Presented priuately, at the Black-Friers; and publiquely at the Globe"and that it is a "perfect and exact Coppy, with diuerse things Printed, that the length of the play would not beare in the Presentment."

23. In the address to the "Courteous Reader" in *The Antipodes* (1640), Richard Brome writes that "You shal find in this Booke more then was presented upon the *Stage*, and left out of the *Presentation*, for superfluous length (as some of the *Players* pretended). . . ." But Brome's desire to see his play published as written rather than as played also reveals the importance of the uncut text for the acting company: "I thoght good it should be inserted according to the allowed original." The uncut text "had a specific identity, an authorising function. It was the players' manuscript that the Master of the Revels had seen and 'allowed' for playing, and to which his signature was appended." See Andrew Gurr, "Maximal and Minimal Texts of Shakespeare," *Shakespeare's Globe Research Bulletin* 4 (April 1998): 3.

24. The foundational texts are Jerome McGann, *A Critique of Modern Textual Criticism* (Chicago: Univ. of Chicago Press, 1983); and D. F. McKenzie, *Bibliography and the Sociology of Texts: The Panizzi Lectures 1985* (London: The British Library, 1986).

25. "Presidential Address: Society for Textual Scholarship, 1985: Unfinished Business," *TEXT* 4 (1988): 8.

26. For a persuasive account of the limitations of fascimiles for scholarly purposes, see G. Thomas Tanselle, "Reproductions and Scholarship," *Studies in Bibliography* 42 (1989): 25–54.

27. Certainly, this is true for Shakespeare, where texts are almost always offered in modernized form. "Old-spelling" editions no doubt offer an illusion of authenticity, but Shakespeare's orthography is unrecoverable from the surviving print record; the early printings record compositorial rather than authorial habits, and their preservation in a modern edition at best registers the inconsistency and idiosyncracy of the publication system. For a more positive view of these same facts see Anthony Hammond's "The Noisy Comma: Searching for the Signal in Renaissance Dramatic Texts," in *Crisis in Editing: Texts of the English Renaissance*, ed. Randall McLeod (New York: AMS Press, 1994), pp. 203–49. Stanley Wells, in both *Modernizing Shakespeare's Spelling, with Three Studies in the Text of "Henry V"* (Oxford: Oxford Univ. Press, 1979) and *Re-editing Shakespeare for the Modern Reader*, has energetically argued for modernization instead of the preservation of archaic and non-authorial accidentals, though somewhat ironically he, with Gary Taylor, has edited an old-spelling edition for Oxford Univ. Press (1986) and there falls prey to the necessity an old-spelling *edition* poses of having to invent old-spelling where the copy-text is considered inadequate.

Chapter 4

1. J. Thomas Looney, *"Shakespeare" Identified in Edward de Vere the Seventeenth Earl of Oxford* (London: Cecil Palmer, 1920).

2. On Battey, see S. Schoenbaum, *Shakespeare's Lives* (Oxford: Oxford Univ. Press, 1970), p. 628; and William F. and Elizabeth S. Friedman, *The Shakespearean Ciphers Examined* (Cambridge: Cambridge Univ. Press, 1958), pp. 7, 181. On Silliman, see Schoenbaum, *Shakespeare's Lives*, p. 625.

3. *Letters of Sir Thomas Bodley to Thomas James, First Keeper of the Bodleian Library*, ed. G. W. Wheeler (Oxford: Oxford Univ. Press, 1926), p. 222.

4. On Brome's contractual relations, see Ann Haaker, "The Plague, the Theater, and the Poet," *Renaissance Drama* n.s. 1 (1968): 283–306. On the general situation of professional playwrighting, see Gerald Eades Bentley, *The Profession of the Dramatist in Shakespeare's Time 1590–1642* (Princeton: Princeton Univ. Press, 1971).

5. *Henslowe's Diary*, ed. R. A. Foakes and R. T. Rickert (Cambridge: Cambridge Univ. Press, 1961), pp. 182, 206.

6. Haaker, "The Plague, the Theater, and the Poet," p. 298.

7. For the Admiral's men, see *Henslowe's Diary*, p. 132. In the case of the King's men, see E. K. Chambers, *William Shakespeare: A Study of Facts and Problems* (Oxford: Oxford Univ. Press, 1930). vol. 1, p. 136. Three different Lords Chamberlain are, of course, involved in the actions of 3 May 1619, 10 June 1637, and 7 August 1641.

8. Here, however, the issue seems more to be an effort to prevent any individual from selling off a property that should benefit the company at large rather than a blanket effort to prevent publication. Indeed, the contract makes an exception of "the booke of Torrismount," holding that this play is "not to be printed by any before twelue months be fully expired," apparently trying to protect it during its current theater run. See James Greenstreet, "Law-

Suit about the Whitefriar's Theatre in 1609," *Transactions of the New Shakespeare Society*, series 1, pt. 3 (1888): 269.

9. See Peter W. M. Blayney's extraordinary essay, "The Publication of Playbooks," *A New History of Early English Drama*, ed. John D. Cox and David Scott Kastan (New York: Columbia Univ. Press. 1997), pp. 383–422.

10. Blayney, "The Publication of Playbooks," p. 394.

11. The pronoun here is self-conscious. Publishers in the period were usually, though not inevitably, male. Widows and daughters on occasion inherited businesses and continued to work (or, more often, sell their inheritance–Dorothy Jaggard, for example, inherited the estate of her husband Isaac but eventually assigned to Thomas and Richard Cotes various titles including "her parte in Shackspheere playes"); but no play of Shakespeare's appearing before 1642 was printed or published by a woman stationer. However, among the twenty-two books Jane Bell published and had available for sale at her shop "at the East-end of Christ Church" was Q3 of *King Lear* (1655), the rights for which, incidently, apparently she did not hold, having instead, but not recognizing the difference, title to the anonymous *King Leir*. See Leo Kirschbaum, "The Copyright of Shakespeare's Plays," *The Library*, 5th series, 14 (1959): 247–49.

12. A. W. Pollard, *Shakespeare Folios and Quartos* (London: Methuen, 1909), esp. pp. 64–88. For the most thorough reconsideration of the idea of the "bad quarto" and its role in our understanding of the printing of early drama, see Laurie E. Maguire, *Shakespearean Suspect Texts: The "Bad" Quartos and their Contexts* (Cambridge: Cambridge Univ. Press, 1996). See also Randall McLeod, "The Marriage of Good and Bad Quartos," *Shakespeare Quarterly* 33 (1982): 421–31.

13. Thomas Heywood, *The Rape of Lucrece* (London, 1608), sig. A2^r.

14. On the Jonson folio, see *Ben Jonson's 1616 Folio,* ed. Jennifer Brady and W. H. Herendeen (Newark: Univ. of Delaware Press, 1991), esp. the essay by Sara van den Berg, "Ben Jonson and the Ideology of Authorship," pp. 111–37. See also Timothy Murray, *Theatrical Legitimation: Allegories of Genius in Seventeenth-Century England and France* (New York and Oxford: Oxford Univ. Press, 1987), esp. pp. 23–104; and Joseph Loewenstein, "The Script in the Marketplace," *Representations* 12 (1985): 101–14.

15. Richard Dutton similarly sees a Shakespeare comfortably working within the collective ethos of the acting company. See his fine essay, "The Birth of the Author," in *Elizabethan Theater: Essays in Honor of S. Schoenbaum*, ed. R. B. Parker and Sheldon Zitner (Newark: Univ. of Delaware Press, 1996), pp. 71–91.

16. *Samuel Johnson on Shakespeare*, ed. Henry Woudhuysen (London: Penguin, 1989), p. 114.

17. Unquestionably the best account of the printing of a playbook in the period (indeed the best account of the very operation of a printing house) is Peter W. M. Blayney's *The Texts of "King Lear" and their Origins: Nicholas Okes and the First Quarto* (Cambridge: Cambridge Univ. Press, 1982). I am throughout obviously and gratefully indebted to Blayney's work on the printing and publication of early drama.

18. Blayney convincingly corrects the usual claim that proofing was not normally done against copy, and notes that Fletcher and Middleton, anyway, seem familiar enough with the practice of authors reading proof that, in act four of *The Nice Valour*, Lepet receives proofs for a soon-to-be published pamphlet. See Blayney, *The Texts of "King Lear" and their Origins: Nicholas Okes and the First Quarto*, pp. 190–97.

19. See, for example, Ben Jonson's epigram, "To My Bookseller," where Jonson dreads the thought of seeing his "title-leaf on posts, or walls, / Or in cleft sticks," hoping, rather, that readers will seek his book without any such promotion.

20. James P. Saegar and Christopher Fassler, "The London Professional Theater, 1576–1642: A Catalogue and Analysis of the Extant Printed Plays," *Research Opportunities in Renaissance Drama* 34 (1995): 106–8.

21. See Blayney's analysis of the printing of the 1608 Lear quarto in *The Texts of "King Lear" and their Origins*, esp. pp. 89–150.

22. See also above p. 37.

23. Peter Stallybrass, "Shakespeare, the Individual, and the Text," in *Cultural Studies*, ed. Lawrence Grossberg, Cary Nelson, and Paula Treichler (New York and London: Routledge, 1992), p. 599.

24. In the following reconstruction of the publishing arrangements for the folio, I am again indebted to Peter Blayney. See his *The First Folio of Shakespeare* (Washington, D.C.: Folger Library, 1991). See also Charlton Hinman, *The Printing and Proof-reading of the First Folio of Shakespeare* (Oxford: Oxford Univ. Press, 1963); W. W. Greg, *The Shakespeare First Folio: Its Bibliographic and Textual History* (Oxford: Oxford Univ. Press, 1955); Edwin Eliott Willoughby, *The Printing of the First Folio of Shakespeare* (Oxford: Bibliographic Society, 1932).

25. See Falconer Madan, *The Original Bodleian Copy of the First Folio of Shakespeare* (Oxford: Oxford Univ. Press, 1905).

26. On 9 November 1609 Smethwick assumed Nicholas Ling's titles to *Love's Labours Lost, Romeo and Juliet*, and *Hamlet* (*SR*, 3, 365); he had earlier acquired the rights to *The Taming of A Shrew* (*SR*, 3, 337), which apparently served to establish title to *Taming of The Shrew*, as that play was not registered by Blount and Jaggard in November in 1623 among those plays without previous entry. Aspley owned the rights to *Much Ado About Nothing* and *2 Henry IV*, both of which he had published in 1600 with Andrew Wise.

27. Oddly, the next to last play entered, "Anthonie & Cleopatra," had already been registered by Blount on 20 May 1608, along with "The booke of Pericles, prynce of Tyre" (*SR*, 3, 378). That Blount thus held the rights to *Pericles*, along with the fact that Jaggard had printed a quarto of it for Pavier in 1619, the very year the King's men performed the play at court, must mean that whatever caused the play's exclusion from the folio, it cannot be an accidental omission; indeed, as all of the principals in the folio's publication were somehow involved with the play, its exclusion may well reveal their skepticism about the play's attribution to Shakespeare.

28. No copyright existed in the collected works as a totality, and, after the folio's publication, rights to the individual plays reverted to their publishers. Arthur Johnson, for example, has clearly retained title to the *Merry Wives of Windsor*, transferring it on 29 January 1630 to Richard Meighan, who publishes the play that year (Q3). Similarly, Thomas Walkley, on 1 March 1628, assigns his title to *Othello* to Richard Hawkins, who publishes an edition in 1630. Smethwick publishes quartos of his four plays—*Love's Labours Lost* (1631), *Taming of the Shrew* (1631), *Romeo and Juliet* (1637), and *Hamlet* (1637)—full title seemingly having reverted to him. And, on 16 November 1630, when Robert Allott acquires the rights to Blount's titles, it is only to the sixteen plays Blount, with Jaggard, had registered in November 1623 that then were without prior entry rather than to Blount's share in the complete volume.

29. Blayney, *The First Folio of Shakespeare*, pp. 21–22.

30. *Records of the Court of the Stationers' Company, 1602 to 1640*, ed. W. A. Jackson (London: Bibliographic Society, 1957), p. 110.

31. On the so-called Pavier quartos, see A. W. Pollard, *Shakespeare Folios and Quartos*, pp. 81–104; W. W. Greg, *The Shakespeare First Folio*, pp. 9–17; and Leo Kirschbaum, *Shakespeare and the Stationers* (Columbus: Ohio State Univ. Press, 1955), pp. 227–42.

32. See Gerald D. Johnson, "Thomas Pavier, Publisher, 1600–25," *The Library*, 6th series, 14 (1992): 12–50.

33. See Margreta de Grazia, *Shakespeare Verbatim* (Oxford: Clarendon Press, 1991), pp. 14–48; and Leah S. Marcus, *Puzzling Shakespeare: Local Reading and its Discontents* (Berkeley: Univ. of California Press, 1988), pp. 2–25, 43–50. See also Stephen Orgel's seminal essay, "The Authentic Shakespeare," *Representations* 21 (1988): 1–25.

34. In E. K. Chambers, *William Shakespeare: A Study of Facts and Problems*, vol. 2, p. 234. The poem, probably by Sir Henry Salisbury of Denbighshire, was first published by Sir Israel Gollancz, "Contemporary Lines to Heminge and Condell," in the *Times Literary Supplement*, January 26, 1922.

35. A. W. Pollard, *Shakespeare's Fight with the Pirates* (Cambridge: Cambridge Univ. Press, 1920), pp. 45–46.

36. See Margreta de Grazia, "The Essential Shakespeare and the Material Text," *Textual Practice* 1 (1988): esp. pp. 72–77; and Paul Werstine, "Narratives about Printed Shakespeare Texts: 'Foul Papers' and 'Bad' Quartos," *Shakespeare Quarterly* 41 (1990): 65–86.

37. While E. K. Chambers, for example, calls Busby "chief of the surreptitious printers" (*The Elizabethan Stage*, [Oxford: Oxford Univ. Press, 1923] vol. 3, p. 191), his practice here seems neither unusual nor improper. See Gerald D. Johnson's "John Busby and the Stationers' Trade," *The Library*, 6th series, 7 (1985): 1–15, one of a series of excellent essays Johnson has written on early modern publishers. Johnson argues that there is nothing irregular about the double entrance of the play: Busby buys and enters the play with the aim only of selling the rights, which he successfully does to Johnson. Only the fact that this sale happens immediately after his own registration of the play produces the unusual double entry and the illusion of some underhanded dealing.

38. *The Plays and Poems of William Shakspear* (London, 1790), vol. 1, p. xii.

39. Though Pollard, for example, puts great weight on the accuracy of this description too (*Shakespeare's Fight with the Pirates*, pp. 59–61), it is worth recalling that Humphrey Moseley in his epistle to the Readers in the 1647 Beaumont and Fletcher folio claims similarly that "Mr. *Fletchers* owne hand, is free from interlining; and his friends affirme he never writ any one thing twice: it seemes he had that rare felicity to prepare and perfect all first in his owne braine; to shape and attire his *Notions*, to adde or loppe off, before he committed one word to writing, and never touched pen till all was to stand as firme and immutable as if ingraven in Brasse or Marble." Even a glance at a page of Fletcher's autograph will reveal the conventional flattery of Moseley's lines.

40. It is, of course, Blount who had the greatest financial vulnerability in the project (Smethwick and Aspley probably having contributed their titles as the greatest part of their investment, and Jaggard still with a thriving printing business) and indeed he may have suffered for it. After a reasonably active publishing career, in the four years following the publication of the Shakespeare folio he publishes nothing. In 1625, he was ordered to assign his share of the English Stock to George Swinhowe in partial fulfillment of an unpaid debt of £160 (see Jackson, *Records of the Court*, p. 180), and in 1627 he sells his bookshop to Robert Allott, though he continues to publish intermittently from 1628 until his death in 1632.

41. Jeffrey Masten writes similarly that "'seventeenth-century authors' did not exist independently of their construction in the textual materials we read" (p. 120). See his remarkable *Textual Intercourse: Collaboration, Authorship, and Sexualities in Renaissance Drama* (Cambridge: Cambridge Univ. Press, 1997), esp. pp. 113–55.

Chapter 5

1. S. Schoenbaum, *William Shakespeare: A Documentary Life* (Oxford: Oxford Univ. Press, 1975), p. 143. James's account appears in the dedicatory epistle to his manuscript edition of Thomas Hoccleve's "The legend and defence of yᵉ Noble knight and Martyr Sir Jhon Oldcastel" (Bodleian Library, MS James 34). The epistle was first published in 1841 by James Orchard Halliwell [–Phillipps], and the entire manuscript was printed in *The Poems Etc., of Richard James, B.D.*, ed. Alexander B. Grosart (London: Chiswick Press, 1880). In his "William Shakespeare, Richard James and the House of Cobham," *RES*, n.s. 38 (1987), Gary Taylor dates the manuscript in "late 1633 or early 1634" (p. 341).

2. Following the DNB, most commentators identify William Brooke and his son Henry as the seventh and eighth Lords Cobham, but see *The Complete Peerage of England, Scotland, and Ireland,* by G. E. C[ockayne], rev. ed. by Vicary Gibbs (London: St. Catherine Press, 1913), vol. 3, pp. 341–51, where they are identified as the tenth and eleventh holders. See also the genealogical tables in David McKeen's *A Memory of Honour: The Life of William Brooke, Lord Cobham* (Salzburg: Universität Salzburg, 1986), vol. 2, pp. 700–2.

3. Nicholas Rowe, "Some Account of the Life, &c. of Mr. William Shakespear," *The Works of Mr. William Shakespeare* (London: Jacob Tonson, 1709), vol. 1, p. ix.

4. Stanley Wells says that this is "the only verse line in which [Falstaff's] name occurs" and notes that it "is restored to a decasyllable if 'Oldcastle' is substituted for 'Falstaff'," in his "Revision in Shakespeare's Plays," in *Editing and Editors: A Retrospect,* ed. Richard Landon (New York: AMS Press, 1988), p. 72. But it is worth observing that at least in the early editions this is not "a verse line" at all. The line appears as verse only following Pope. In all the early quartos, as well as in the folio, the line appears in a prose passage. In "'This is not the man': On Calling Falstaff Falstaff," in *Analytical and Enumerative Bibliography,* n.s. 4 (1990): 59–71. Thomas A. Pendleton contests the assertion that the missing syllable argues for a merely perfunctory revision, pointing out how metrically rough the entire section is (and recognizing that it is printed as prose in the earliest editions), and how many simple ways there are to regularize the line if one only sought to substitute "Falstaff" for "Oldcastle" (pp. 62–63).

5. The text's "Old." could, however, stand for "Old man" ("I know thee not, old man") rather than "Oldcastle."

6. There has, of course, been much discussion of the name change, most notably Gary Taylor's "The Fortunes of Oldcastle," *Shakespeare Survey* 38 (1985): 85–100; Taylor's "William Shakespeare, Richard James and the House of Cobham," *RES,* n.s. 38 (1987): 334–54; E.A.J. Honigmann, "Sir John Oldcastle: Shakespeare's Martyr," in *"Fanned and Winnowed Opinions": Shakespearean Essays Presented to Harold Jenkins,* ed. John W. Mahon and Thomas A. Pendleton (London: Routledge, 1987), pp. 118–32; Pendleton's "'This is not the man': On Calling Falstaff Falstaff," Jonathan Goldberg, "The Commodity of Names: 'Falstaff' and 'Oldcastle' in *1 Henry IV*" in *Reconfiguring the Renaissance: Essays in Critical Materialism,* ed. Jonathan Crewe (Lewisburg: Bucknell Univ. Press, 1992), pp. 76–88; and Eric Sams, "Oldcastle and the Oxford Shakespeare," *Notes and Queries,* n.s. 40 (1993): 180–85. See also Rudolph Fiehler, "How Oldcastle Became Falstaff," *MLQ* 16 (1955): 16–28; and Alice-Lyle Scoufus, *Shakespeare's Typological Satire: A Study of the Falstaff-Oldcastle Problem* (Athens: Univ. of Ohio Press, 1978).

7. See E. K. Chambers, *William Shakespeare: A Study of Facts and Problems* (Oxford: Oxford Univ. Press, 1930), vol. 1, p. 382. Though it is perhaps worth noting that *The Famous Victories of Henry the fifth,* in which Oldcastle appears, was published by Thomas Creede also in 1598.

8. See *Henslowe's Diary*, ed. R. A. Foakes and R. T. Rickert (Cambridge: Cambridge Univ. Press, 1961), p. 216. Gary Taylor (in "Fortunes," p. 90) has similarly suggested that the performance for the ambassador [reported in a letter of 8 March 1599/1600 to Robert Sydney, *Letters and Memorials of State*, ed. Arthur Collins (London, 1746), vol. 2, p. 175] must be Shakespeare's play, but Eric Sams ("Oldcastle and the Oxford Shakespeare") has, energetically if not entirely convincingly, argued that "there is no objective reason to suppose that the text was not copied, or borrowed, or indeed commandeered, by the court company, the Lord Chamberlain's men" (p. 182).

9. The reference from Jane Owen's *An Antidote Against Purgatory* (1634) is reported by R. W. F. Martin in "A Catholic Oldcastle," *Notes and Queries*, n.s. 40 (1993): 185–86.

10. Stanley Wells and Gary Taylor, *William Shakespeare: A Textual Companion* (Oxford: Clarendon Press, 1987), p. 330. John Jowett has argued, on somewhat similar grounds, that Peto and Bardolph were names "introduced at the same time as Falstaff," and that their original names, Harvey and Russell (present in Q1 at 1.2.158), like Falstaff's, should be restored in modern editions. See his "The Thieves in *1 Henry IV*," *RES* 38 (1987): 325–33.

11. *Henry IV, Part 1*, ed. David Bevington (Oxford: Oxford Univ. Press, 1987), p. 108.

12. See, for example, J. Dover Wilson, "The Origin and Development of Shakespeare's *Henry IV*," *Library* 26 (1945): 13, who argues that Cobham was "a man puritanically inclined and inimical to the theatre." See also E. K. Chambers, *The Elizabethan Stage* (Oxford: Oxford Univ. Press, vol. 1, p. 297. William Green, however, in *Shakespeare's "Merry Wives of Windsor"* (Princeton: Princeton Univ. Press, 1962), has demonstrated that during Cobham's term as Lord Chamberlain "not one piece of legislation hostile to the theater was enacted" and, in fact, between 1592 and his death in 1597, Lord Cobham "was absent from every meeting of the Council at which a restraining piece of theatrical legislation was passed" (pp. 113–14).

13. William Warburton, *The Works of Shakespear* (1747), vol. 4, p. 103.

14. See Robert J. Fehrenbach, "When Lord Cobham and Edmund Tilney 'were att odds': Oldcastle, Falstaff, and the Date of *1 Henry IV*," *Shakespeare Studies* 18 (1986): 87–101. But see also E.A.J. Honigmann, "Sir John Oldcastle: Shakespeare's Martyr," who argues that the play was intended "to annoy the Cobhams" and "to amuse Essex" (pp. 127–28), and suggests that the play "was written—or at least begun" in the first half of 1596 "before Lord Cobham became Lord Chamberlain" (p. 122).

15. *The Church History of Britain* (London, 1655), book 4, p. 168.

16. George Daniel, *Trinarchodia*, in *The Poems of George Daniel, esq. of Beswick, Yorkshire*, ed. Alexander B. Grosart (privately printed, 1878), vol. 4, p. 112.

17. The best account of the life of Oldcastle's life is still W. T. Waugh's "Sir John Oldcastle," *English Historical Review* 20 (1905): 434–56, 637–58. See also the entry on Oldcastle in the DNB written by James Tait. The following paragraphs are indebted to both.

18. See DNB, vol. 14, p. 986. Stow, in his *Annales of England* (1592), reports that "the last words that he spake, was to sir Thomas of Erpingham, adjuring him, that if he saw him rise from death to life again, the third day, he would procure that his sect might be in peace and quiet" (p. 572).

19. Quoted in David McKeen, *A Memory of Honour: The Life of William Brooke, Lord Cobham*, vol. 1, p. 22. Thynne's "treatise of the lord Cobhams" was written to honor Lord Cobham's admission to the Privy Council on 2 February 1586 for inclusion in the 1586/87 edition of Holinshed's *Chronicles*, but was excised from the edition along with other parts that touched on contemporary political events. Thynne presented an elegant manuscript version (British Museum MS add. 37666) to William's son, Henry, in December of 1598. See David Carlson, "The Writings and Manuscript Collections of the Elizabethan Alchemist,

Antiquary, and Herald Francis Thynne," *Huntington Library Quarterly* 52 (1989), esp. pp. 210–11 and 235–36.

20. John Foxe, *Acts and Monuments*, ed. Josiah Pratt, in *The Church Historians of England* (London: Seeleys, 1855), vol. 3, p. 350.

21. "Presbyterianism, the Idea of a National Church and the Argument from Divine Right," in *Protestantism and the National Church in Sixteenth Century England*, ed. Peter Lake and Maria Dowling (London: Croom Helm, 1987), p. 195.

22. See Annabel Patterson, "Sir John Oldcastle as a Symbol of Reformation Histriography," in *Religion and Literature in Post-Reformation England, 1540–1658*, ed. Donna B. Hamilton and Richard Stie (Cambridge: Cambridge Univ. Press, 1996), pp. 6–26.

23. P. T., "Observations on Shakespeare's Falstaff," *Gentleman's Magazine* 22 (October 1752): 459–61. Rudolph Fiehler, in "How Oldcastle Became Falstaff," has suggested that it is "not inconceivable" that P. T. was actually William Warburton (p. 19).

24. I remain unpersuaded that Shakespeare was a Catholic, though for a provocative argument making a case for a "Catholic Shakespeare" (p. 126), see E. A. J. Honigmann, *Shakespeare: The "Lost Years"* (Manchester: Manchester Univ. Press, 1985).

25. D. R. Woolf, *The Idea of History in Early Stuart England* (Toronto: Univ. of Toronto Press, 1990), p. 109. The two parts of Hayward's *Life and Raigne of King Henrie IIII* have recently been published by the Camden Society, ed. John J. Manning (London: Royal Historical Society, 1991), and the quoted material is on pp. 90–91. For an account of the association of Lollards with sedition, see Margaret Aston's "Lollardy and Sedition 1381–1431," *Past and Present* 17 (1960): 1–44.

26. Quoted in John Booty, "Tumult in Cheapside: The Hacket Conspiracy," *Historical Magazine of the Protestant Episcopal Church* 42 (1973): 293.

27. "That Fraunces Johnson For His Writing Is Not Under The Danger Of The Statute Of 35 Elizabeth, Chapter I . . .", in *The Writings of John Greenwood and Henry Barrow*, ed. Leland H. Carlson (London: George Allen and Unwin, 1970), p. 463. An incomplete version of the document (Lansdowne MSS. 75, item 25, ff. 52–53) appears in John Strype, *Annals of the Reformation* (Oxford: Clarendon Press, 1824), vol. 4, pp. 192–94.

28. See J. E. Neale, *Elizabeth I and her Parliaments 1584–1601* (New York: Norton, 1966), esp. pp. 58–83; and Patrick Collinson, "John Field and Elizabethan Puritanism," in *Godly People: Essays on English Protestantism and Puritanism* (London: Hambledon Press, 1983), pp. 335–70. The quotation from Elizabeth appears in Neale, p. 163.

29. Quoted in Patrick Collinson, *The Elizabethan Puritan Movement* (1967; rpt. Oxford: Clarendon Press, 1990), p. 388.

30. 35 Eliz. c. 1; in J.R. Tanner, *Tudor Constitutional Documents* (1922; Cambridge: rpt. Cambridge Univ. Press, 1951), pp. 197–200. Neale sees the harsh turn against the Protestant sectaries, equating schism with sedition, "as a revolution in parliamentary policy" accomplished by Whitgift and his party. See *Elizabeth I and her Parliaments, 1584–1601*, pp. 280–97.

31. *Church and People 1450–1660: The Triumph of the Laity in the English Church* (Glasgow: Fontana, 1976), p. 152. Nonetheless, if "further reformation of the Church of England was, for the moment, out of the question," we must recognize what Patrick Collinson has called "the paradox that the miscarriage of the further reformation coincided with the birth of the great age of puritan religious experience" (*The Elizabethan Puritan Movement*, p. 433).

32. Quoted in Neale, *Elizabeth I and her Parliaments*, vol. 2, p. 163. For a different account of Falstaff/Oldcastle's relation to contemporary religious anxieties, see Kristen Poole's "Saints

Alive! Falstaff, Martin Marprelate, and the Staging of Puritanism," *Shakespeare Quarterly* 46 (1995): 47–75.

33. Jonathan Goldberg, in his essay in *Reconfiguring the Renaissance*, similarly argues that the restoration of the name "Oldcastle" works to "remove the traces of the history that produced the earliest texts of *1 Henry IV*" (p. 83).

34. "The Theory of the Text," in *Untying the Text: A Post-Structural Reader*, ed. Robert Young (Boston and London: Routledge, 1981), p. 39.

35. In this regard it is notably different from the expurgation of profanity in the folio text. The uncensored forms exist in the 1598 quarto as readings that can be *restored*.

36. James Thorpe, in a seminal essay, "The Aesthetics of Textual Criticism," *PMLA* 80 (1965): 465–82, argued that in every work of art "the intentions of the person we call the author . . . become entangled with the intentions of all the others who have a stake in the outcome." Jerome J. McGann offers perhaps the most influential and sustained account of the literary text as a "social product," first in *A Critique of Modern Textual Criticism* (Chicago: Univ. of Chicago Press, 1983) and later in his *The Textual Condition* (Princeton: Princeton Univ. Press, 1991). See, however, the essay by G. Thomas Tanselle, "Historicism and Critical Editing," *Studies in Bibliography* 39 (1986): 1–46, esp. pp. 20–27.

37. See G. Thomas Tanselle, "The Editorial Problem of Final Authorial Intention," *Studies in Bibliography* 32 (1979): 309–54.

38. Gary Taylor and John Jowett, *Shakespeare Reshaped: 1606–1623* (Oxford: Clarendon Press, 1993), p. 237.

39. Gary Taylor, *Reinventing Shakespeare: A Cultural History from the Restoration to the Present* (New York: Weidenfeld & Nicolson, 1989), p. 311.

40. It is worth wondering about how much weight to attach to Rowe's "confirmation." Rowe follows Richard Davies in recording the apocryphal story about Shakespeare's "frequent practice of Deer-stealing" in "a Park that belong'd to Sir *Thomas Lucy* of *Cherlecot*"; and the very passage that comments on the alteration of the name of "Oldcastle" includes the probably fanciful account, derived from John Dennis, of Queen Elizabeth's delight with the "Character of Falstaff" and her order to Shakespeare to write "one Play more, and to shew him in Love" ("Some Account of the Life, &c. of Mr. William Shakespear," *Works*, vol. 1, pp. v, viii–ix).

41. T. H. Howard-Hill has claimed, for example, that Tilney's "relationship with the players although ultimately authoritarian was more collegial than adversarial," in "Buc and the Censorship of *Sir John Olden Barnavelt* in 1619," *RES*, n.s. 39 (1988): 43. For a full account of the mechanisms of dramatic censorship, see Richard Dutton, *Mastering the Revels: The Regulation and Censorship of English Renaissance Drama* (Iowa City: Univ. of Iowa Press, 1991). See also Annabel Patterson, *Censorship and Interpretation; The Conditions of Writing and Reading in Early Modern England* (Madison: Univ. of Wisconsin Press, 1984), who, while less interested in the processes of control than in its effects, sees the necessity for "assuming some degree of cooperation and understanding on the part of the authorities themselves" (p. 11); and Janet Clare, "*Art made tongue-tied by authority*" : *Elizabethan and Jacobean Dramatic Censorship* (Manchester and New York: Univ. of Manchester Press, 1990), who similarly understands that censorship "is perhaps the most potent external force which interacts with the creative consciousness" (p. 215).

42. Gerald Bentley writes: "Falstaff was clearly most famous of all the characters of Shakespeare and Jonson in the seventeenth century. This fact ought to surprise no reader familiar with the literature of the time, but the overwhelming dominance of his position has perhaps not been so obvious." *Shakespeare and Jonson: Their Reputations in the Seventeenth Century Compared* (1945; rpt. Chicago and London: Univ. of Chicago Press, 1969), vol. 1, p. 119; see also pp. 120 and 126.

43. Thomas Palmer, "Master John Fletcher his dramaticall Workes now at last printed," in *Comedies and Tragedies, written by Francis Beaumont and John Fletcher, Gentlemen* (London, 1647), sig. f2^{v}.

44. "Upon Master William Shakespeare, the Deceased Authour, and his Poems," in *Poems. written by Wil. Shake-speare. Gent.* (London, 1640), sig.*4^{r}.

45. Joseph Quincy Adams, ed., *The Dramatic Records of Sir Henry Herbert, 1623–1673* (New Haven: Yale Univ. Press, 1917), p. 52. That this was not an entirely anomalous practice is revealed by a notation on a scrap of paper from the Revels Office that has been dated *ca.* 1619: "nd part of Falstaff . . ." See Bentley, *Shakespeare and Jonson*, vol. 2, p. 1.

46. "To the great Variety of Readers," *The Norton Facsimile: The First Folio of Shakespeare*, ed. Charlton Hinman (New York: Norton, 1968), p. 7.

Chapter 6

1. Freud, *Wit and its Relation to the Unconscious*, in *The Basic Writings of Sigmund Freud*, ed. A. A. Brill (New York: Random House, 1938), p. 650.

2. Pauline Gregg, *King Charles I* (Berkeley and Los Angeles: Univ. of California Press, 1981), p. 444.

3. *The Political Works of James I*, ed. Charles Howard McIlwain (Cambridge, Mass.: Harvard Univ. Press, 1918), p. 12

4. Gregg, *King Charles I*, pp. 437–40.

5. "Venetian Ambassador at Munster to the Doge and Senate, 26 February 1649," in *The Puritan Revolution: A Documentary History*, ed. Stuart E. Prall (London: Routledge and Kegan Paul, 1969), p. 193.

6. Quoted in Perez Zagorin, *The Court and the Country: The Beginning of The English Revolution* (New York: Atheneum, 1970), p. 312.

7. "The Sentence of the High Court of Justice Upon the King [27 January 1649]," in *The Puritan Revolution: A Documentary History*, p. 192.

8. E. M. W. Tillyard, *Shakespeare's History Plays* (London: Chatto & Windus, 1944); and Stephen Greenblatt, "Invisible Bullets," *Shakespearean Negotiations: The Circulation of Social Energy in Renaissance England* (Berkeley: Univ. of California Press, 1988), pp. 21–65; this influential piece was first published in *Glyph* 8 (1981): 40–61. For an important challenge to the assumptions of both Tillyard and Greenblatt about the functioning of the popular theater and royal spectacle, however, see the suggestive essay of Franco Moretti, "'A Huge Eclipse': Tragic Form and the Deconsecration of Sovereignty," in *The Power of Forms in the English Renaissance*, ed. Stephen Greenblatt (Norman: Pilgrim Books, 1982), pp. 7–40; see also Christopher Pye, "The Sovereign, the Theater, and the Kingdome of Darknesse: Hobbes and the Spectacle of Power," *Representations* 8 (1984): 85–106.

9. See Jonas A. Barish, *The Antitheatrical Prejudice* (Berkeley: Univ. of California Press, 1981), esp. pp. 80–131. The case demonstrating the inadequacy of the label "Puritan" for all antitheatrical sentiment is well made in Margot Heinemann's *Puritanism and Theatre: Thomas Middleton and Opposition Drama under the Early Stuarts* (Cambridge: Cambridge University Press, 1980), pp. 18–48. Also see below, pp. 202–3.

10. Phillip Stubbes, *The Anatomie of Abuses* (London, 1583), sig. H2^v.

11. *Histrio-Mastix* (London, 1633) sig. X2^r.

12. Stubbes, *The Anatomie of Abuses*, "A Preface to the Reader," does recognize "some kind of playes, tragedies and enturluds," as being "very honest and very commendable exercyses."

13. *Records of Early English Drama: Chester*, ed. Lawrence M. Clopper (Toronto and Buffalo: Univ. of Toronto Press, 1979), p. 247.

14. Quoted in Harold C. Gardiner, *Mysteries' End* (New Haven: Yale Univ. Press, 1946), p. 78. See also Michael O'Connell's suggestive essay, "The Idolatrous Eye: Iconoclasm, Antitheatricalism, and the Image of the Elizabethan Theater," *ELH* 52 (1985): 279–310.

15. Quoted in *The Elizabethan Stage*, ed. E. K. Chambers (Oxford: Oxford Univ. Press, 1923), vol. 2, p. 75.

16. *The Elizabethan Stage*, vol. 2, p. 419.

17. *Tudor Royal Proclamations: The Later Tudors*, ed. Paul L. Hughes and James F. Larkin (New Haven: Yale Univ. Press, 1969), vol. 2, p. 240–41.

18. *Acts of the Privy Council of England: 1596–7* (London: Mackie and Co., 1902), pp. 26, 69.

19. Roy C. Strong, *Portraits of Queen Elizabeth I* (Oxford: Clarendon Press, 1963); and Marianna Jenkins, "The State Portrait, Its Origin and Evolution," *Monographs on Archeology and Fine Arts* 3 (1947): 23–24.

20. *The Elizabethan Stage*, vol. 4, p. 247.

21. Quoted in Virginia Crocheron Gildersleeve, *Government Regulation of the Elizabethan Drama* (New York: Columbia Univ. Press, 1908), p. 119.

22. *Collections, Part III* (Oxford: Malone Society, 1909), p. 263.

23. *Vox Regis* (London, 1622), pp. 34–35.

24. This paragraph is indebted to David Bevington, *Tudor Drama and Politics* (Cambridge, Mass: Harvard Univ. Press, 1968), p. 9. He quotes all three examples that I use here, though I have used additional material from Rowland White's letter to Sir Robert Sidney, 22 November 1595, in *Letters and Memorials of State . . . Written and Collected by Sir Henry Sidney, Sir Philip Sidney, Robert Earl of Leicester, and Viscount Lisle,* ed. Arthur Collins (London, 1746), vol. 1, p. 362.

25. Bevington, *Tudor Drama and Politics, passim.* For the politics of Stuart drama, see Martin Butler, *Theater and Crisis 1632–1642* (Cambridge: Cambridge Univ. Press, 1984); and Albert H. Tricomi, *Anti-Court Drama in England, 1603–1642* (Charlottesville: Univ. Press of Virginia, 1989).

26. *Apology for Actors* (London, 1612), sig. F3^v.

27. *The Elizabethan Stage*, vol. 4, p. 321.

28. Stephen Gosson, *Playes Confuted in Fiue Actions* (London, 1582), sig. E5^r.

29. *The Elizabethan Stage*, vol. 4, p. 258.

30. *The Education of a Christian Prince*, ed. Lester K. Born (New York: Columbia Univ. Press, 1936), p. 152.

31. See Jonas A. Barish, "*Perkin Warbeck* as Anti-History," *Essays in Criticism* 20 (1970): 151–171; and Jackson I. Cope, *The Theater and the Dream: From Metaphor to Form in Renaissance Drama* (Baltimore and London: The Johns Hopkins Univ. Press, 1973), pp. 122–33.

32. See chapter 7 notes, pp. 239–42.

33. Richard Bancroft, *Daungerous Positions and Proceedings* (London, 1593), sig. E3^{v}.

34. *Fragmenta Regalia*, ed. John C. Cerovski (Washington, D.C.: Folger Shakespeare Library, 1985), p. 44.

35. In *Elizabethan Backgrounds: Historical Documents of the Age of Elizabeth I*, ed. Arthur F. Kinney (Hamden: Archon Books, 1975), p. 16. On royal entries, see R. M. Smuts, "Public ceremony and royal display: the English royal entry in London, 1485–1642," in *The First Modern Society: Essays in English History in Honour of Lawrence Stone*, ed. A. L. Beier, David Cannadine, and James M. Rosenheim (Cambridge: Cambridge Univ. Press, 1989), pp. 65–94. For a suggestive analysis of Elizabeth's entry see Mark Breitenberg, "' . . . the hole matter opened': Iconic Representation and Interpretation in 'the Quenes Majesties Passage,'" *Criticism* 28 (1986): 1–26.

36. See Stephen Orgel, *The Illusion of Power: Political Theater in the English Renaissance* (Berkeley: Univ. of California Press, 1975); and Roy Strong, *Art and Power: Renaissance Festivals 1450–1650* (Berkeley and Los Angeles: Univ. of California Press, 1984).

37. "Invisible Bullets," *Shakespearean Negotiations*, p. 64.

38. *The Elizabethan Stage,* vol. 4, p. 263.

39. *The Quene's Majesty's Passage,* in *Elizabethan Backgrounds*, ed. Kinney, p. 37.

40. *Plays Confuted in Fiue Actions*, sig. D1^{r}. Ann Jennalie Cook has argued, in her *The Privileged Playgoers of Shakespeare's London* (Princeton: Princeton Univ. Press, 1981), that the audience of Shakespeare's theater was drawn mainly "from the upper levels of the social order"; but see appendix 2 of Martin Butler's *Theater and Crisis 1632–1642*, pp. 293–306, which effectively challenges Cook's conclusions. See also Cook's recent reconsideration, "Audiences: Investigation, Interpretation, Inventions," in *A New History of Early English Drama*, ed. John D. Cox and David Scott Kastan (New York: Columbia Univ. Press, 1997), pp. 305–20.

41. *The Gull's Hornbook*, in *Thomas Dekker: Selected Writings*, ed. E. D. Pendry (Cambridge, Mass: Harvard Univ. Press, 1968), p. 98.

42. Robert Weimann, *Shakespeare and the Popular Tradition in the Theater*, ed. Robert Schwartz (Baltimore and London: The Johns Hopkins Univ. Press, 1978), pp. 208–52.

43. Quoted in the Arden *King Richard II,* ed. Peter Ure (London: Methuen, 1954), p. lix.

44. Stephen Orgel, "Making Greatness Familiar," *The Power of Forms in the English Renaissance*, ed. Stephen Greenblatt (Norman: Pilgrim Books, 1982), p. 45.

45. William Camden, *The History of . . . Elizabeth, Late Queen of England* (London, 1688), pp. 607–8.

46. Camden, *The History of . . . Elizabeth*, pp. 610, 609, 606.

47. Quoted in Corinne Comstock Weston and Janelle Renfrow Greenberg, *Subjects and Sovereigns: The Grand Controversy over Legal Sovereignty in Stuart England* (Cambridge: Cambridge Univ. Press, 1981), p. 8.

48. Alvin Kernan, "The Henriad: Shakespeare's History Plays," in *Modern Shakespearean Criticism*, ed. Alvin Kernan (New York: Harcourt, Brace and World, 1970), p. 245. See also my "'To Set a Form upon that Indigest': Shakespeare's Fictions of History," *Comparative Drama* 17 (1983): 1–15, from which I have borrowed a few phrases.

49. *The Life and Letters of Sir Henry Wotton*, ed. L. Pearsall Smith (Oxford: Oxford Univ. Press, 1907), vol. 1, p. 350.

50. For provocative accounts of Spenser's complex relation with Elizabeth, see Louis Adrian Montrose, "The Elizabethan Subject and the Spenserian Text," in *Literary Theory/Renaissance Texts*, ed. Patricia Parker and David Quint (Baltimore and London: The Johns Hopkins

Univ. Press, 1986), pp. 303–40; and Richard Helgerson, *Self-Crowned Laureates: Spenser, Jonson, Milton, and the Literary System* (Berkeley, Los Angeles, and London: Univ. of California Press, 1983), pp. 55–100. Frank Whigham, in his *Ambition and Privilege: The Social Tropes of Elizabethan Courtesy Theory* (Berkeley, Los Angeles, and London: Univ. of California Press, 1984), provides an interesting analysis of the tensions and anxieties of the Elizabethan courtier.

51. "Invisible Bullets," *Shakespearean Negotiations*, pp. 53, 65.

52. "Making Greatness Familiar," p. 45. Greenblatt, however, sensitive to the charge of totalization, has, as his work developed, notably shifted his understanding of culture from one structured by a Foucauldian notion of power inhabiting all social relations to one shaped by the "the circulation of social energy" (the subtitle of *Shakespearean Negotiations*), which produces not "a single, coherent, totalizing system" but one that is "partial, fragmentary, conflictual" (p. 19).

53. *King Richard II*, ed. Peter Ure, p. ix.

54. "Calendar of the Contents of the *Baga de Secretis*," in *Fourth Report of the Deputy Keeper of the Public Records*, Appendix II, (London, 1843), p. 293.

55. See John Bellamy, *The Tudor Law of Treason: An Introduction* (London: Routledge and Kegan Paul, 1979), esp. pp. 30–33.

56. In *Apophthegms New and Old*, in *The Works of Francis Bacon*, ed. James Spedding, Robert Leslie Ellis, and Douglas Denon Heath (Boston: Brown and Taggard, 1860), p. 341. As Jonathan Dollimore writes, in his *Radical Tragedy: Ideology and Power in the Drama of Shakespeare and his Contemporaries* (Chicago: Univ. of Chicago Press, 1984), "what makes an idea subversive is not so much what is intrinsic to it or the mere thinking of it, but the context of its articulation–to whom, and to how many and in what circumstances it is said and written" (p. 10). It was precisely on these grounds that Hayward was found guilty. See Annabel Patterson, *Censorship and Interpretation: The Conditions of Writing and Reading in Early Modern England* (Madison: Univ. of Wisconsin Press, 1984), esp. pp. 44–48.

57. Martin Butler, in his rejection of Ann Jennalie Cook's assertion of an audience of "privileged playgoers" (see fn. 40), not only cites the numerous references to "unprivileged" playgoers by contemporary theatergoers, but also challenges Cook's statistical analyses. For Butler, "the ratio between population and theater capacity seems to point in the opposite direction from Cook's conclusions, towards inclusiveness rather than exclusiveness" (p. 298).

58. See Stephen Mullaney's *The Place of the Stage: License, Play, and Power in Renaissance England* (Chicago: Univ. of Chicago Press, 1988); and Louis Montrose, *The Purpose of Playing: Shakespeare and the Cultural Politics of the Elizabethan Theatre* (Chicago: Univ. of Chicago Press, 1996), esp. pp. 19–108. Montrose had anticipated some of this work in his groundbreaking essay, "The Purpose of Playing: Reflections on a Shakespearean Anthropology," *Helios* n.s. 7 (1980): 53–76.

59. *The Elizabethan Stage*, vol. 3, p. 500. Stephen Orgel, in "Making Greatness Familiar," calls attention to the implications of Venner's notorious fraud which, he says, "actualizes one of the deepest corporate fantasies of the Elizabethan theater and its audience" (p. 46).

Chapter 7

1. Lily B. Campbell, in her *Shakespeare's "Histories": Mirrors of Elizabethan Policy* (1947; rpt. London: Methuen, 1970), provocatively called attention to the ways in which Shakespeare's

presentation of the events of the reign of Henry IV necessarily recalled for "an English audience of the last years of the sixteenth century" recent English history and contemporary concerns (pp. 229–44). While her sense of the political meanings of Shakespeare's play seems to me unduly prescriptive, her reconstruction of the contemporary resonances of the events of the reign of Henry IV provides a useful corrective to almost exclusive focus of more recent historicist critics on the parallel provided by Elizabeth's notorious "I am Richard II, know ye not that?"

2. Recently, a number of studies of English colonialism have insisted that "the cultural products which celebrated the supremacy of Englishness were based upon difference and discrimination and ensure that the positional superiority of the English was produced through the 'otherness' and inferiority of alien people of which the Irish were one." See, for example, David Cairns and Shaun Richards, *Writing Ireland: Colonialism, Nationalism and Culture* (Manchester: Manchester Univ. Press, 1988), p. 7.

3. For extensive discussion of these mythological identifications, see Elkin Calhoun Wilson, *England's Eliza* (Cambridge, Mass.: Harvard Univ. Press, 1939), as well as Frances A. Yates, *Astraea: The Imperial Theme in the Sixteenth Century* (London: Routledge and Kegan Paul, 1975), pp. 88–111.

4. *The Works in Verse and Prose of Nicholas Breton,* ed. Alexander B. Grosart (London: Edinburgh Univ. Press, 1879), vol. 2, n.p.

5. Thomas Fuller, *Worthies of England,* ed. John Freeman (London: George Unwin, 1952), p. 408.

6. Stephen J. Greenblatt, *Shakespearean Negotiations: The Circulation of Social Energy in Renaissance England* (Berkeley: Univ. of California Press, 1988), p. 30. See also C. L. Barber's argument, in his *Shakespeare's Festive Comedies* (Princeton: Princeton Univ. Press, 1952) that "misrule works . . . to consolidate rule" (p. 205) and Leonard Tennenhouse's assertion, in *Power on Display: The Politics of Shakespeare's Genres* (New York and London: Methuen, 1986) that in the history plays "the figures of carnival will play a particularly instrumental role in the idealizing process that proves so crucial in legitimizing political power" (p. 83).

7. Roy Strong, *Splendour at Court: Renaissance Spectacle and the Theater of Power* (Boston: Houghton Mifflin, 1973). Among the fine studies of the politics of early modern spectacle are Sydney Anglo, *Spectacle, Pageantry, and Early Tudor Policy* (Oxford: Oxford Univ. Press, 1969); David Bergeron's *English Civic Pageantry, 1558–1642* (Columbia and London: Univ. of South Carolina Press, 1971); Stephen Orgel, *The Illusion of Power: Political Theater in the English Renaissance* (Berkeley and London: Univ. of California Press, 173); and Graham Parry, *The Golden Age Restor'd: The Culture of the Stuart Court* (Manchester: Manchester Univ. Press, 1981).

8. It is important to note, however, that Greenblatt, in the various revisions of his argument, has gradually modified his sense of the unity and stability of early modern England. The diverse cultural activity which once seemed to him to be part of an irresistible strategy of ideological reproduction has come to seem more clearly marked by stresses and conflict: "Even those literary texts that sought most ardently to speak for monolithic power could be shown to be the sites of institutional and ideological contestation" (*Shakespearean Negotiations,* p. 3). Nonetheless, his phrase, "could be shown," does perhaps reveal some lingering doubt about the possibilities of actual resistance or subversion.

9. Robert Weimann, *Shakespeare and the Popular Tradition in the Theater,* ed. Robert Schwartz (Baltimore and London: The Johns Hopkins Univ. Press, 1978), pp. 208–55.

10. Mikhail Bakhtin, *Rabelais and his World,* trans. Hélène Iswolsky (Bloomington: Indiana Univ. Press, 1984), p. 465.

11. *Miscellaneous Prose of Sir Philip Sidney,* ed. Katherine Duncan-Jones and J. A. Van Dorsten (Oxford: Oxford Univ. Press, 1973), p. 114.

12. *The Poems of Joseph Hall*, ed. Arnold Davenport (Liverpool: Liverpool Univ. Press, 1969), p. 5.

13. Edward Forset, *A Comparative Discourse of the Bodies Natural and Politique* (London, 1606), sig. E1^r.

14. Thomas Hobbes, *Leviathan*, ed. Michael Oakeshott (New York: Collier, 1962), p. 129. Christopher Pye has provocatively used Hobbes to consider the nature of political and theatrical representation in the Renaissance, finding in Hobbes's account of the constitution of sovereignty a means to explore "the vulnerability and the terrifying power of the monarch's visible presence." See his *The Regal Phantasm: Shakespeare and the Politics of Spectacle* (London and New York: Routledge, 1989), esp. pp. 43–81. See also chapter 6, above.

15. Pye, *The Regal Phantasm: Shakespeare and the Politics of Spectacle*, p. 43.

16. Sidney, *Miscellaneous Prose*, p. 52.

17. Raphael Holinshed, *The First and Second Volumes of Chronicles* (London, 1586), sig. Eee2^r.

18. Jacques Derrida, *Margins of Philosophy*, trans. Alan Bass (Chicago: Univ. of Chicago Press, 1982), p. 241.

19. Hobbes, *Leviathan*, p. 125.

20. *Political Works of James I*, ed. C. E. McIlwain (Cambridge, Mass.: Harvard Univ. Press, 1918), p. 3.

21. *Political Works of James I*, p. 69. On the theory of succession, see Howard Nennar, *The Right to be King: The Succession to the Crown of England* (Chapel Hill: Univ. of North Carolina Press, 1995), esp. pp. 1–71.

22. Jean Bodin, *The Six Bookes of a Commonweale*, trans. Richard Knolles (London, 1606), sig. E6^r.

23. *Political Works of James I*, pp. 61–62.

24. *Leviathan*, p. 506.

25. William Segar, *Honor, Military and Ciuill, contained in foure Bookes* (London, 1602), sig. S6^r.

26. ". . . *si un homme qui se croit un roi est fou, un roi qui se croit un roi ne l'est pas moins*," in Jacques Lacan, *Ecrits* (Paris: Editions du Seuil, 1966), p. 170. See also the discussion by Slavoj Žižek, in *The Sublime Object of Ideology* (London and New York: Verso, 1989), who invokes Lacan in considering the "fetishistic misrecognition" by both king and subject that "the king is already in himself, outside the relationship to his subjects" (p. 25).

27. Raymond Williams, *Writing in Society* (London: Verso, 1984), p. 15.

28. George Puttenham, *The Art of English Poesie* (London, 1589), sig. X4^r. Sir Anthony Weldon claimed disparagingly in his "Court and Character of King James" that this, rather than the more familiar *Beati pacifici*, was actually the King's motto. See Sir Walter Scott, *The Secret History of James the First* (Edinburgh: J. Ballantyne, 1811), vol. 1, p. 421.

29. Mikhail Bakhtin, *Problems of Doestoevski's Poetics*, trans. Caryl Emerson (Minneapolis: Univ. of Minnesota Press, 1984), p. 318.

30. See David Wiles's excellent account of Falstaff and clowning, in his *Shakespeare's Clowns* (Cambridge: Cambridge Univ. Press, 1987), esp. pp. 116–35. Wiles argues that Falstaff's role "is structurally the clown's part" and that the part was written specifically for Kemp (p. 116). The epilogue or jig, Wiles sees, as part of a convention of clowning which when understood would force us "to discard the old critical notion of the unity of the text, and seek instead the unity of the theatrical experience" (p. 56). John Cox has also suggestively recognized Falstaff as the dramatic heir of the stage clown, particularly Tarlton. See his *Shakespeare and the Dramaturgy of Power* (Princeton: Princeton Univ. Press, 1989), pp. 121–24.

31. Richard Helgerson, *Forms of Nationhood: The Elizabethan Writing of England* (Chicago and London: Univ. of Chicago Press, 1992), p. 227.

32. Jean Bodin, *Six Bookes of a Commonweal*, trans. Richard Knolles (London, 1606), sig. Iii iii3^r; *Everyman Out of His Humor*, London, 1600), sig. E3^v; *The Poems of Sir John Davies*, ed. Robert Krueger (Oxford: Oxford Univ. Press, 1975), p. 136. The fullest account of the jig remains Charles Read Baskerville, *The Elizabethan Jig and Related Song Drama* (1929; rpt. New York: Dover, 1965).

33. *Middlesex County Records*, vol. 2, pp. 83–4. Quoted in Baskerville, *The Elizabethan Jig*, p. 116. It isn't entirely clear how effective this order was, though Shirley in 1632 has a character in his *Changes* say that many gentlemen "Are not, as in the dayes of understanding, / Now satisfied without a Iigge, which since / They cannot, with their honour, call for, after / The play, they looke to be serv'd up ith' middle" (sig. H2^{r-v}). Whether this means that it was illegal to do so or merely that it was considered socially inappropriate, certainly sometime in the 1630s the jig again became a familiar afterpiece of the popular drama.

Chapter 8

1. See, for example, the valuable discussions on the language of social ordering in early modern England by Peter Burke, "The Language of Orders in Early Modern Europe," *Social Orders and Social Classes in Europe Since 1500: Studies in Social Stratification*, ed. M. L. Bush (London and New York: Longman, 1992), pp. 1–12; David Cressy, "Describing the Social Order of Elizabethan and Stuart England," *Literature & History* 3 (1976): 29–44; and Keith Wrightson, "Estates, Degrees, and Sorts: Changing Perceptions of Society in Tudor and Stuart England," in *Language, History and Class*, ed. Penelope J. Corfield (Oxford: Blackwell, 1990), pp. 30–52.

2. Even beyond the question of the historical specificity of a notion of class, the issue of its conceptual availability is of consequence, because unlike the familiar (and obviously silly) argument about the applicability of Freudian concepts to people living before Freud, class, it could be argued, needs to be available within the cognitive system of the people as a condition of its existence. If there is such a thing as the unconscious, it exists with or without an individual's awareness of its existence; a class, however, may be said to exist not as an *a priori* category waiting to be filled but only when people discover themselves as a class. Among the many influential considerations of class consciousness, see Georg Lukács, *History and Class Consciousness*, trans. R. Livingstone (London: Merlin, 1971); *Aspects of History and Class Consciousness*, ed. István Mészáros (New York: Herder and Herder, 1972), esp. E.J. Hobsbawm's "Class Consciousness in History," pp. 85–127; and E. P. Thompson, "Eighteenth-Century English Society: Class Struggle without Class?," *Social History* 3 (1978): 133–65.

3. Even Marx is inconsistent in his usage, sometimes identifying class as a historically specific concept as in *The German Ideology*, ed. C. J. Arthur (London: Lawrence and Wishart, 1970), where the pre-industrial system of estates is contrasted with a true class system "which is itself a product of the *bourgeoisie*" (p. 87), while at other times using class as a universal category referring to discrete social groups in relations of domination and subjection, as in *Manifesto*, where notoriously "the history of class struggle" is identified as "the history of all hither-to existing society."

4. See Mary Jacobus's fine article, "Is There a Woman in This Text," *New Literary History* 14 (1982): 117–42. Jacobus's essay, like my own, obviously finds its title in a play upon Stanley Fish's *Is There a Text in this Class?: The Authority of Interpretive Communities* (Cambridge, Mass.: Harvard Univ. Press, 1980).

5. For a wonderfully rich account of the representation of popular energies on the

Shakespearean stage, see Annabel Patterson's *Shakespeare and the Popular Voice* (Oxford: Blackwell, 1989). But if Patterson effectively disrupts the elitist notions of both art and politics that have dominated the critical account of Shakespeare to reinstate the popular as a productive category and concern, she nonetheless largely ignores the mediations of the theater that permit the popular voice to be heard. Although she brilliantly recognizes the "ventriloquism" by which the popular voice speaks "through Shakespeare's playtext" (p. 50), she resists seeing this as the inescapable nature of class representation on the stage. Powerfully opposing the political and ethical implications of the claims for the autonomy of discourse made by various post-structuralisms, Patterson insists that "it does indeed matter . . . who speaks," and she notes that the plays are "obsessed" with "questions of voice (or political representation)" (p. 97). But dramatic representation is no less the issue. Patterson writes, for example, that *Coriolanus* "allows the people to speak *for themselves* as a political entity" (p. 127, emphasis hers), but if in the playtext they may speak "for themselves," in the playhouse actors always must speak for them.

6. E. K. Chambers, *The Elizabethan Stage* (Oxford: Oxford Univ. Press, 1923), vol. 3, p. 500.

7. There have been, of course, many influential studies of cross-dressing on the Elizabethan stage, but see especially, in this regard, Catherine Belsey, "Disrupting Sexual Difference: Meaning and Gender in the Comedies," *Alternative Shakespeares*, ed. John Drakakis (London: Methuen, 1985), pp. 166–90; Jean E. Howard, *The Stage and Social Struggle in Early Modern England* (London: Routledge, 1994), esp. pp. 93–128; Laura Levine, *Men in Women's Clothing: Antitheatricality and Effeminization, 1579–1642* (Cambridge: Cambridge Univ. Press, 1994); and Phyllis Rackin, "Androgyny, Mimesis, and the Marriage of the Boy Heroine on the English Renaissance Stage," *PMLA* 102 (1987): 29–41.

8. Howard, *The Stage and Social Struggle*, p. 95.

9. Phillip Stubbes, *The Anatomie of Abuses* (London, 1583), sig. C2^v.

10. On sumptuary legislation in early modern England, see N. B. Hart, "State Control of Dress and Social Change in Pre-Industrial England," in *Trade, Government and Economy in Pre-Industrial England*, ed. D. C. Coleman and A. H. John (London: Weidenfeld & Nicolson, 1976), pp. 132–65; and two useful earlier studies: Wilfrid Hooper, "The Tudor Sumptuary Laws," *English Historical Review* 30 (1915): 433–49; and Frances Elizabeth Baldwin, *Sumptuary Legislation and Personal Regulation in England* (Baltimore: The Johns Hopkins Univ. Press, 1926). The quotation comes from a proclamation of 6 July 1597, in *Tudor Royal Proclamations*, ed. Paul L. Hughes and James F. Larkin (New Haven and London: Yale Univ. Press, 1969), vol. 3, p. 175.

11. Hughes and Larkin, *Tudor Royal Proclamations*, vol. 2, p. 136.

12. William Perkins, *The Whole Treatise of the Cases of Conscience* (Cambridge, 1608), sig. GG2^v.

13. Stephen Gosson, *Playes Confuted in Fiue Actions* (London, 1582), sig. G7^v.

14. Fynes Moryson, *An Itinerary* (1617; Glasgow: Maclehose, 1907), vol. 4, p. 233–34.

15. For example, in *1 Henry VIII.* c. 14. "Players in enterludes," along with "ambassatures Hencemen," "Harroldes of armes," "Mynstrelles," and men "weryng any apparrell of the Kyngs lyverey geven hym by the King, for the tyme beyng of his Attendance aboute the Kyngs Grace" are specifically exempted from the act's provisions. In Elizabethan England, however, dispensations again are made to "henchmen, heralds, pursuivants at arms, runners at jousts, tourneys, or such martial feats, or such as wear apparel given by the Queen's majesty" (*Tudor Royal Proclamations*, vol. 3, p. 180), but the specific dispensation for players has disappeared.

16. Philip Henslowe, *Diary*, ed. R. A. Foakes and R. T. Rickert (Cambridge: Cambridge Univ. Press, 1961), pp. 291–92.

17. *Tudor Royal Proclamations*, 3, 176)

18. William Rankins, *A Mirrour of Monsters* (London, 1587), sig. C3^r.

19. Stephen Greenblatt, *Shakespearean Negotiations: The Circulation of Social Energy in Renaissance England* (Berkeley: Univ. of California Press, 1988), p. 88.

20. Jonas A. Barish, "The Antitheatrical Prejudice," *Critical Quarterly* 8 (1966): 331.

21. Sir Walter Ralegh, *Selected Writings*, ed. Gerald Hammond (Harmondsworth: Penguin, 1986), p. 147.

22. Among the many useful studies of the status of players in Elizabethan England, see Jean-Christophe Agnew, *Worlds Apart: The Market and the Theatre in Anglo-American Thought, 1550–1700* (Cambridge: Cambridge Univ. Press, 1986), pp. 101–48; M. C. Bradbrook, *The Rise of the Common Player: A Study of the Actor and Society in Shakespeare's England* (Cambridge, Mass.: Harvard Univ. Press, 1964), pp. 17–66; and Philip Edwards, *Threshold of a Nation: A Study of English and Irish Drama* (Cambridge: Cambridge Univ. Press, 1979), pp. 17–39.

23. Chambers, *The Elizabethan Stage*, vol. 4, pp. 204, 197.

24. Ibid., 269.

25. Gamaliel Ratsey, *Ratseis Ghost* (London, 1605), sig. A4^r.

26. For a full account of the specificities surrounding the grant of arms, see S. Schoenbaum, *William Shakespeare: A Documentary Life* (New York: Oxford Univ. Press, 1975), pp. 167–73.

27. Chambers, *The Elizabethan Stage*, vol. 4, p. 269–70.

28. *Malone Society Collections* 1, pts. 4 & 5, ed. W. W. Greg (Oxford: Oxford Univ. Press, 1911), pp. 348–49.

29. Chambers, *The Elizabethan Stage*, vol. 4, p. 256. On the theater as "a proxy form of the new but partly fathomable relations of a nascent market society," see Agnew, *Worlds Apart* (pp. 1–148, quotation, p. 11); and Kathleen E. McLuskie, who suggestively argues that the complex shift from patronage to commerce, a shift for the drama from "use value to exchange value," was "often confused with a shift from élite to popular culture," in her "The Poets' Royal Exchange: Patronage and Commerce in Early Modern Drama," in *Patronage, Politics, and Literary Traditions in England, 1558–1658*, ed. Cedric C. Brown (Detroit: Wayne State Univ. Press, 1991), pp. 125–34, quotation, p. 127.

30. Ibid., 299.

31. Ibid., 300.

32. Ibid., 237.

33. Ibid., 276.

34. Ibid., 200.

35. [Anthony Munday], *A Second and Third Blast of Retrait from Plaies and Theaters* (London, 1580), sig. H7^{r-v}; see also William Prynne, *Histrio-Mastix* (London, 1633), sig. X3^r.

36. Quoted in Bradbrook, *The Rise of the Common Player*, p. 95.

37. Quoted in David Mann, *The Elizabethan Player: Contemporary Stage Representations* (London: Routledge, 1991), p. 97.

38. Chambers, *The Elizabethan Stage*, vol. 4, pp. 198–99.

39. Quoted in Andrew Gurr, *The Shakespearean Stage, 1574–1642*, 3rd ed. (Cambridge: Cambridge Univ. Press, 1992), p. 132; *Annales* (London, 1631), p. 1004.

40. Fynes Moryson, *Shakespeare's Europe . . . Being Unpublished Chapters of Fynes Moryson's "Itinerary,"* ed. Charles Hughes (New York: Blom, 1967), p. 476.

41. Robert Greene, *Greenes Neuer Too Late: or, a Powder of Experience sent to all youthfull Gentlemen* (London, 1590), sig. I4^r.

42. Chambers, *The Elizabethan Stage*, vol. 2, pp. 208–9.

43. Chambers, *The Elizabethan Stage*, vol. 4, p. 255.

44. *Acts and Ordinances of the Interregnum, 1642–1660*, ed. C. H. Firth and R. S. Rait (London: HMSO, 1911), p. 1070.

45. For a full discussion of the closing, see chapter 11 below.

46. *A Groats-worth of Witte*, ed. G. B. Harrison (New York: Barnes and Noble, 1966), p. 33.

47. Stephen Gosson, *The S[c]hoole of Abuse, Conteining a Pleasaunt Inuectiue against Poets, Pipes, Plaiers, Iesters, and such like Caterpillers of a Commonwealth* (London, 1579), sig. C6^r.

48. *Thomas Platter's Travels in England, 1599*, trans. Clare Williams (London: Cape, 1937), p. 167. For another account of a gift of clothing to players, see Henry Herbert's report that "many rich clothes were given" to a troupe of French actors in 1635 in *The Dramatic Records of Sir Henry Herbert, Master of the Revels, 1623–1673*, ed. Joseph Quincey Adams (New Haven: Yale Univ. Press, 1917), p. 61. See also *The Earl of Strafforde's Letters and Dispatches*, ed. William Knowler (London, 1739), vol. 2, p. 150.

49. *Documents Relating to the Office of the Revels in the Time of Queen Elizabeth*, ed. Albert Feuillerat (Louvain Uystpruyst, 1908), pp. 21–28.

50. *Documents*, ed. Feuillerat, pp. 409–10.

51. See, for example, the agreement between Henslowe and the actor, Robert Davies in *Henslowe Papers, Being Documents Supplementary to Henslowe's Diary*, ed. W. W. Greg (London: Bullen, 1907), p. 125.

52. See, for example, the excellent account by William Carroll, in his *Fat King, Lean Beggar: Representations of Poverty in the Age of Shakespeare* (Ithaca and London: Cornell Univ. Press, 1996), esp. pp. 180–207.

53. In *Rogues, Vagabonds, and Sturdy Beggars*, ed. Arthur F. Kinney (Amherst: Univ. of Massachusetts Press, 1990), p. 91.

54. Agnew, *Worlds Apart*, pp. 63–69, 125–35.

55. *Tudor Royal Proclamations*, vol. 3, p. 196.

56. Quoted in James Winny, *The Frame of Order* (Folcroft: Folcroft, 1969), p.106.

57. On the social dislocation in the play, see Raman Selden, "King Lear and True Need," *Shakespeare Studies* 19 (1988): 143–70; Judy Kronenfeld, "'So distribution should undo excess, and each man have enough': Shakespeare's *King Lear*–Anabaptist Egalitarianism, Anglican charity; Both, Neither?," *ELH* 59 (1992): 755–84; and Daniel Vitkus's as yet unpublished paper, "Poverty and Ideology in *King Lear*."

58. Jonathan Dollimore, *Radical Tragedy: Religion, Ideology, and Power in the Drama of Shakespeare and his Contemporaries* (Chicago: Univ. of Chicago Press, 1984), p. 191.

Chapter 9

1. Lawrence Danson, *Tragic Alphabet: Shakespeare's Drama of Language* (New Haven: Yale Univ. Press, 1974), p. 141.

2. Leonard Tennenhouse, *Power on Display: The Politics of Shakespeare's Genres* (New York and London: Methuen, 1986), p. 132.

3. Marilyn L. Williamson, "Violence and Gender Ideology in *Coriolanus* and *Macbeth*," in *Shakespeare Left and Right*, ed. Ivo Kamps (New York and London: Routledge, 1991), p. 150.

4. *Characters of Shakespear's Plays* (1817; rpr. London: Dent, 1969), p. 191.

5. "Speculations: *Macbeth* and Source," in *Reproducing Shakespeare*, ed. Jean E. Howard and Marion F. O'Connor (London: Methuen, 1987), p. 249.

6. Jonathan Goldberg, "Speculations: *Macbeth* and Source"; Harry Berger, Jr., "The Early Scenes of *Macbeth*: Preface to a New Interpretation," *ELH* 47 (1980): 1–31; rpt. in *Making Trifles of Terrors: Redistributing Complicities in Shakespeare* (Stanford: Stanford Univ. Press, 1997), pp. 70–97; Alan Sinfield, "*Macbeth*: History, Ideology and Intellectuals," *Critical Quarterly* 28 (1986); rpt. in *Faultlines: Cultural Materialism and the Politics of Dissident Reading* (Berkeley: Univ. of California Press, 1992), pp. 95–108; David Norbrook, "*Macbeth* and the Politics of Historiography," in *Politics of Discourse: The Literature and History of Seventeenth-Century England*, ed. Kevin Sharpe and Stephen N. Zwicker (Berkeley and Los Angeles: Univ. of California Press, 1987), pp. 78–116.

7. Berger, "The Early Scenes of *Macbeth*: Preface to a New Interpretation"; see also Stephen Booth, *King Lear, Macbeth, Indefinition, and Tragedy* (New Haven and London: Yale Univ. Press, 1983), pp. 96–101.

8. Edmund Malone, "An Attempt to Ascertain the Order in which the Plays of Shakespeare were Written," in *The Plays of William Shakespeare*, (London, 1778), vol. 1, p. 324.

9. E. B. Lyle, "The 'Twofold Balls and Treble Scepters' in *Macbeth*," *Shakespeare Quarterly* 28 (1977): 516–19.

10. *Power on Display*, p. 131.

11. See *The Chronicles of Scotland, compiled by Hector Boece*, trans. into Scots by John Bellendon (1531) and ed. Edith C. Batho and H. Winifred Husbands (Edinburgh: William Blackwood and Sons, 1941), vol. 2, pp. 154–5. On the use of fictional "history" to underpin the Scottish monarchy, see Colin Kidd, *Subverting Scotland's Past: Scottish Whig Historians and the Creation of an Anglo-British Identity, 1689–c. 1830* (Cambridge: Cambridge Univ. Press, 1993), esp. pp. 18–23.

12. George Buchanan, *The History of Scotland* (London, 1690), sig. Qq3^r.

13. Arthur Kinney, in one of several interesting essays on the historical contexts of the play, discusses this show, though he assumes that the eighth "King" must have been James himself, remarking this "singularly striking moment . . . when . . . suddenly the representation of the audience's own king appears on stage." It is unlikely that the eighth monarch in the show would be explicitly identified as James; such representation would be prohibited, and, in any case, James was the ninth of the Stewarts. It is, of course, possible that Mary, actually the eighth monarch in the Stewart line, was excluded as she was not a *king* but a queen, but if so her exclusion is no less unsettling. See Arthur F. Kinney's "Scottish History, The Union of the Crowns, and the Issue of Right Rule: The Case of Shakespeare's *Macbeth*," in *Renaissance Culture in Context*, ed. Jean R. Brink and William F. Gentrup (Aldershot: Scolar Press, 1993), p. 21.

14. Louis Knafla, *Law and Politics in Jacobean England: The Tracts of Lord Chancellor Ellesmere* (Cambridge: Cambridge Univ. Press, 1972), p. 22. James was the ninth consecutive Stuart monarch to rule in Scotland; the longest unbroken post-Conquest English reign lasted only five generations.

15. No doubt this is a contested term and is often used imprecisely. Nonetheless, the claim of a number of recent historians of seventeenth-century England that the Stuarts ruled within and through the law and cannot therefore be thought of as "absolutist" seems to run the risk of losing a useful distinction in considering not only the centralization of power in the crown but more crucially how the monarchy conceived of the sources and sanctions of its authority. James, for example, saw himself sitting "in the Throne of God," and if he ruled within the law clearly thought himself "above the law, as both the author and giver of strength thereto" (*The Political Works of James I*, ed. Charles Howard McIlwain [Cambridge, Mass: Harvard Univ. Press, 1918], pp. 326, 63). Charles I also could be said to have ruled through the law (though that, of course, is not an uncomplicated claim), but he had no doubt that the court that tried him for treason in 1649 had no right to sit in judgment on a king. For important considerations of the concept, see Nicholas Henshall, *The Myth of Absolutism: Change and Continuity in Early Modern European Monarchy* (London: Longman, 1992); *Absolutism in Seventeenth-Century Europe*, ed. John Miller (London: Macmillan, 1990), esp. the essay by J. H. Burns, "The Idea of Absolutism," pp. 21–42; Howard Nenner, *By Colour of Law: Legal Culture and Constitutional Politics in England 1660–1689* (Chicago: Univ. of Chicago Press, 1977); and Glenn Burgess, *Absolute Monarchy and the Stuart Constitution* (New Haven: Yale Univ. Press, 1996); but see also Perry Anderson's *Lineages of the Absolutist State* (London: Verso, 1974).

16. "An Act for the establishment of the King's succession" (1534; 25 Henr. VIII, c. 22). Rpt. in *Tudor Constitutional Documents, A.D. 1485–1603, with Historical Commentary*, ed. J. R. Tanner (Cambridge: Cambridge Univ. Press, 1930), pp. 382–85.

17. *Les Reportes del Cases in Camera Stellata, 1593–1609*, ed. William Paley Baildon (London: privately printed, 1894), pp. 163–64.

18. "A Speach to the Lords and Commons of the Parliament at White-Hall" (21 March 1609), in *The Political Works of James I*, p. 307.

19. Quoted in Max Weber, *From Max Weber: Essays in Sociology*, trans. and ed. H. H. Gerth and C. Wright Mills (1946; rpt. New York: Oxford Univ. Press, 1958), p. 78. Weber is here arguing about the state's "monopoly" on legitimate violence.

20. [William Covell], *Polimanteia* (London, 1595), sig. C4^r.

21. *The Jacobean Union: Six Tracts of 1604*, ed. Bruce R. Galloway and Brian P. Levack (Edinburgh: Scottish History Society, 1985), p. 196.

22. *The Case of the Commonwealth of England, Stated*, ed. Philip. A. Knachel (Charlottesville: Univ. of Virginia Press, 1969), p. 15.

23. Quoted in William M. Lamont, *Richard Baxter and the Millennium* (London: Croom Helm, 1979), p. 97.

24. *The Trew Law of Free Monarchies*, in *Political Works of James I*, p. 61.

25. Ibid., 62–63.

26. *Basilikon Doron*, in *Political Works of James I*, p. 18. A Scottish coin of 1591, the silver helf merk, had as its motto on the reverse, *his differet rege tyrannus*. See Adam R. Richardson, *Catalogue of Scottish Coins in the National Museum of Antiquities* (Edinburgh: Society of Antiquaries, 1905), p. 253. Alan Sinfield, in *Faultlines*, similarly observes the theoretical polarization of tyrant and legitimate king that is demanded to legitimize the state's monopoly on violence (pp. 95–108).

27. Jean Bodin, *The Six Bookes of a Commonweale*, trans. Richard Knolles (London, 1606), sig. V2^v.

28. "The Fourth Part of the Sermon for Rogation Week," in *Certain Sermons and Homilies* (London: Society for Promoting Christian Knowledge, 1908), p. 530. See also the proverbial "Ill-gotten goods thrive not to the third heir," in Morris Palmer Tilly's *Dictionary of Proverbs in England in the Sixteenth and Seventeenth Century* (Ann Arbor: Univ. of Michigan Press, 1950), p. 267.

29. *Conscience Satisfied* (London, 1643), sig. D4^v.

30. J. G. A. Pocock, *The Ancient Constitution and the Feudal Law: A Study of English Historical Thought in the Seventeenth Century* (1957; rpt. Cambridge: Cambridge Univ. Press, 1987), p. 149.

31. *The Trew Law of Free Monarchies*, in *Political Works of James I*, pp. 62–63.

32. *Ius Regis* (London, 1612), sig. Ff8^v.

33. Roger Widdrington [i.e., Thomas Preston], *Last Reioynder to Mr Thomas Fitz-Herberts Reply . . .* (London, 1619), sig. L4^r.

34. Ecclesiastical Canons of 1606, in *Synodalia*, ed. Edward Cardwell (Oxford: Oxford Univ. Press, 1842), vol. 1, p. 346. On the political theory of absolutism, see n. 15, as well as J. P. Sommerville, *Politics and Ideology in England, 1603–1640* (London: Longman, 1986), esp. pp. 9–56; and James Daly, *Sir Robert Filmer and English Political Thought* (Toronto: Univ. of Toronto Press, 1979).

35. Raphael Holinshed, "The Historie of Scotland," *Chronicles of England, Scotland and Ireland* (London, 1587), vol. 2, sig. O1^r.

36. See, for example, Henry N. Paul, *The Royal Play of "Macbeth"* (New York: Macmillan, 1950): "He might have learned it from Buchanan's history, with which he certainly had some acquaintance; but this seems unlikely because of the meagerness of what Buchanan says on the subject. Or—and this is more likely—he may have sought the aid of some well informed Scot to keep him from falling into errors about the history of Scotland" (p 155).

37. Holinshed, *Chronicles*, vol. 2, sig. P2^r.

38. Ibid.

39. "*Macbeth* and Witchcraft," in *Focus on "Macbeth,"* ed. John Russell Brown (London: Routledge and Kegan Paul, 1982), p. 193.

40. See Arthur F. Kinney, "Scottish History, the Union of the Crowns and the Issue of Right Rule: The Case of Shakespeare's *Macbeth*," in *Renaissance Culture in Context*, esp. pp. 18–20.

41. "Speculations: *Macbeth* and Source," p. 242.

42. Philip Sidney, *The Defence of Poesie* (London, 1595), sig. E4^v.

43. Sinfield, "*Macbeth*: History, Ideology and Intellectuals," p. 100.

44. Norbrook, "*Macbeth* and the Politics of Historiography," p. 104.

45. Holinshed, *Chronicles*, vol. 2, sig. P3^v.

46. Norbrook, "*Macbeth* and the Politics of Historiography," p. 104.

47. *The Right of Magistrates*, in *Constitutionalism and Resistance in the Sixteenth Century*, ed. and trans. Julian Franklin (New York: Pegasus, 1969), pp. 105, 107, 129.

48. *A sermon preached at the last general assize holden for the county of Sommerset at Taunton* (London, 1612), sig. A4^v.

49. *The Trew Law of Free Monarchies*, in *Political Works of James I*, p. 66.

50. Ibid.

51. Ibid., 60.

52. See Francis Barker, *The Culture of Violence: Essays on Tragedy and History* (Chicago: Univ. of Chicago Press, 1993), p. 66.

53. Karin S. Coddon, "'Unreal Mockery': Unreason and the Problem of Spectacle in *Macbeth*," *ELH* 56 (1989): 499.

54. *The Trew Law of Free Monarchies*, in *Political Works of James I*, p. 64.

55. *A Remonstrance for the Right of Kings*, in *Political Works of James I*, p. 206.

56. *The Trew Law of Free Monarchies*, in *Political Works of James I*, p. 65.

57. Tennenhouse, *Power on Display*, p. 132.

58. *Daphnis Polystephanus* (London, 1605), sig. A3r.

59. Holinshed, *Chronicles*, vol. 2, sig. P8ᵛ.

60. Boece remarks that Malcolm's introduction of the "maners, langage, and superflew chere of Inglishmen" was felt by many to contribute to the "perdicioun of his pepill" (p. 172); and Buchanan similarly comments on the unfortunate "reforming of the publick Manners" and notes that Donald Bane felt that English values were "corrupting the Discipline of his Ancestry" (sig. Ee3ᵛ–4ʳ) and were what led to his revolt.

61. *The Progresses, Processions, and Magnificent Festivities of James I*, ed. John Nichols (London, 1828), 1, 331.

62. *Stuart Royal Proclamations*, ed. J. F. Larkin and L. P. Hughes (Oxford: Clarendon Press, 1973), vol. 1, p. 95–9.

63. *Journals of the House of Commons* (London, 1803), vol. 1, p. 183. On the idea of the *plenitudo potestatis*, see J. H. Burns, "The Idea of Absolutism," in *Absolutism in Seventeenth-Century Europe*, ed. John Miller, pp. 21-42.

64. This is, of course, not to say that there is no difference between a humane ruler and a brutal one, or, as the play writes this difference, between Duncan and Macbeth. Such a claim would be silly at best. It is, however, to say that the significant differences that do exist in the political relations that their kingship structures should not be sought in an idea of legitimacy, which works, I have argued, to mystify rather than clarify the distinction that would be made, and is a mystification that itself functions insidiously to make the effective power relations ever more invisible and beyond remedy.

Chapter 10

1. *The Comedy of Errors*, 3.2.133–35. It is worth noting that "America," perhaps inevitably for a play written in the early 1590s, is here associated with a Spanish colonial interest rather than an English one.

2. Edmond Malone, *An account of the incidents from which the title and part of the story of Shakespeare's "Tempest" were derived and its true date determined* (London: C. and R. Baldwin, 1808).

3. *The Tempest*, ed. Morton Luce (London: Methuen, 1901), pp. xii, xlii.

4. John Gillies, *Shakespeare and the Geography of Difference* (Cambridge: Cambridge University Press, 1994), p. 149. On Shakespeare's relations with the Virginia Company, see Charles Mills Gayley, *Shakespeare and the Founders of Liberty in America* (New York: Macmillan, 1917).

5. The phrase, now a staple of *Tempest* criticism, derives from Antonio de Nebrija's justification to Queen Isabella for his Spanish grammar: "language is the perfect instrument of empire" (quoted from Louis Hanke, *Aristotle and the American Indians* [Bloomington: Indiana University Press, 1959], p. 8). Nebrija (or, more properly, Lebrija) was, however, a bit less explicit about the instrumental relation of language and empire; "siempre la lengua fue compañera del imperio" (sig. a2^r) is what he wrote in his *Grammatica Castellana* (1492). For the play's "implication" in the English colonial project, see, for example, Paul Brown, "'This thing of darkness I acknowledge mine'": *The Tempest* and the Discourse of Colonialism," *Political Shakespeare: New Essays in Cultural Materialism*, ed. Jonathan Dollimore and Alan Sinfield (Ithaca: Cornell Univ. Press, 1985), esp. pp. 56 and 64.

6. *Narrative and Dramatic Sources of Shakespeare* (London: Routledge and Kegan Paul, 1975), vol. 8, p. 245.

7. *Coleridge on Shakespeare: The Text of the Lectures of 1811–1812*, ed. R. A. Foakes (Charlottesville: Univ. Press of Virginia, 1971), p. 106.

8. Greenblatt, *Shakespearean Negotiations: The Circulation of Social Energy in Renaissance England* (Berkeley and Los Angeles: Univ. of California Press, 1988), p. 156; and Hulme, "Hurricanes in the Caribbees: The Constitution of the Discourse of English Colonialism," in *1642: Literature and Power in the Seventeenth Century*, ed. Francis Barker, et al. (Colchester: Univ. of Essex, 1981), p. 74.

9. Ralph Berry, *On Directing Shakespeare: Interviews with Contemporary Directors* (London: Croom Helm, 1977), p. 34.

10. Leslie A. Fiedler, *The Stranger in Shakespeare* (New York: Stein and Day, 1972), p. 238.

11. Epistle Dedicatory to *The Second Volume of Chronicles* in *The First and Second Volumes of Chronicles,* ed. Raphael Holinshed, et al. (London, 1586), sig. A3^v.

12. Francis Barker and Peter Hulme, "Nymphs and reapers heavily vanish: The Discursive Con-texts of *The Tempest*," in *Alternative Shakespeares*, ed. John Drakakis (London: Routledge, 1985), p. 198. Richard Halpern similarly says that "colonialism has established itself as a dominant, if not the dominant code for interpreting *The Tempest*," in his "'The Picture of Nobody': White Cannibalism in *The Tempest*," in *The Production of English Renaissance Culture*, ed. David Lee Miller, Sharon O'Dair, and Harold Weber (Ithaca: Cornell Univ. Press, 1994), p. 265.

13. "Certain Fallacies and Irrelevancies in the Literary Scholarship of the Day," *Studies in Philology* 24 (1927): 484.

14. *Narrative and Dramatic Sources of Shakespeare*, vol. 8, p. 241.

15. Barker and Hulme, "Nymphs," p. 204. Greenblatt, while basing his account of *The Tempest* upon its relation to the Virginia Company narratives, does see the play's "swerve away from these materials," though he sees this swerve as evidence "of the process by which the Bermuda material is made negotiable"; that is, even as the play transforms the source material, for Greenblatt, it remains centrally grounded in the new world and "colonial discourse" (*Shakespearean Negotiations*, pp. 154–55).

16. Dennis Kay identifies the allusion here to the pillars of Hercules, adopted as an imperial emblem first by Charles V and then by other European rulers, including Elizabeth. See his "Gonzalo's 'Lasting Pillars': *The Tempest*, V.i.208," *Shakespeare Quarterly* 35 (1984): 322–24.

17. See E. K. Chambers, *William Shakespeare: A Study of Facts and Problems* (Oxford: Clarendon Press, 1930), vol. 2, p. 342.

18. *Parliamentary Debates in 1610*, ed. S. R. Gardiner (London: Camden Society, 1861), p. 53.

19. See Roger Lockyer, *The Early Stuarts: A Political History of England* (London and New York:

Longman, 1989), esp. p. 15. It is perhaps of interest here that Pembroke and Southampton, to both of whom Shakespeare had connections, were proponents of an aggressive pro-Protestant foreign policy. See Thomas Cogswell, *The Blessed Revolution: English Politics and the Coming of War, 1621–1624* (Cambridge: Cambridge Univ. Press, 1989), esp. pp. 12–50.

20. John Nichols, *Progresses of King James the First* (1828; rpt. New York: AMS Press, n.d.), vol. 2, 601–2.

21. Henry Wotton wrote in May 1611 of how Rudolf was forced "to make Matthias King of the Romans." Commenting on the treatment of Rudolf by the supporters of Matthias, Wotton notes, "having first spoiled him of obedience and reverence, next of his estates and titles, they have now reduced him to so low a case, that he is no longer patron of his voice." See *Life and Letters of Sir Henry Wotton*, ed. Logan Pearsall Smith (Oxford: Clarendon Press, 1907), vol. 1, p. 507.

22. *Life and Letters of Sir Henry Wotton*, vol. 1, p. 268.

23. Quoted in R. J. W. Evans, *Rudolph II and his World* (Oxford: Clarendon Press, 1973), p. 196. See also Hugh Trevor-Roper, *Princes and Artists: Patronage and Ideology at Four Habsburg Courts 1517–1633* (London: Thames and Hudson, 1976), esp. pp. 122–23.

24. Michael Srigley's *Images of Regeneration: A Study of Shakespeare's "The Tempest" and its Cultural Background* (Uppsala: Academiae Upsaliensis, 1985) does make an argument for such topical allegory, though, of course, we should remember that as early as *Loves Labor's Lost* Shakespeare had begun thinking about rulers who preferred the study to the affairs of state.

25. *Daemonologie (1597) and Newes From Scotland*, ed. G.B. Harrison (London: Bodley Head, 1924), pp. 24–25.

26. *The Political Works of James I*, ed. Charles Howard McIlwain (Cambridge, Mass.: Harvard Univ. Press, 1918), p. 38.

27. Even Marc Ferro's ambitious synthesis, *Colonization: A Global History* (London and New York: Routledge, 1997), admits that "it is true that one colonization was different from another" (p. viii).

28. *The Original Writings and Correspondence of the Two Richard Hakluyts*, ed. Eva G. R. Taylor (London: Hakluyt Society, 1935), p. 243. See Jeffrey Knapp's fine *An Empire Nowhere: England, America, and Literature from "Utopia" to the "The Tempest"* (Berkeley: Univ. of California Press, 1992), esp. pp. 231–34.

29. *Soundings in Critical Theory* (Ithaca: Cornell Univ. Press, 1989), p. 193.

30. Richard E. Palmer, *Hermeneutics* (Evanston: Northwestern Univ. Press, 1969), p. 120.

31. The terms here are familiar. Jonathan Culler writes, "meaning is context-bound, but context is boundless" in his *On Deconstruction: Theory and Criticism after Structuralism* (Ithaca: Cornell Univ. Press, 1982), p. 123. But, for example, Susan Horton invokes the same wordplay ("although meaning itself may be 'context bound' . . . context itself is boundless") in her *Interpreting Interpreting: Interpreting Dickens's "Dombey"* (Baltimore: The Johns Hopkins Univ. Press, 1979), p. x.

32. Hans-Georg Gadamer, *Truth and Method*, trans. Garrett Barden and John Cumming (London: Sheed and Ward, 1975), p. 269.

33. It is in the work of George Lamming, Roberto Fernández Retamar, Aimé Césaire, and others writing from within the anticolonial struggles of the mid-twentieth century that *The Tempest* suffers its sea-change and becomes the paradigmatic drama of colonialism.

34. Howard Felperin has recently argued similarly that "the colonialism of the New World" has been overemphasized. Its traces in the play, he argues, have been "overread," mistaking "the part for the whole." Felperin, however, wants finally to see the "whole" not as a larger

historical picture but "as a projection of nothing less than a historical totality" itself, or, as he says, "a vision of history as a cycle of repetition." This, however, seems to me to return the play to the very idealism that historical criticism has tried to counter. See his "Political Criticism at the Crossroads: The Utopian Historicism of *The Tempest*," in *The Tempest*, ed. Nigel Wood (Buckingham and Philadelphia: Open University Press, 1995), esp. pp. 47–55. For a different relocation of *The Tempest* in relation to new world colonial activity, see Meredith Anne Skura's "Discourse and the Individual: The Case of Colonialism in *The Tempest*," *Shakespeare Quarterly* 40 (1989): 42–69 and reprinted in *Critical Essays on Shakespeare's "The Tempest"*, ed. Alden and Virginia Vaughan (New York: G. K. Hall, 1998).

Chapter 11

1. *Acts and Ordinances of the Interregnum, 1642–1660*, ed. C. H. Firth and R. S. Rait (London: HMSO, 1911), vol. 1, pp. 26–27.

2. Margot Heinemann, *Puritanism and Theatre: Thomas Middleton and Opposition Drama under the Early Stuarts* (Cambridge: Cambridge Univ. Press, 1980).

3. Thomas White, *A Sermo[n] Preached at Pawles Crosse on Sunday the thirde of Nouember 1577, in the time of the Plague* (London, 1578), sig. C8^r.

4. Brian Morris, "Elizabethan and Jacobean Drama," in *English Drama to 1710*, ed. Christopher Ricks (London: Sphere Books, 1971), p. 65.

5. Widdowes, *The Schysmatical Puritan* (London, 1631), sig. A3^r.

6. [Henry Parker], A Discourse Concerning Puritans," in *Images of English Puritanism: A Collection of Contemporary Sources, 1589–1646*, ed. Lawrence A. Sasek (Baton Rouge: Univ. of Louisiana Press, 1989), p. 130.

7. *Calendar of State Papers and Manuscripts Relating to English Affairs, Existing in the Archives and Collections of Venice and in other Libraries of North Italy*, ed. R. Brown, et al. (London: Historical Manuscript Commission, 1864–), vol. 14, p. 245. Hereafter referred to as *CSPV*.

8. See C. H. Frith, "Sir William Davenant and the Revival of Drama under the Protectorate," *English Historical Review* 18 (1903): 319–21; and James R. Jacob and Timothy Raylor, "Opera and Obedience: Thomas Hobbes and *A Proposition for Advancement of Moralitie* by William Davenant," *Seventeeth Century* 6 (1991): 205–50.

9. Barish, *The Antitheatrical Prejudice* (Berkeley: Univ. of California Press, 1981), p. 83.

10. H. C. Grierson, *Cross Currents in English Literature of the XVIIth Century* (1929; rpt. London: Chatto & Windus, 1965), p. 69.

11. John Moore, 26 January 1641/42, in *The Private Journals of the Long Parliament, 3 January to 5 March*, ed. Willson H. Coates, Anne Steele Young, and Vernon F. Snow (New Haven: Yale Univ. Press, 1982), p. 182.

12. John Milton, *A Treatise of Civil Power in Ecclesiastical Causes* (London, 1659), sig. B12^v.

13. Philip Edwards, "The Closing of the Theatres," in *The Revels History of Drama in English, 1613–1660*, ed. Philip Edwards, Gerald Eades Bentley, Kathleen McLuskie, and Lois Potter (London: Methuen, 1981), p. 63.

14. Heinemann, *Puritanism and Theatre*; and Martin Butler, *Theatre and Crisis, 1632–1642* (Cambridge: Cambridge Univ. Press, 1984).

15. James Shirley, "Prologue at the Black-Fryers," in *The Sisters* (London, 1652), sig. A3^r.

16. *Journal of the House of Lords*, vol. 5, pp. 334–37 (hereafter *LJ*); *Journal of the House of Commons*, vol. 2, pp. 749–50 (hereafter *CJ*). See also newsbooks like *A True and Perfect Diurnall of the passages in Parliament*, 29 August to 6 September 1642.

17. The most convincing accounts of the closing are Butler's compact and compelling treatment in *Theatre and Crisis*, pp. 136–40; and a fine essay by Rick Bowers: "Players, Puritans, and Theatrical Propaganda, 1642–1660," *Dalhousie Review* 67 (1987–88): 463–79. Both understand, in Bowers's words, that "closing the theatres was a significant gesture in the direction of public order" (p. 465); and, though the earliest form of this chapter was presented at the Renaissance Society of America in 1984, before either work had appeared, I am deeply indebted to both accounts in my understanding of the events of the 1640s.

18. Edwards, "The Closing of the Theatres," p. 63.

19. "The Prologue to his Majesty," in *The Poetical Works of John Denham*, ed. Theodore Howard Banks (New Haven: Yale Univ. Press, 1928), p. 94.

20. *The Last News in London: Or, A Discourse Between a Citizen and a Country-Gentleman* (London, 1642), p. 2.

21. [Samuel Butler], *The Loyal Satyrist: Or, Hudibras in Prose* (London, 1682), p. 21.

22. *The Stage-Players Complaint. In A pleasant Dialogue betweene Cain of the Fortune, and Reed of the Friers. Deploring their sad and solitary conditions for want of Imployment. In this heavie and Contagious time of the plague in London* (1641). In *The English Drama and Stage under the Tudor and Stuart Princes, 1543–1664*, ed. W. C. Hazlitt (1869; rpt. New York: Burt Franklin, 1964), pp. 256–57.

23. "To my honoured Friend M. *Ja.* Shirley," in James Shirley, *Poems &c.* (London, 1646), sig. A5^r.

24. Quoted in Gerald Eades Bentley, *The Jacobean and Caroline Stage* (Oxford: Oxford Univ. Press, 1968), vol. 6, p. 42.

25. Berry, "Folger MS V.b.275 and the Deaths of Shakespearean Playhouses," *Medieval and Renaissance Drama in England* 10 (1998): 62–93.

26. Edmund Gayton, *Pleasant Notes Upon Don Quixot* (London, 1654), sig. Mm4^r.

27. Heinemann, *Puritanism and Theatre*, p. 235.

28. Leonard Tennenhouse, *Power on Display: The Politics of Shakespeare's Genres* (New York and London: Methuen, 1986), p. 39.

29. See chapter 6.

30. Sir Ralph Winwood, *Memorials of Affairs of State in the Reigns of Q. Elizabeth and K. James*, ed. E. Sawyer (London, 1725), vol. 1, p. 271.

31. Nigel Bawcutt, *The Control and Censorship of Caroline Drama: The Records of Sir Henry Herbert, Master of the Revels 1623–73* (Oxford: Oxford Univ. Press, 1996), p. 46.

32. *Letters of John Chamberlain*, ed. Norman Egbert McClure (Philadelphia: American Philosophical Society, 1939), vol. 2, p. 578.

33. Quoted in Bentley, *The Jacobean and Caroline Stage*, vol. 4, p. 871.

34. Butler, *Theatre and Crisis*; see also Albert H. Tricomi, *Anticourt Drama in England, 1603–1642* (Charlottesville: Univ. of Virginia Press, 1989).

35. *Brennoralt*, 3.2.38–39; in *The Works of Sir John Suckling*, ed. L. A. Beaurline (Oxford: Oxford Univ. Press, 1971), vol. 2, p. 210.

36. William D'Avenant, *The Fair Favourite*, in *The Dramatic Works of Sir William D'Avenant*, ed.

James Maidment and W. H. Logan (1874; rpt. New York: Russell & Russell, 1964), vol. 4, pp. 223, 232.

37. Bawcutt, *The Control and Censorship of Caroline Drama*, p. 208; Butler, *Theatre and Crisis*, p. 200. Bawcutt notes that Butler and others assume somewhat too confidently that Herbert's comment refers to *The Court Beggar*.

38. James Wright, *Historia Histrionica: A Historical Account of the English-Stage* (London, 1699), sig. B3^r.

39. Quoted in William Haller's *Liberty and Revolution in the Puritan Revolution* (New York: Columbia Univ. Press, 1955), p. 9.

40. *The Debates on the Grand Remonstrance*, ed. John Foster (London: John Murray, 1866), p. 292.

41. Quoted in Glynne Wickham, *Early English Stages, 1300–1600* (New York: Columbia Univ. Press, 1963), vol. 2, part 1, p. 67.

42. *Ideology and Politics on the Eve of Restoration: Newcastle's Advice to Charles II*, ed. Thomas P. Slaughter (Philadelphia: American Philosophical Society, 1984), p. 84.

43. Henry Crosse, *Vertues Common-Wealth: Or, The High-way to Honour* (London, 1603), sig. Q1^r; Montaigne, "Of the Institution and Education of Children; to the Ladie Diana of Foix, Countess of Gurson," *The Essayes of Michael Lord of Montaigne*, trans. John Florio (London: Henry Frowde, 1904), vol. 1, p. 207.

44. Peter Stallybrass and Allon White, *The Politics and Poetics of Transgression* (Ithaca: Cornell Univ. Press, 1986).

45. E. K. Chambers, *The Elizabethan Stage* (Oxford: Oxford Univ. Press, 1930), vol. 4, p. 341.

46. Rous, Pym's step-brother, was a committed Calvinist, having undergone a conversion while preparing for a legal career, but one that led him to take an active political role to advance a further reformation. See Nicholas Tyacke, *Anti-Calvinists: The Rise of English Arminianism c. 1590–1640* (Oxford: Oxford Univ. Press, 1987), pp. 138–89.

47. Butler, *Theatre and Crisis*, p. 138.

48. *CJ*, vol. 2, p. 84. On the regulation of print in this period, see Fredrick Seaton Siebert, *Freedom of the Press, 1476–1776* (Urbana: Univ. of Illinois Press, 1952), esp. pp. 165–91.

49. *CJ*, vol. 2, p. 514.

50. *CJ*, vol. 2, p. 739; see also *LJ*, vol. 5, p. 322.

51. *CJ*, vol. 2, p. 747.

52. Unquestionably the most important voice urging this awareness of the inadequacy of homogenizing the notion of "Parliament" is Conrad Russell. In a series of studies Russell emphasizes the inevitable fractures within that group and the need to inquire more specifically into the individuals and groups that urged specific actions. See, in particular, his *Parliaments and English Politics 1621–1629* (Oxford: Oxford Univ. Press, 1979), esp. pp. 1–84.

53. Quoted in R. W. Harris, *Clarendon and the English Revolution* (London: Chatto & Windus, 1983), p. 132. This idea of the war, or at least of its first phase from 1642–46, as a struggle between aristocratic elites has led "revisionist" historians to repudiate the older, Whiggish view of the war as a crucial event in the progress toward democracy and toleration, and see it instead as a largely accidental conflict with short-term causes and few, if any, long term effects. They see England in 1642 as a culture largely in agreement on constitutional principles (and divided mainly along religious lines). The radicalism of the early phase of the war, a radicalism evident not only discursively but also, and arguably more crucially, in the visible presence of the common people as political agents, forcing a redefinition of the political nation, has, however, been too easily dismissed. An anti-revisionist position has emerged in

response, more subtle than the earlier progressive histories, reaffirming the revolutionary implications of these years. See R. C. Richardson's survey, *The Debate on the English Revolution Revisited* (London: Routledge, 1988); and Richard Cust and Ann Hughes, "Introduction: After Revisionism," in *Conflict in Early Stuart England: Studies in Religion and Politics 1603–1642* (London: Longman, 1989), pp. 1–46.

54. *A Declaration of the Valiant Resolution of the Famous Prentices of London* (London, 1642), sig. A3ʳ.

55. Quoted in Anthony Fletcher, *The Outbreak of the English Civil War* (New York: New York Univ. Press, 1981), p. 379.

56. Quoted in Conrad Russell, *The Crisis of Parliaments: English History, 1509–1660* (Oxford: Oxford Univ. Press, 1971), p. 348.

57. Quoted in H. N. Brailsford, *The Levellers and the English Revolution* (Stanford: Stanford Univ. Press, 1961), p. 35.

58. Quoted in *Freedom in Arms: A Selection of Leveller Writings*, ed. A. L. Morton (New York: International Publishers, 1975), p. 239.

59. In *Leveller Manifestoes of the Puritan Revolution*, ed. D. M. Wolfe (1944; rpt. New York: Humanities Press, 1967), p. 237.

60. In Brailsford, *The Levellers and the English Revolution*, p. 93.

61. Thomas Hobbes, *Behemoth: or, The Long Parliament*, ed. Ferdinand Tönnies (Chicago: Univ. of Chicago Press, 1990), p. 64.

62. Edward Hyde, Earl of Clarendon, *The History of the Rebellion and Civil Wars in England*, ed. W. D. Macray (Oxford Univ. Press, 1888), vol. 1, p. 269.

63. *The Diurnall Occurrences, or Dayly Proceedings of Both Houses . . . From the third of* November, *1640, to the third of* November *1641* (London, 1641), sig. B4ᵛ.

64. Clarendon, *The History of the Rebellion*, vol. 1, p. 270.

65. Thomas May, *The History of the Parliament of England* (London, 1647), p. 79. For the most compelling account of the role of the common people in the civil war, see Brian Manning, *The English People and the English Revolution*, and his more recent *Aristocrats, Plebeians and Revolution in England 1640–1660* (London: Pluto Press, 1996). See also Valerie Pearl, *London and the Outbreak of the Puritan Revolution* (Oxford: Oxford Univ. Press, 1961), esp. pp. 210–36.

66. *The Third Speech of The Lord George Digby, To the House of Commons* (London, 1641), sig. B1ᵛ–B2ʳ.

67. *CSPV*, vol. 25, p. 128–29.

68. Quoted in Manning, *The English People and the English Revolution*, p. 58.

69. Ibid., 64.

70. *CSPV*, vol. 25, p. 148.

71. Sir Philip Warwick, *Memoires of the Reigne of Kinge Charles I* (London, 1701), p. 163

72. *CSPV*, vol. 25, p. 129.

73. Quoted in Keith Lindley, "London and Popular Freedom in the 1640s," in *Freedom and the English Revolution*, ed. R. C. Richardson and G. M. Ridden (Manchester: Manchester Univ. Press, 1986), p. 120. See also Terence Kilburn and Anthony Milton, "The Public Context of the Trial and Execution of Strafford," in *The Political World of Thomas Wentworth, Earl of Strafford, 1621–1641*, ed. J.F. Merritt (Cambridge: Cambridge Univ. Press, 1996), pp. 230–52.

74. *Calendar of State Papers: Domestic Series, 1641–43*, p. 188.

75. *CSPV*, vol. 25, p. 284. The Venetian ambassador, of course, cannot be thought to offer an entirely objective account of the events he witnessed, and here, as always with his reports, the oligarchical bias must be factored in.

76. Sir Thomas Aston, *A Remonstrance against Presbitery* (London, 1641), sig. K1^v.

77. Quoted in Clarendon, *The History of the Rebellion*, vol. 4, p. 114.

78. In John Rushforth, *Historical Collections* (London, 1721), vol. 5, p. 307.

79. Quoted in Lindley, "London and Popular Freedom in the 1640s," p. 121.

80. John Corbet, *An Historicall Relation of the Military Government of Gloucester* (London, 1645), sig. B3^v.

81. A facsimile of the Declaration is included in the collection of *Commonwealth Tracts, 1625–50*, ed. Arthur Freeman (New York and London: Garland, 1975).

82. Chambers, *The Elizabethan Stage*, vol. 4, p. 308.

83. Ibid., 271.

84. Ibid., 273.

85. Ibid., 317.

86. Ibid., 294.

87. *The Actors Remonstrance, or Complaint* (1643), in *The English Drama and the Stage under the Tudor and Stuart Princes*, ed. W. C. Hazlitt, p. 261.

88. *Craftie Cromwell: Or, Oliver ordering our New State* (London, 1648), sig. A1v. See also important studies of this aspect of what Dale Randall calls "the paper war": Susan Wiseman, *Drama and Politics in the English Civil War* (Cambridge: Cambridge Univ. Press, 1998), pp. 19–79; Dale B. J. Randall, *Winter Fruit: English Drama 1642–1660* (Lexington: Univ. Press of Kentucky, 1995), pp. 51–65; Nigel Smith, *Literature and Revolution in England, 1640–1660* (New Haven and London: Yale Univ. Press, 1994), esp. pp. 70–92; and Lois Potter, *Secret Rites and Secret Writing: Royalist Literature, 1641–1660* (Cambridge: Cambridge Univ. Press, 1989), esp. pp. 90–93.

89. See Louis B. Wright, "The Reading of Plays during the Puritan Revolution," *Huntington Library Bulletin* 6 (1934): 73–108.

90. See Hyder E. Rollins, "A Contribution to the History of the English Commonwealth Drama," *Studies in Philology* 18 (1921): 302–3.

91. *Comedies and Tragedies,* written by Francis Beaumont and John Fletcher, Gentlemen, (London, 1647).

92. *Mercurius Melancholias* (4 September 1647), sig. A2v. Quoted in Bentley, *The Jacobean and Caroline Stage*, vol. 7, p. 176.

93. *CSPV*, vol. 30, p. 165. See also *The State Papers of John Thurloe*, ed. Thomas Birch (London, 1742), vol. 4, pp. 107–17, where district commanders are shown to receive instructions to forbid public gatherings, including at stage plays because "treason and rebellion is (sic) usually hatched and contrived against the state on such occasions."

94. *LJ*, vol. 5, p. 234.

95. Wright, *Historia Histrionica*, sig. B4^r. Wright, however, it should be remembered, is not above special pleading; cf. *Mercurius Britannicus*, 11 August 1645: "the Players; who now in these sad times, have most of them turn'd Lieutenants, and Captains, as their fellowes on the other side, have turn'd *Deacons*, and Lay-elders."

96. Arendt, *Between Past and Future* (1954; rpt. London: Penguin, 1977), p. 4.

97. Chambers, *The Elizabethan Stage*, vol. 4, p. 318.

98. *Weekley Account*, quoted in Bentley, *The Jacobean and Caroline Stage*, vol. 6, p. 174; the proposition from The Treaty of Uxbridge is cited from the *Constitutional Documents of the Puritan Revolution, 1625–1660*, ed. Samuell Rawson Gardiner (Oxford: Oxford Univ. Press, n.d.), p. 277; for the parliamentary prohibitions of 22 October 1647 and of 11 February 1647/48, see Firth and Rait, *Acts and Ordinances*, vol. 1, pp. 1027 and 1070–72.

99. Thomas Edwards, *The Third Part of Gangraena* (London, 1646), p. 187.

100. See Nigel Smith, "Popular Republicanism in the 1650s: John Streater's 'Heroick Mechanicks,'" in *Milton and Republicanism*, ed. David Armitage, Armand Himy, and Quentin Skinner (Cambridge: Cambridge Univ. Press, 1995), pp. 137–55, esp. p. 151; for Hall, see Smith, *Literature and Revolution in England, 1640–1660*, p. 71.

101. *Mercurius Pragmaticus* (18–25 January 1648), sig. T4^r. See also Butler, *Theatre and Crisis*, p. 139.

Index